We've got MAJIC, STAN AND THE KING OF JAPAN

GORDON STRACHAN'S FIRST SEASON AT CELTIC

2005 ★ 2006

MATT CORR

Foreword by Neil Lennon

THE CELTIC STAR

Majic, Stan And The King of Japan
Gordon Strachan's first season at Celtic
by Matt Corr

Published by The Celtic Star
in cooperation with Matt Corr Media.

First Published in the UK in 2023 by The Celtic Star.

ISBN 978-1-8380207-7-4

A catalogue for this book is available from
the British Library and the Irish Library in Dublin.

Cover & page design and typesetting by Stephen Cameron.

Publisher - David Faulds: email editor@thecelticstar.co.uk

Printed by CPI.

Bookstore website – https://celticstarbooks.com

Dedication

Dedicated to the memory of David Potter, who now takes his own richly deserved place in the story of his beloved Celtic.

A wonderful historian, an inspirational author and teacher.

And a dear friend who will be hugely missed.

Acknowledgements

Special thanks to Stephen Cameron and David Faulds for editorial guidance and design input, and to Martin Gorman for many much-appreciated hours of proof reading.

Contents

Foreword

Celtic Park back in the summer of 2005 had a very different feel about it.

That spring we had endured a bittersweet week where we saw our League title snatched away in the cruellest, most dramatic of circumstances, won the Scottish Cup for the second consecutive year then bade farewell to our charismatic and hugely successful manager. I had worked closely with Martin for the best part of a decade, firstly at Leicester then at Celtic, and we enjoyed our fair share of silverware and incredible memories during that period.

But now it was time for a new chapter for me at Celtic, under Gordon Strachan. It was a huge honour when Gordon asked me to be his captain, to skipper MY club, but we both realised that there was a huge amount of work to be done.

Many of the experienced players and backroom staff involved in those trophy-laden years, which immediately preceded that summer, had moved on. There were a few of us left, Big John and Sutty up front. Thommo and Stan beside me in midfield and Bobo and Didier at the back and of course the much-loved and missed Tommy Burns was still around to add to that sense of continuity. Nevertheless, the huge turnaround in personnel required made it a daunting task to make 2005/06 a successful season. Our optimism was tinged with caution.

But this is Celtic, and success is exactly what was achieved, despite an horrendous start on a crazy, balmy evening in Bratislava, where anything that could possibly go wrong on the night decided to do just that. Even at that, our new team was an agonising goal away from creating European history six days later. I was hugely proud of the way the boys fought that night, then recovered from that setback to go on a run which blew our opposition away domestically.

There were some wonderful highlights along the way, back-to-back victories over traditional rivals Rangers in November were followed by a stunning comeback in the pivotal match of the season, the New Year's Day triumph at Tynecastle. New signing Roy Keane watched from the stand that day, but we were together in midfield at Ibrox the next month as the man they call 'Majic' scored the winner. Oh, and I made my own contribution to the goals tally around the same time, on that East End pitch where I was bordering on prolific!

There was sadness of a different kind during the season, as we lost one of our own, Jimmy Johnstone, one of my boyhood heroes. And so the script was written, for a Celtic team all wearing the number seven on our shorts to win the Jinky Final. He would have loved that, and it was a poignant way for me to lift my first trophy as Celtic captain. We also had the first signs of illness to Tommy, another great Celt, albeit none of us really expected what was to follow.

We won the League title in early April, beating our closest challengers Hearts before 60,000 supporters on a memorable night at Celtic Park, Big John scoring the winner on his birthday. We got to celebrate that in some style as the trophy was presented against the side from the other half of Edinburgh a week or so later. Some of us had been down that road many times before but it was brilliant to see the expressions on the faces of the boys who were experiencing that champion feeling as a Celt for the first time. I know from experience that winning cups and titles simply gives you that hunger to go again, and the team would indeed build on that success moving forward.

Anyway, that's for another day. This story is all about the remarkable, rollercoaster campaign that was Celtic's 2005/06 season, from the depths to the heights and everything in between.

Sit back, relive the memories and enjoy.

Neil Lennon

PROLOGUE

The last march with O'Neill

The fallout from Black Sunday, when the League title was surrendered at Fir Park, Motherwell, to two last-gasp Scott McDonald goals, was still being painfully endured and analysed by those with Celtic in their hearts, when the worst-kept secret in Scottish football was confirmed in the mainstream media. It was Wednesday, 25 May 2005. Lisbon Day, as if the knife required twisting. After five years at the helm, Martin O'Neill would be leaving Celtic after Saturday's Scottish Cup Final against Dundee United.

The news was neither unexpected nor welcome. Martin's wife, Geraldine, had been battling a serious illness, lymphoma, for some time and he had decided to take some time away from football to focus on supporting her and the rest of his family through this most worrying of periods.

For once, the normally-expansive O'Neill kept his statement brief and succinct.

"I am leaving Celtic purely for personal reasons and I am extremely sorry to be departing in such circumstances. We have had discussions for some weeks, as we awaited certain biopsy results. We have had suspicions in recent weeks, and that has taken it to a different level but she [Geraldine] wouldn't like me to go into too much detail. We had some good news at the back end of last year, but she is not so clever at the moment. I don't have a monopoly of bad news, but it is the correct thing to do. She has stood with me for quite some time, so this is the right thing. I would like to thank sincerely Dermot Desmond and the Celtic board

for giving me the opportunity to manage this fantastic club five years ago. It has been an honour and a privilege to have served the club and its supporters during that time and [to have] been a part of Celtic's history."

Celtic chairman Brian Quinn spoke of his "great disappointment, reluctance and regret, whilst fully respecting the reasons behind the decision," whilst Peter Lawwell commented on the "consummate professionalism" of O'Neill and his backroom team, the Parkhead chief executive then adding;

"Martin has taken Celtic on a remarkably thrilling and successful adventure over the past five years and, as well as achieving tremendous domestic success, has helped put Celtic back where it belongs - on the European stage."

It was difficult to disagree with those sentiments, as somewhat bucking the normal trend, a manager left his post at Celtic Park without acrimony. Whilst the previous week had ripped the heart and soul out of the Celtic family, for the most part it had been a very special journey with the man from Derry.

Three days later, the Martin O'Neill era drew to a close with an uninspiring 1-0 victory over Dundee United at Hampden, courtesy of an early Alan Thompson free-kick. The goal was in keeping with the rest of the game, untidy and instantly forgettable, the ball eventually going into the net off defender Gary Kenneth, after Bobo Balde had either dummied or missed Thompson's original cross, depending on your view of the big Guinean. Late on in the match, there was another less-than-memorable Cup Final moment, as we had to share the indignity of Chris Sutton as he slipped before shanking his spot-kick high over Tony Bullock's crossbar. Twelve years down the line, a cruel twist of fate would see a big Australian midfielder replicate Sutton's feat at the same end of Hampden, triggering the end of another managerial regime at Parkhead.

Future Partick Thistle manager Alan Archibald then blasted a long-range shot off the Celtic crossbar to be denied his own 'Roy of the Rovers' moment, the last action of the 2005 Scottish Cup final. Seconds later, referee John Rowbotham signalled the end of the match and Martin's tenure at Parkhead.

Archibald would later succeed winning Celtic captain Jackie McNamara in the Firhill dugout, having worked under him there as a player-coach until January 2013, when Jackie resigned to take up the manager's job at, rather ironically, Tannadice. Gordon Chisholm's beaten United side that day was skippered by current Kilmarnock boss Derek McInnes and included two future Celts, Mark Wilson and Barry Robson.

Twelve months earlier, McNamara had deputised for injured Hoops skipper Paul Lambert, leading the dark-green-clad Celts out at Hampden for the 2004 Scottish Cup Final for the great Henrik Larsson's last competitive match for the club. Jackie then shared the winners' podium with the two-goal Swede, as Martin O'Neill's second League and Cup Double was secured. Today, poignantly, by now appointed Celtic captain as Lambert turned his sights on a coaching career post-Parkhead, Jackie stood aside to allow O'Neill, John Robertson and Steve Walford the opportunity to display the famous old trophy to the massed ranks of the Celtic support. All four men would enjoy a last hurrah at Celtic Park just 24-hours later, as the Republic of Ireland provided the opposition in McNamara's testimonial game, the only goal of that match scored in stoppage-time by another future Celt, Robbie Keane. I guess only Jackie himself will know if his own farewell was expected. I remember being surprised when it was announced that he had joined Glenn Hoddle's Wolverhampton Wanderers the following week.

In 50 years of attending Scottish Cup Finals, I cannot recall an atmosphere such as this one after a win. When Celtic lift a trophy, without exception, I find myself shedding a tear as I think about my dad and how much I wish he was sitting beside me to share this moment. To make it even more special. To see him look into the eyes of my kids and think, "I started this." Whilst that dagger pierced, as it always did, this was a different kind of sadness. For those of us of a certain vintage, that 'Celtic sixth-sense' was already kicking in. As we watched Martin and his backroom staff take a final, emotional walk around the Hampden track, the Irishman's hand in the air in acknowledgement of the outpouring of love and support, there was that horrible, ominous feeling that something very special was ending. The era of Larsson, Sutton and Hartson taking on Europe's finest defenders, of 6-2 against 'the benchmark' on the day the world changed, of the genius Lubo scoring incredible goals with both feet, and of marching with O'Neill into the Champions League then all the way to Seville, my dad, the veteran of Lisbon, hanging on for a third and last European final. There was a chapter inevitably closing on all of this, Celtic and life as always tied together in an unbreakable bond. There was a feeling of fear and dread in my heart at what next season would bring, in comparison to such magical heights.

It would take time before I was ready to contemplate the future with real positivity.

With enthusiasm.

To understand and remember that Celtic FC has previous, in terms of recovering from major setbacks to go in search of new glories.

We idolise the great legends of the past, enjoy the stars of the present then await the emergence of the next generation, those who will thrill us and leave their own mark for the supporters of the future. The Celtic rite of passage, on the pitch, just as it is with the support.

There would be a time for reflection, as we regrouped and re-organised post-O'Neill.

Then it would be a time for new heroes as, once again, we willed those wearing the green-and-white Hoops of our beloved Celtic to make new memories and take on that history, to remain the dominant force in Scotland in the third millennium.

CHAPTER 1

A rather surprising Gordon for us

Although the departure of Martin O'Neill was widely expected, the name repeatedly being touted as his replacement was something of a surprise to many of us. None of the usual boxes could be ticked. Gordon Strachan had neither played for nor been connected to Celtic prior to his announcement as the next manager of the club. Conversely, for many years he had been a thorn in our side, a figure who created antagonism within elements of the Celtic support, which on a couple of occasions strayed into the unacceptable. However, that could all have been very different but for some twists of fate.

Rejecting overtures from both Hibernian - his boyhood club - and Manchester United, Strachan made his debut for Dundee as a substitute in a Drybrough Cup victory over Raith Rovers at Dens Park in July 1973. He then missed out in midweek, as the Dark Blues were beaten 4-0 by champions Celtic in the semi-final of the pre-season brewery-sponsored tournament, returning from the bench at Firhill in a League Cup sectional match two weeks later, still just 16-years-old, as the visitors ran out 3-0 winners.

He would remain on the periphery as Dundee went all the way to Hampden that December, where they would face a Celtic side playing in their tenth successive League Cup Final, albeit having lost the previous three. The game dredges up some miserable memories for those of us Celts unfortunate enough to have shivered in the 'crowd' of under 28,000 - a record low for the event at the time - but remains a red-letter day for those of a Dark Blue persuasion. Horrendous weather and playing conditions combined with a grey, sparsely-populated stadium, lunchtime kick-off and the general depression surrounding 'three-day-week Britain' to make this the most surreal cup final I ever witnessed. A late Gordon Wallace goal gave Dundee a deserved victory, their first trophy since the League Championship of 1962 and their last major success to this day. For the Celtic faithful, now four-time losers in a tournament we were winning for fun just a few years previously, the sight of Lisbon hero Tommy Gemmell, now the Dundee captain, rather sheepishly holding the League Cup aloft at the end, as we prepared to shuffle home and cancel Christmas, pretty much summed up our day.

Whilst the teenage Strachan would struggle to make his first-team breakthrough at Dundee over the next 18 months, he was earning rave reviews in the second-string, twice voted Scottish Reserve Player of the Year. His time duly arrived in the early part of the 1975/76 season, as the new 10-club Scottish Premier League got underway. Missing from the Dens side who once again lost 4-0 away to Celtic, in the second week of the new season as Bobby Lennox hit the first Hoops hat-trick of the SPL era and Jackie McNamara Senior scored a rare goal, he was a regular by the time the sides met again in early November. A late goal from Bobby Robinson gave the home side victory, as Strachan excelled. Whilst his career was on the up, it was a different story for Celtic. It was a long drive home on the road and the miles from Dundee, as we contemplated how things had changed in less than 12 months.

In December 1974, I had sat in the main stand at Dens Park, watching in awe as Jinky and Kenny terrorised the Dark Blues, both running riot in a 6-0 victory. A few yards away, Rod Stewart was falling in love with Celtic, his most enduring relationship. The fans were belting out the old Pilot hit, 'Magic', signifying the inevitable march to 10-in-a-row. It was a great time to be alive. All was as it should be.

Then 'La Decima' never arrived, as the title was inexplicably lost. The Scottish Cup *was* won, however, even that was tinged with sadness, as Billy McNeill called time on his wonderful career. Some of the old guard followed. Jimmy Johnstone, released just six months after that virtuoso performance in Dundee, and the late Jim Brogan, who retired. Then two who left before their time, Steve Murray succumbing to injury and the incredible George Connelly to personal pressures. Worst of all, we very nearly lost Jock, the legendary Celtic manager involved in a serious road accident in July, which left him fighting for his life. Football was temporarily put into some perspective whilst we dealt with that.

The performances of the talented, diminutive redhead Strachan on the right flank for Dundee were drawing inevitable comparisons with Jimmy Johnstone. There were strong rumours that he was on the radar of Sean Fallon, managing the Parkhead first team whilst Stein recovered from his injuries. Gordon did actually manage to wear the Hoops, on the first day of December 1975 at Dens Park, just three weeks after that Robinson goal had given his Dundee side victory over Celtic at the same venue. Long-serving full-back Bobby Wilson had been granted a testimonial and, as was often the case, Celtic were invited to provide the opposition. Technically, it was a Celtic select, with current stars Harry Hood and Paul Wilson lining up beside former Bhoys Tommy Gemmell, Billy McNeill, Davie Hay and Bertie Auld, together with a couple of guest players who would later represent Celtic with very different results, Pat Stanton and Frank Munro. Thomson Allan, Dundee's Scottish international goalkeeper, was between the sticks for Celtic, as his young team-mate Strachan made his one and only appearance in the Hoops from the bench. The 'home side' won 5-1.

Gordon Strachan made an impressive 31 League starts that season, scoring six goals. He made his Celtic Park debut on 3 January 1976, just two days after a first-half Derek Johnstone header had ruined my first visit to Ibrox. Celts had recovered well from an Andy Lynch own goal against Dundee to lead 3-1 early in the second half, thanks to the dynamic duo of Deans and Dalglish, the latter with a double, however, the relegation-haunted visitors responded with two goals from Wilson Hoggan and Dave McIntosh to inflict yet more damage on Celtic. It was Strachan's corner-kick which set up the late equaliser, the little redhead's display described as 'outstanding' in the following day's *Sunday Mail*.

20

The fourth and final meeting of the clubs that season took place at Dens Park on Saturday, 20 March 1976. Three days earlier, Celtic, with the 'adopted' Roy Aitken in tow, had lost in East Germany to Sachsenring Zwickau in the quarter-final of the European Cup-Winners' Cup. The Dundee game was made memorable for being the Hoops debut of Johnny Doyle, signed earlier that week from Ayr United in a club-record £90,000 deal. I recall being under the covered enclosure opposite the main stand as the teams ran out that afternoon, a friend of my dad stating that "we had signed the new Jinky," before being roundly scorned for such sacrilege. Sadly, Johnny's boyhood dream lasted only half-an-hour, the late winger carried off after one crunching Dundee tackle too many.

Few, if any, would have been aware of another contender for such a compliment sitting in the home dugout, where he would remain for the rest of the afternoon, an unused substitute as a solitary goal from King Kenny provided some relief for the under-pressure Fallon. There would be no such respite forthcoming for Davie White, the former Ibrox manager now in charge of Dundee. Despite the three points gained at Celtic's expense in those two earlier matches, White's season would end in bitter disappointment as the Dens men finished agonisingly just below the safety line, level on the 32-point mark with both Aberdeen and city rivals Dundee United, only to be relegated with bottom club St. Johnstone on the final day, due to an inferior goal difference.

There would be no visits to Celtic Park the following season, as Strachan and Dundee adapted to life in the new 14-club First Division. However, they did face the Hoops at Hampden, in the semi-final of the Scottish Cup, after a thrilling run which included victory at Pittodrie on a night which would have life-changing implications for the young midfielder. That ride would come to an end in Mount Florida, two late goals from Joe Craig pointing Celts towards Jock Stein's final Double, the following month.

There were many other positives in a season which saw the Dark Blues hit 90 League goals across the imbalanced 33 fixtures, including 36 from top-scorer Billy Pirie and eight from Gordon Strachan. Dundee could consider themselves unfortunate to face the two outstanding teams in the Division - Alex Ferguson's exciting young St Mirren colts and a Davie Cooper-inspired Clydebank - twice away from home. Nevertheless, they contrived to lose all six matches against those sides, ultimately trailing in a distant third to miss out on the craved promotion. That perceived failure would cost manager Davie White his job in May 1977.

Dundee would meet Celtic again in the Scottish Cup in February 1978, a third-round tie at Celtic Park. The 7-1 home victory was a rare highlight in a dismal Hoops season, as the great Jock Stein went out on an unprecedented and undeserved low, however, by that time, Gordon Strachan was no longer at Dens Park. The managerial merry-go-round in May 1977 had involved two of Jock's Lions, Billy McNeill moving from his first managerial post at Clyde to replace new Scotland boss Ally MacLeod at Pittodrie, whilst Dundee skipper Tommy Gemmell moved to the dugout in the wake of White's departure from Dens, the former Celtic legend immediately installing his 19-year-old midfield star as his own successor, by making Strachan the Tayside club's youngest-ever captain.

There was a poignant cameo in the developing career of his protege, as Gemmell brought his friend and fellow Lion Jimmy Johnstone to Dens Park. Despite the Edinburgh-born midfielder's leanings towards Easter Road, 'Jinky' had long been a hero of the schoolboy Strachan. Now he would have the opportunity to play beside and learn from the Celtic icon. Sadly, those teachings would not all be on the field, the two redheads unwittingly but unwisely bumping into Gemmell during a drinking session in the manager's Errol hotel. Johnstone would make only three appearances at Dens, his life and career sadly continuing in a downwards trajectory, whilst his young colleague recovered from both the hangover and the lesson to make his own way in the game.

The new Dundee manager/captain partnership would also have a brief life. Things had become increasingly difficult at Dens Park following the club's relegation from the inaugural Premier League in May 1976, the fiscal situation then exacerbated by Dundee's failure to secure immediate promotion. Gordon Strachan paints a dismal picture of this period in his autobiography, My Life in Football.

"There was nothing remotely glamorous about Dundee Football Club behind the scenes, especially when it ran into serious financial difficulty following relegation. There were fears we would have to go part-time. It was like the footballing equivalent of I'm a Celebrity, Get Me Out of Here. The players' training kit – including our pants – was only washed once a week, on a Friday. After we had trained in it on Tuesday, Wednesday and Thursday, often in terrible conditions, you can imagine what sort of state it was in by the end of the week!"

By October 1977, the club was in crisis. Tommy Gemmell was advised by Dundee chairman Ian Gellatly that £50,000 was required to prevent the bank closing the Dens Park doors by the end of the week. There was only one way that kind of money was coming in so quickly. Tommy picks up the story in his own autobiography, Lionheart.

"Billy [McNeill] *had being doing a bit of sniffing after Gordon but I told him Strachan was not available because I knew that if we won promotion to the Premier Division, he would be able to shine at that level. So, I phoned Billy up, told him the situation at Dundee and said I would sell Strachan to raise the necessary funds but made it clear he would not be getting him for £50,000. He would need a lot more to purchase the player. After some negotiations, we received £85,000 plus Jim Shirra. The money went straight into the bank and Dundee survived to fight another day."*

Timing in football is everything. A few months later, that phone call to Billy would have been picked up in the manager's office at Celtic Park. Instead, McNeill and Mike Jackson, his trusted sidekick from their playing days together at Celtic, made the long journey down from Aberdeen to Dumfries on the evening of Wednesday, 26 October 1977, to watch Gordon Strachan and his Dundee teammates take on Queen of the South in the second leg of their third-round League Cup tie. The teams had drawn a blank at Dens Park three weeks earlier, however, the return match would be a night to forget for those supporting the Dark Blue cause, the Doonhamers running riot in handing Dundee a 6-0 mauling. Nevertheless, McNeill had seen enough to believe the young midfielder could enhance his Dons side and despite continued links with Parkhead, Strachan would be heading up the A90. A 1-1 draw with Hearts three days later would be his Dens Park swansong. After 91 appearances and 51 goals, he was an Aberdeen player, swapping one Lisbon legend for another as he jumped back into the elite League.

The fortunes of Billy McNeill and his former mentor Jock Stein could hardly have been further apart as Gordon Strachan signed up at Pittodrie. Cesar had built impressively on the success achieved by Ally MacLeod the previous season, his Dons team tucked in just two points behind leaders Rangers at the top of the table. In contrast, the defending champions were toiling, Stein's men edging just ahead of the relegation slots after a 3-2 victory over fellow-strugglers Ayr United at Celtic Park. The two sides met at Parkhead just a few weeks later, Celts again edging a five-goal thriller thanks to a late winner from their versatile Icelandic star Johannes Edvaldsson, in front of 27,000 spectators. Strachan actually played in central midfield that afternoon, with Dom Sullivan and Davie Robb on either side of him. The Dons would take their revenge with a Sullivan double in January at Pittodrie, Andy Lynch missing a late spot kick for Celtic with Strachan an unused substitute. And the midfielder remained on the bench at Celtic Park in April, future-Bhoy Sullivan amongst the goals again, scoring the equaliser in a 2-2 draw which kept Aberdeen at the top of the table with just five games remaining. The Dons would ultimately fall just short, two points behind Rangers in the final analysis, the Ibrox side also beating McNeill's young Reds 2-1 in the Scottish Cup Final in May to complete the Treble. It was a disappointing end to a first season in the Granite City for Gordon, who failed to make the Hampden squad.

Cesar's performances in the Pittodrie hotseat had alerted the men in charge at Parkhead, now on the lookout for a successor as Jock Stein's last season as manager of Celtic fell apart. There was one obvious name in the frame when the sad but inevitable parting of the ways took place, Billy McNeill returning to his spiritual home. Gordon Strachan's new boss at Pittodrie would be the volatile but successful Alex Ferguson, who had transformed St Mirren before being sacked, allegedly, for breach of contract. There were suggestions that he had already agreed to join Aberdeen, the club he had reputedly rejected just 12 months earlier. Ferguson did take up the reins at Pittodrie in June 1978, as McNeill settled in at Celtic Park. That season of 1978/79 would ultimately be a disappointing one for Strachan and Aberdeen, whilst Billy would work his magic in Glasgow, as Ten Men Won the League. However, those of us on the buses heading home from the newly all-seated Pittodrie in early October would have required some convincing of those outcomes, having watched Gordon Strachan and Dom Sullivan dominate proceedings in a 4-1 home victory, the return of Cesar and his assistant John Clark quickly turning into one best forgotten.

There was an interesting recollection from Strachan on that 1978 Pittodrie reunion on 23 April 2019, the day the sad news broke that the legendary Lions' captain had passed away the previous night. In my opinion, his comments actually spoke volumes about the character and integrity of both men, even if Gordon's memory of both the score and timing of his first-born son may require some refreshment!

"What does Billy McNeill mean to me? The man changed my life. I mean, I have always believed you make your own way in life but there is no question he was a major contributor to the way mine worked out. He signed me a couple of days after we got beat 6-1 – Dundee versus Queen of the South. Between him and Mike Jackson, they decided to take a chance on me and take me to Aberdeen. From there, when I went to Aberdeen, I was absolutely useless and felt like I was letting him down. I mean I was seriously useless. I was one of those guys who got booed whenever his number came up! But Billy was very strong in the way he supported me, and I have never really been able to shake this feeling I let him down."

"But here's the thing about Billy. He then left Aberdeen for Celtic and the first time we played against them at home we beat them 4-1. But guess who then turned up at my door at six o'clock that night? It was Billy and his wife, Liz, with a gift for my son, Gavin, who had just been born [Current Celtic coach Gavin Strachan was actually born on 23 December 1978, some eleven weeks

later!]. That sticks in my memory more than anything else. Here was a guy who'd just been beaten 4-1, turning up at my house to deliver a present. And, when you consider I hadn't played well for him, it just tells you about the kind of guy you're talking about here. The kind of family you're talking about."

The spoils would be shared in the remaining clashes between the sides that season. There was a goalless draw in December and a 1-0 Celtic win in March, both League games played in Glasgow due to fixture complications, before the teams met again at Pittodrie in the Scottish Cup quarter-final the following week. Gordon Strachan was a key figure as the match finished 1-1, however, on this occasion it was for his defensive heroics, the little midfielder twice heading goal-bound Johannes Edvaldsson efforts off the line to keep his side in the cup. Strangely, he was missing for the ill-tempered replay four days later, the Dons scoring twice in the opening 12 minutes following Peter Latchford errors to reach the last four. Strachan's boyhood team Hibernian would then end Aberdeen's hopes of Scottish Cup glory in the semi-final at Hampden the following month with a 2-1 win.

There had been heartbreak for Gordon at the National Stadium just a few weeks before that semi-final defeat, as he took his place in the Aberdeen side against Rangers in the League Cup Final on the last day of March 1979. Early in the second half, he provided the cross for Duncan Davidson to nod the Dons in front, and things were looking good for his first senior trophy. However, it all fell apart in the last 15 minutes. Firstly, a shot from Alex MacDonald was deflected out of the reach of goalkeeper Bobby Clark to level the match. Then, as the clock ticked down, Aberdeen centre-half Doug Rougvie was given his marching orders by referee Ian Foote after a joust with Rangers striker Derek Johnstone. The 10-man Pittodrie side bravely held on until the dying seconds before veteran defender Colin Jackson looped his header over Clark to keep the cup at Ibrox.

The final League clash that season between Aberdeen and Celtic, played at Pittodrie three weeks later, saw Gordon Strachan score his first goal against the Hoops, the little midfielder knocking the ball home at the far post from a Dom Sullivan cross to give the Dons the lead. Andy Lynch equalised with a penalty before the interval, as Celts picked up the point which kept them marginally ahead of Aberdeen in third place, just one point behind defending champions Rangers but trailing leaders Dundee United by a less-than-magnificent seven. Remarkably, Cesar's Celts would storm through the remaining eight games to eventually snatch the title in glorious style with *that* 4-2 win over Rangers, whilst the Dons retained their fourth spot. But their time was coming.

Having broken his scoring duck against Celtic, Gordon Strachan would spend the next few seasons inflicting pain on the Hoops support, as he developed into one of the finest midfield players in Europe. The 1979/80 season saw both clubs in a dogfight for the major Scottish honours. The first meeting took place at Pittodrie in September, dramatically described in the next day's *Sunday Mail* as the 'game of shame.' Strachan had looked miles offside as he gave the home side the lead within two minutes, the Hoops' sense of injustice apparent as Tommy Burns was sent off on the half-hour for a ridiculous and out-of-character challenge on his fellow redhead, something which I am sure would be the subject of conversation in another, later chapter of their lives. Playing with 10 men, a goal down and away from home to their nearest challengers, all looked lost. However, just as they had done on that memorable night the previous May, Celts turned it around. Roy Aitken equalised before half-time, The Bear the first in the posse of Hoops to react after Bobby Clark had saved Murdo MacLeod's spot kick. The veteran Dons keeper then made a hash of a throw-out, which was intercepted by the ever-alert Bobby Lennox and quickly dispatched to Johnny Doyle, who gleefully won the match for Celtic.

Aberdeen took an early opportunity for revenge the following month, a Halloween hat-trick from Steve Archibald, a player ironically signed from Clyde by Billy McNeill whilst Dons boss, giving them a slender 3-2 advantage to take to Celtic Park for the second leg of their League Cup semi-final. This time it was the Hoops who had scored in the opening minutes, through Johannes Edvaldsson, a superb late free-kick from Davie Provan giving Celts genuine hope of reaching the final after the blond Dons striker had claimed the match ball. Severe weather conditions then delayed the return until the end of November, the game kicking off late to allow almost 40,000 fans to pack into the old ground. Despite dominating possession and providing the bulk of the attacking play, Celtic were suckered five minutes after the break, the goal having a real 'future Celt' connection. Gordon Strachan's corner was headed back by defender Willie Garner, for substitute Mark McGhee to open his own Parkhead scoring account and knock the Bhoys out of the League Cup.

Two weeks later, Strachan and Aberdeen lined up at Hampden for their second League Cup Final in that calendar year of 1979. This time the opponents were Jim McLean's Dundee United, in the first tangible sign that the long-discussed 'threat to the established order' from the North-East had arrived. Just over 27,000 were inside the National Stadium for the first game, beating the unwelcome record for the lowest attendance at this fixture set by Dundee and Celtic six years earlier. The match finished goalless, for once the powers-that-be then displaying some common sense by fixing the midweek replay for Dens Park. A 29,000 crowd created an excellent atmosphere for the players to thrive on, United rising to the occasion by winning 3-0, the Tangerines thus claiming their first-ever major trophy on the home ground of their neighbours and fiercest rivals. There is nothing quite like football for throwing up a story like that.

Three weeks into the new decade, Aberdeen and Celtic fought out a goalless draw at Pittodrie, the hard-earned point ensuring the Bhoys remained four clear of Morton at the top of the Premier League. The scheduled November clash at Parkhead had been postponed, allowing the League Cup semi-final second leg tie between the clubs at the same venue to take precedence, meaning that the Pittodrie side still had to visit Glasgow's East End twice before the end of the season. These games would be critical in determining the eventual destination of the League flag and they would both take place within 18 days in April. Over 40,000 basked in the sunshine at Celtic Park on the afternoon of Saturday, 5 April 1980, most hoping that the Bhoys would extend their seven-point lead over the Dons and take another giant step towards the successful defence of their title. Billy McNeill's men had bounced back from a crushing 3-0 defeat to Real Madrid in the Estadio Santiago Bernabeu in mid-March, by scoring five goals without reply against Hibernian and Rangers, the latter thanks to a late header from new record signing Frank McGarvey. With the title challengers locked at 1-1, Drew Jarvie's early opener cancelled by a Johnny Doyle header shortly afterwards, two decisive second-half moments settled the game, allowing the first signs of nerves to creep into the Celtic psyche. Firstly, Mark McGhee put the Dons in front for the second time from close-range, then, 10 minutes later, Bobby Lennox, the last of the Lisbon Lions, in the final weeks of his wonderful two-decade Celtic career, had a glorious chance to equalise from the spot, after McGarvey had been fouled in the box. Sadly, Bobby's effort was weak, Aberdeen goalkeeper Clark making up for his initial error by pulling off a save which would have huge implications by the season's end as the Dons held out for a crucial 2-1 win. Alex Ferguson's Aberdeen were now just five points behind with a game in hand.

Celts had suffered two crushing defeats in Dundee, 3-0 at Tannadice then, incredibly, 5-1 at Dens Park, by the time Aberdeen next rolled up to Parkhead, on the evening of Wednesday, 23 April 1980. The Dons were now just two points behind Celtic with that match still up their sleeve. The pressure was on. Big time. The crowd matched the occasion, 48,000 in the house for the most important game of the season. The early sparring produced a goal apiece, George McCluskey's penalty cancelling out Steve Archibald's opener, with Gordon Strachan then missing an opportunity from the spot as Peter Latchford produced perhaps his only positive contribution on the night. The turning point came on the half-time whistle, Mark McGhee yet again breaking Celtic hearts as he nodded home, and on the hour-mark, his partner-in-crime, Strachan added a killer third, as the Dons went to the top of the table for the first time, albeit on goal difference. As we suspected then, it was a lead they would not relinquish.

On Saturday, 3 May 1980, the title was finally won or conceded, depending on your viewpoint. The scheduled final-day fixtures had not been kind to Celtic. They were away to a St Mirren side enjoying their finest League season that century, eventually finishing third. In contrast, former Love Street manager Alex Ferguson's Aberdeen simply required a win at Easter Road against already-relegated Hibernian to claim a first Scottish League Championship in 25 years, and only a second ever title. The sides were level on 46 points going into the games that afternoon, with Aberdeen ahead by four goals and having a midweek fixture against Partick Thistle at Firhill still to play, a welcome safety net should things not go to plan in Leith. It would not be required. As Celts drew a rare blank in Paisley, the Dons won 5-0 to become Scottish champions, the first club outside Glasgow to do so for 15 years, since the against-the-odds triumph of Willie Waddell's vintage '65 Kilmarnock at Tynecastle.

Six years to the day, another 5-0 final-day victory, this time *by* Celtic at Love Street, would produce an extraordinary chapter in the Bhoys' own incredible history. For now, though, the power base would temporarily transfer north. It was a first senior honour for the 23-year-old Gordon Strachan and would quickly be followed by his international call-up for Scotland in Belfast, then a prestigious personal award, as he was voted the Scottish Football Writers' Association Player of the Year. These would be the first of many such accolades for Gordon over the coming years.

Season 1980/81 was a largely frustrating one for Strachan, despite signing a new four-year deal at Pittodrie which reflected his status as the creative spark of the Scottish champions. He was troubled with a stomach injury, causing him to miss the second-half of the campaign. He did feature in the first clash between Aberdeen and Celtic, a 2-2 League draw at Pittodrie in September, as the Dons came back from two goals down to salvage a point in the final 20 minutes. Earlier in the game, Charlie Nicholas, Celtic's latest young star, had created a club record by scoring in his ninth successive match.

Gordon probably wishes he had been somewhere else when the sides next came together, at Celtic Park in early November, three days after the Pittodrie side's first-ever European Cup campaign had come to an end at the hands of eventual winners Liverpool at Anfield. Aberdeen were a Walker McCall goal in front early in the second half, when a spectator ran from the 'Jungle' enclosure and knocked him to the ground, the intruder then lashing out at several policemen before being arrested. The game continued after this appalling incident, a second strike from the beanpole Dons striker soon afterwards sealing the two points for the defending champions and a miserable day all round for Celts.

There was a third match between the sides at Pittodrie two days after Christmas, perhaps Strachan's finest hour against Celtic. The little maestro was unstoppable, setting up three Aberdeen goals before making it 4-0 himself from the spot with 20 minutes remaining. A late Charlie Nicholas counter was scant consolation as we trudged towards the convoy of supporters' buses for the long journey home, convinced that our title hopes had disappeared for another season, Celts three points behind the Dons having played one game more. However, as the song suggests, 'night is darkest just before the dawn.'

Aberdeen's midfield dynamo had succumbed to a muscle-tear by the time the Dons visited Celtic Park for the final meeting of the title contenders in late March 1981. A tremendous run since the December defeat at Pittodrie had earned the Bhoys an eight-point advantage with just seven League games to play. It was a must-win for the visitors, chasing a sixth consecutive victory at Parkhead. Andy Harrow's strike in the opening quarter provided some hope for the Red Army contingent within the 35,000 crowd, however, the game turned with the introduction of George McCluskey for Charlie Nicholas midway through the second half. Firstly, George teased Willie Miller into a desperate challenge which resulted in the award of a Celtic penalty, Murdo MacLeod's effort being saved by Dons' keeper Jim Leighton to further frustrate the huge home support. Then with just five minutes remaining, McCluskey beat the Scotland stopper with a superb flick, after some Davie Provan wing magic, to make it 1-1. He was then controversially denied a last-gasp winner by the linesman's flag, a decision that could tactfully be described as harsh at best. Whilst two points would have all but wrapped up the flag, Cesar's Celts would not look back, reclaiming their championship crown at Tannadice on a memorable Wednesday night with a 3-2 victory just three weeks later.

31

Season 1981/82 would see the battle between the two title rivals go all the way to the wire. Sadly, the aggression was not confined to the players, Gordon Strachan attacked for a second time in this fixture as the teams met at Pittodrie in September. He had just put his side in front from the spot in the second minute, Tommy Burns then heading a quick equaliser before Frank McGarvey struck either side of the interval in a thrilling 3-1 Celtic win. That dynamic Hoops form was carried into the second League clash, at Parkhead in early November. This time the obligatory Strachan strike came in the final minute, by which time Celtic were two goals ahead, courtesy of tremendous efforts from Frank McGarvey and George McCluskey. Whilst the win would ultimately be crucial in terms of flag retention, this was also a huge result psychologically for Celtic, providing a first home victory over the Dons in eight attempts, spanning a painful 20-month period.

The next meeting of the sides, at Pittodrie in January 1982, saw the arrival of another incredible young Celtic talent on the big stage. The previous week, 17-year-old Paul McStay had made his senior Hoops debut in a 4-0 Scottish Cup win over Queen of the South at Celtic Park, a game also memorable for the 'JFK moment' of a goal from Daniel Fergus McGrain. Seven days later, he was thrown into the cauldron in the Granite City, emerging with honours with a debut League goal, Celtic's third in another 3-1 win at the home of their closest challengers. George McCluskey and Murdo MacLeod had earlier cancelled out a first-minute opener from John McMaster. Looking back now, it was quite remarkable how often that Pittodrie fixture between the clubs produced an early goal. In fairness, none of those goals were scored earlier than that by John Hewitt at Fir Park on 23 January 1982, the day of young McStay's debut at Celtic Park. The Aberdeen striker notched the only goal of the Scottish Cup-tie against Motherwell in an incredible 9.6 seconds, the fastest in the competition's long history, the ball hitting the net before the legendary Jamaican sprinter Usain Bolt would reach the 100m tape. Hewitt would repeat his scoring feat three weeks later, against champions Celtic in the next round at Pittodrie, albeit dragging his heels until the 19th minute before hooking the ball past Pat Bonner for the only goal.

Gordon Strachan's Dons would then march all the way to the 1982 Scottish Cup Final, where they faced holders Rangers. With the game level at 1-1 after 90 minutes, the Scotland midfielder came alive, setting up Mark McGhee for 2-1 before accepting his return gift for a tap-in third. He then sent Neale Cooper through to make it 4-1, as Aberdeen won the old trophy for the first time since that infamous Robert Holley Davidson episode of May 1970, sadly my first personal Hampden cup final experience. They would not have quite so long to wait for a repeat success.

Back in the bread-and-butter of the Scottish Premier League, the Dons had kept the title race alive with a somewhat fortunate victory over Celtic at Parkhead in March 1982, a Stuart Kennedy cross drifting over stranded Irishman Pat Bonner to drop into the net, after he had received a short corner from Gordon Strachan. Minutes later, Jim Leighton saved yet another Celtic penalty attempt, this time from George McCluskey, as Aberdeen held out for a first League win in three over the reigning Scottish champions. This cut their deficit to four points, as we entered the final furlong. Dropped points at Greenock and Tannadice, then at home to St Mirren, meant that lead had been reduced to just two points as the final set of League fixtures was played out on Saturday, 15 May 1982. Just as they had been two years earlier, the Paisley side were Celtic's last-day opponents, albeit this time in the east end of Glasgow, having drawn 0-0 there just 12 days previously on a wet Bank Holiday Monday as the opportunity to clinch the title went a-begging following a nervous home display. The following Saturday, a 3-0 defeat at Tannadice sparked terror amongst the Hoops support, recalling an identical scenario in 1980 which had ultimately cost us our flag. It couldn't happen again, could it?

To add to the intrigue, closest challengers Aberdeen would face Rangers at Pittodrie, the Ibrox side trailing hopelessly in third place and making noises about resting key players ahead of their Scottish Cup Final meeting with the Dons at Hampden the following week. Conspiracy theories abounded as to exactly how the points and goal difference swing would come about. As Alex Ferguson himself often quoted, it was 'squeaky-bum time' as the big day beckoned. Aberdeen required to win by five goals and for Celtic to drop something against St Mirren. Whilst that may have appeared to have been a bit of a stretch at kick-off, by half-time it was most definitely on the cards. Celts had struggled to break down a stubborn Paisley defence and a storm of booing erupted from the 40,000 crowd as news came through that the Dons were already 4-0 ahead at Pittodrie. Finally, two of the stars of Celtic's season came to the fore after the interval, Tommy Burns and George McCluskey twice combining brilliantly for the striker to fire the Hoops ahead then clinch the game and the title at 3-0, a Tom McAdam header just about crossing the line between those two strikes, as the party started in the Jungle around me. Amongst the celebrations, there was yet another example of that extra-special bond between fans and players, as the late Johnny Doyle was remembered. The Jungle rose as one as the chant rang out, *'We won the League for Doyle, oh yes we won the League for Doyle.'* It was a poignant Celtic moment.

The popular 'Celtic-daft' winger had tragically died whilst working in his Kilmarnock home the previous October. He was only 30-years-old. He had been on the bench at Tannadice on that memorable night in April 1981, celebrating like a fan as goals from Murdo MacLeod, Frank McGarvey and Tommy Burns clinched a title that had been all over bar the shouting after a sublime Charlie Nicholas winner at Ibrox, four days earlier. Doyle had then found it increasingly difficult to secure a first-team slot in an attack consisting of some frightening firepower, the chosen three normally some combination of Davie Provan, McGarvey, Nicholas and George McCluskey. Against those odds, still he refused offers to move on from his beloved Celtic, rejecting approaches from Motherwell and Hearts amongst others. I always felt that tragic as his untimely death was, there was something so right about the fact that he left this world as Johnny Doyle of Celtic. Rest in peace, Johnny, a man who lived his dream…and ours.

You may recall that Doyle had made his Celtic debut back in March 1976 at Dens Park, as a young Gordon Strachan cooled his heels in the home dugout. Whilst the now-Aberdeen midfielder would not witness the Parkhead championship party, no doubt facing the famous 'Fergie Hairdryer' after his side's failure to wrest the championship from Celtic, the football fates would conspire to send him 200 yards along Tannadice Street some 26 years later. On that occasion, he would be managing his Celtic side to another emotional title, as Tommy Burns, the star performer of that 1981/82 campaign, was in every hooped heart and thought as Jan Vennegoor of Hesselink's header secured an unlikely three-in-a-row for Strachan's Bhoys. The much-loved Burns, by now a first-team coach at Celtic, had succumbed to illness on 15 May 2008, just seven days earlier, still only 51-years-old. From my corner seat above the Tannadice tunnel that Thursday evening - the Scottish League season having been unusually extended to accommodate Rangers' European run – I watched on as the little Scot walked around the ground, bedecked like his players in a white T-shirt depicting Tommy in his iconic 'praying' image, taking in the sights and sounds of the massed Celtic ranks. If ever there was a moment when someone 'got' our club, it was Gordon Strachan that night, as we thought about Tommy Burns and his former friend and team-mate, Phil O'Donnell, who had tragically collapsed and died at Fir Park the previous December whilst playing for Motherwell against, ironically enough, Dundee United. Two great Celts and, more importantly, two lovely men, both sadly missed. *'They never die who live in the hearts of those they leave behind.'*

Whilst the 1982 League Championship had ultimately alluded him, it had been a fine return from injury for Gordon Strachan, a Scottish Cup-winner, the top-scoring player at Pittodrie with 20 goals overall and a key figure in Jock Stein's Scotland side, heading for the Costa del Sol to take on the Brazilians in the World Cup that summer. I often reflected back then that a side composed of Aberdeen's defence and Celtic's attacking players, with McGrain and Strachan retaining their own positions, would have been well-nigh unbeatable in Europe in the early 1980's. Forty years or so later, it is a view I stand by.

Strachan would continue to inspire Aberdeen and inflict damage on Celtic for two final seasons. The 1982/83 campaign would see the Dons soar to new heights, as Europe got the message about the new kid in town. Having eliminated holders Ipswich Town from the UEFA Cup the previous autumn, before falling to German giants SV Hamburg, who would become European champions the following season, hopes were high in the Granite City that their boys could do well in the Cup-Winners' Cup. Those hopes were not misplaced. Memorable victories over European aristocrats Bayern Munich and Real Madrid saw the Dons lift the trophy in Gothenburg on 11 May 1983, a first continental success for the club.

Domestically there were mixed outcomes. Attempts to win a first League Cup of the Alex Ferguson era had begun well, Gordon Strachan's return to Dens Park when he scored four of Aberdeen's goals in a 5-1 rout being an early highlight. But defeat in both quarter-final legs against Fergie's nemesis, Jim McLean, meant that would have to wait for another year. It would remain the one trophy to elude both manager and star player in those respective careers. Celtic would beat United in the two-legged semi-final before seeing off Rangers at Hampden in the Rain in December to claim a first League Cup success in eight long years, a wonderful 57th birthday gift for my dad.

The Premier League race of 1982/83 was unforgettable, as three tremendous sides jostled for the right to be crowned champions. Aberdeen's campaign had started with defeat at Tannadice, although they later took retribution with a 5-1 victory over Jim McLean's men in November, thanks to a ruthless exhibition from Gordon Strachan. Likewise, the Dons had claimed a 3-1 victory at Parkhead in October, the customary Strachan and Mark McGhee goals in there, of course, together with Danny McGrain's only red card in senior football, before losing 2-1 to Celtic at Pittodrie just before Christmas, the late Neale Cooper infamously taking out Charlie Nicholas three seconds after the kick-off! Dundee United and Celtic shared four goals at Tannadice in October, just a few days after both had enjoyed wonderful victories in the Netherlands, defeating PSV Eindhoven and Ajax respectively. These were heady times.

And so it would continue, into the new year. Strachan remained on the bench as Ferguson opted for power rather than guile at Parkhead in February 1983, Eric Black hitting the first visiting hat-trick there in 15 years to cancel out Charlie Nicholas' opener, his 36th goal of a magical season, in front of 43,000 spectators. By winning 3-1, the Dons had removed Celtic from the Premier League summit for the first time in two years, as the Race for the Flag intensified.

April was the crunch month, Celtic facing two games against each of their title rivals. And it started well, a 2-0 home victory over Dundee United sending the Hoops three points clear of both sides with just six games remaining in the quest for three-in-a-row, albeit Aberdeen still had a game in hand. Ten days later, the Bhoys met Aberdeen in the semi-final of the Scottish Cup at Hampden. The Dons had surprisingly lost at Ibrox the previous week, to seriously undermine their title bid, however, they received a pre-match boost with the news that both 46-goal Nicholas and inspirational skipper Danny McGrain would be missing from the Celtic team. The match was settled in controversial fashion, the on-form Black clearly handling the ball before crossing for Peter Weir to head the only goal. Things then got even worse for Celtic in midweek, against Dundee United in a re-arranged fixture at Parkhead. Tied at 2-2 as the end of the match drew close and playing against 10-men – Richard Gough dismissed after a clash with Davie Provan - Celts only had to see out the match to retain their advantage. Then Ralph Milne lobbed the ball over Pat Bonner and suddenly the Tayside men were back in the title race.

Three days later, Gordon Strachan excelled as Mark McGhee scored the only goal to defeat Celtic at Pittodrie, reviving the Dons' own challenge whilst, crucially, enabling United to edge one point clear of the Hoops at the summit, with just three games to play. The teams then remained nip and tuck until the final day, the third time in four years that the SPL title race had gone right to the wire.

The Scottish Fixture Gods had done their job well once again as the three top teams in the country awaited their fate on Saturday, 14 May 1983. Title favourites Dundee United would have to travel just 200 yards along Tannadice Street to face neighbours Dundee at Dens Park, scene of their only two major trophy triumphs in a 60-year history, the League Cups of 1979 and 1980 won against Gordon Strachan's former and current sides. The Arabs would certainly not get it easy there.

Celtic too had a city derby, a visit to Ibrox where they had broken a 62-year hoodoo in January, goals from Paul McStay and Charlie Nicholas producing a first Celts win there in the traditional Ne'erday fixture since 1921. The speculation around Charlie's future had been intense for months now. The smart money said that this would be his last appearance in the famous green-and-white Hoops.

Aberdeen had been the only one to blink in the final run-in, dropping a point in a goalless midweek draw at Easter Road. Remarkably, they would face the same side on the last day, just as they had on that glorious occasion for them three years earlier, this time at home. The Dons were level on points with Celtic - with an inferior goal difference – and one behind United, and would go into the final day as outsiders, requiring both Celtic and Dundee United to slip up to lay claim to a third Scottish crown.

Celtic's task was more straightforward. Achieve a better result at Ibrox than the Tannadice side could secure at Dens Park and a third consecutive flag would be flying proudly above the Jungle in August, for the first time since Jock Stein's great team of the late 1960s and early 1970's.

The objective for Jim McLean's young team was even clearer. Simply match the results of the others for the title. And they set about their task with relish, Ralph Milne's delicious chip, fit to win a championship in itself, was followed by Eamonn Bannon's penalty rebound, putting United two goals up within 10 minutes. Ian Ferguson pulled a goal back for a defiant Dundee on the half-hour, however, with one more home strike required to take the race to a title decider, unprecedented in the modern era, Dundee United would hold on at 2-1 to become Scottish Champions for the first time.

At Ibrox, Billy McNeill's Celtic side had emerged from the interval two deflected goals down to a sea of green-and-white and an incredible version of *'You'll never walk alone'* from three sides of the stadium, a spine-tingling moment for those of us who witnessed that. And it worked, goals from Tom McAdam and Frank McGarvey, book-ended by two spot-kick conversions from the departing Charlie Nicholas, turning the game around completely. There was a brief moment of hope, as word spread in the Broomloan Road Stand that Dundee had equalised. I will never understand the folk who do this, or why. Sadly, but predictably, it was a false alarm, and our title fate was known long before Charlie said goodbye with his parting penalty goal for a most bittersweet 4-2 victory.

Three days after their Gothenburg glory, Aberdeen had produced another sparkling display, defeating Hibernian by the traditional final-day 5-0 at a packed Pittodrie, Gordon Strachan on target again for his second successive 20-goal season. Any sense of Dons disappointment would be banished the following Saturday, a solitary Eric Black strike enough for Aberdeen to beat Rangers in extra-time in the Scottish Cup final for the second successive season, bringing the trophy back to the Granite City. One man was disappointed, Alex Ferguson famously slaughtering his players live on TV for their poor performance, surely a first for a cup-winning manager. Yes, 1982/83 would be a difficult act to follow.

As Gordon Strachan prepared for one final assault on the Scottish footballing community, there were major changes taking place at Celtic Park. As expected, Charlie Nicholas had gone, surprisingly and in my view erroneously, to Arsenal rather than the English champions Liverpool. Sadly, Billy McNeill had also headed south, in his case to Manchester City, citing 'differences' with the Parkhead board. His replacement would be David Hay, who had enjoyed success in his first managerial post at Motherwell, winning the Scottish First Division title the previous season before heading to the USA. Cesar had won three titles in five seasons, whilst agonisingly losing the two others on the final day to two of the best teams Scotland has ever produced. He had also won a Scottish Cup and a League Cup, his sides playing some of the best attacking football I would witness in more than 50 years following the club. I had grown up with his team and, like most supporters, I could relate to them. Billy would be greatly missed.

Aberdeen and Celtic clashed for the first time in the David Hay era at Pittodrie in October 1983. The Dons were already two goals to the good when Gordon Strachan stepped up to take yet another penalty against Pat Bonner, this time the Irishman denying him with a brilliant save. Two minutes later, there was a second chance for the Dons talisman from the spot, and this time he made no mistake to finish the match as a contest at 3-0. Job done, Strachan was replaced minutes later by Neil Simpson, Roy Aitken's late consolation strike then making it 3-1.

The sides met again at Celtic Park in December, just three days after Brian Clough's Nottingham Forest had counter-attacked Hay's Hoops out of the UEFA Cup, winning 2-1 in front of 67,000 mostly-disappointed supporters. In contrast, the Dons had achieved an excellent goalless draw against European champions SV Hamburg in Germany, in the first leg of their European Super Cup tie. They would win the return leg and the trophy at Pittodrie by 2-0. Aberdeen produced a similar defensive performance in Glasgow, Celts lacking that creative spark to prise them open as again the match finished 0-0, with new signing Jim Melrose dismissed late on for using an elbow on Doug Rougvie.

The third League fixture of the season took place in early February 1984 at Pittodrie, yours truly posted missing as I was involved in a different type of match back in Glasgow. My 'best man' brother thought it would be a good laugh to present a signed photograph from Alex Ferguson and his squad as part of his speech. Sadly, the joke was on us, Gordon Strachan setting up John Hewitt for the only goal of the game, the Dons thus moving six points clear at the top and Celtic's flag hopes already looking distinctly forlorn. The boys from the Cairn CSC made for a sorry sight as they filed into the Renfrew hotel evening reception on their return from the long and fruitless trip north.

There was an early opportunity for revenge, as the sides clashed again at the same venue just three weeks later, in the first leg of their League Cup semi-final. This time the much-maligned Celtic defence held firm, the Bhoys dominating the game after Gordon Strachan had smacked the crossbar in the opening minutes and unlucky only to return with a 0-0 draw. There were over 41,000 fans packed in for the decider, played a fortnight later, at Celtic Park. The game of few chances was decided early in the second half, Tommy Burns chopped down and Mark Reid dispatching the spot kick expertly past Jim Leighton, as Aberdeen's hopes of a first-ever Treble were crushed in the east end of Glasgow. The Double was very much on though. The last day of March 1984 saw the teams meet again in the final League clash at Celtic Park, a paltry 19,000 crowd perhaps reflecting the home support's view of our fading title challenge. Melrose scored the game's only goal in the first half, a second successive 1-0 home victory over the Dons being merely a temporary blip in their march to the Premier flag.

There would be one more clash between Aberdeen and Celtic before Gordon Strachan left Pittodrie. Almost fittingly, the great rivalry would be contested at Hampden in the final of the Scottish Cup. The Dons were massive favourites, having finished seven points clear of Hay's Celts in the League. But this was the Scottish Cup. Our Cup. The Hoops were already trailing to a controversial Eric Black opener when the pivotal moment of the final occurred, just before half-time. Roy Aitken charged in on Mark McGhee, referee Bob Valentine, with not a little help from the chirping Strachan, eventually sending the big defender for the proverbial 'early bath,' the first player to suffer that fate in the season's showpiece in 55 years. It was the harshest of calls, however, Valentine had previous. Two months earlier, the Dundee official had awarded Rangers not one but two debatable penalty kicks as they won a five-goal thriller against Celtic to lift the League Cup, in David Hay's first cup final as Celtic manager.

As the 1984 Scottish Cup final edged towards its conclusion, there was a sting in the tail from the 10-man Celts, Paul McStay rifling the ball home at the far end to take the match unexpectedly into extra-time. Despite that brief stay of execution, the last word would go to the two players who had caused so much damage to Celtic over the preceding seven years. In the 98th-minute, Gordon Strachan picked the ball up on the left and floated in a cross which Pat Bonner fatally misjudged, leaving

Mark McGhee free to rifle home the winner. As the seconds ticked down on both the final and Strachan's playing career north of the border, there was a final defiant shot from the little redhead, which crashed back off the Irishman's bar, before the famous old cup was handed to Willie Miller for an impressive third consecutive season. It would signal the end of an incredible era for Gordon Strachan at Aberdeen.

Mark McGhee had impressed SV Hamburg sufficiently in their four recent meetings for the Bundesliga giants to offer him a lucrative contract, the powerful striker beginning a new life in Germany. He should have been joined there by his good friend Gordon Strachan, a deal apparently agreed between Aberdeen and 1FC Koln for the transfer of Scotland's talented playmaker, however, that would not come to pass. Out of left-field, Manchester United manager Ron Atkinson came in for him at the eleventh hour and, after a protracted struggle, the midfielder duly signed up at Old Trafford instead.

I recall thinking that it would be great to see the back of the pair of them, particularly Gordon Strachan, who through a combination of great skill, countless goals and a general tendency to 'wind us up' had not endeared himself to the Celtic support over a number of years. Grudging respect comes to mind.

But as the late Jimmy Greaves used to say, "football is a funny old game sometimes."

Mark McGhee would spend less than 18 months in northern Germany before returning to Scotland in November 1985…to sign for David Hay at Celtic! He would be part of Hay's title-winning side at the end of that first season in the Miracle on Love Street, then taste success again under the returning Cesar as a Centenary Bhoy in that never-to-be-forgotten League and Cup Double of spring 1988.

And on Wednesday, 1 June 2005, 21 years after leaving Aberdeen to progress his career south of the border, his friend Gordon Strachan became the 14th person chosen to manage Celtic Football Club.

CHAPTER 2

The long and winding road to Paradise

Despite almost 30 years of involvement in top-flight football, first in Scotland then south of the border, the appointment of Gordon Strachan as Celtic manager would surely represent the toughest challenge of his career. Following his move from Aberdeen in the summer of 1984, he had enjoyed success at the end of his first season at Old Trafford, part of the first-ever FA Cup-winning team comprising entirely of senior international players. Norman Whiteside's glorious curling effort in extra-time had beaten Neville Southall to deny Howard Kendall's Everton an unique treble. Three nights earlier, on Wednesday, 15 May 1985, the new English champions had defeated Rapid Vienna 3-1 in Rotterdam, to win their first European trophy, the Cup-Winners' Cup. There was a banner memorably displayed in the De Kuip for the watching viewers, proclaiming 'Celtic should have been here!', reflecting the infamous events involving the Austrians the previous winter in both Glasgow and Manchester.

David Hay's side had bounced back from a 3-1 first-leg defeat in Vienna to win by three clear goals at Celtic Park, only to find that an appeal by the Austrian side to have the Bhoys punished for a missile-throwing incident had been upheld, a complete about-turn from UEFA, who had initially punished Rapid for an assault on Tommy Burns by one of its players, Reinhard Kienast. The match was ordered to be replayed more than 100 miles from Celtic Park, with Old Trafford, now Gordon Strachan's home ground, the preferred choice of the Parkhead club. Thus, on Wednesday, 12 December 1984, the biggest movement of Celtic supporters outside

Scotland to that point headed for Manchester, over 51,000 turning the stadium into an absolute cauldron, the likes of which I have never since witnessed.

Just opposite me, to the left of the current players' tunnel, a small section of Manchester United fans cheered and booed throughout the evening, out of alignment with the on-field action. They were tuned into a UEFA Cup second-leg tie involving the two United's at Tannadice, the sides having drawn 2-2 at Old Trafford two weeks earlier. Gordon Strachan would return to a ground which had not been kind to him as an Aberdeen player, to set up all three goals as the English side edged a five-goal thriller to qualify. Celtic would then become the second Scottish side to exit Europe that icy night, doing so amidst disgraceful scenes, as two Rapid players were, this time, genuinely attacked on the pitch. The football was almost incidental, the match turning in a critical 60 seconds early on, Roy Aitken's shot crashing off the crossbar only for Peter Pacult to race the length of the field to score the only goal of the game. In addition to our hard-earned and prized reputation, it would cost Celtic a second European campaign the following autumn, an excellent 1-1 away draw with Atletico Madrid negated by a 2-1 home defeat at a closed-doors Parkhead a fortnight later, a sanction imposed as a consequence of the events in Manchester in December 1984. It had been a bitter experience in every sense for Celtic.

Neither Manchester United nor Everton would be competing in Europe that 1985/86 season, following the Heysel tragedy of Wednesday, 29 May 1985, as English clubs commenced a five-year ban from UEFA competitions imposed after events surrounding the European Cup Final between Liverpool and Juventus in Brussels. Gordon Strachan's next continental appearance would actually be in the white of United's Yorkshire rivals Leeds United, seven years later, in the autumn of 1992. He had moved there in March 1989, a little over two years after his old Pittodrie boss Alex Ferguson replaced Ron Atkinson as the manager of Manchester United. By all accounts the pair had not parted Aberdeen on good terms back in 1984, Ferguson accusing the player of going behind his back to sign a pre-contract deal with 1FC Koln, and their earlier Scottish success was not replicated in a disappointing, trophyless period for both. It was therefore no huge surprise when Strachan left Old Trafford, however, his next destination raised a few eyebrows. Rejecting an approach from former 'gaffer' Atkinson to join Sheffield Wednesday, he accepted an offer from Howard Wilkinson to become the pivot for his plans to resurrect the fortunes of Leeds, then an ailing Second Division club. He was immediately installed as captain at Elland Road.

The move paid instant dividends, Leeds winning the title to return to the top-tier after an eight-year absence. They then finished a lofty fourth in the First Division the following season, their Scottish skipper picking up the Football Writers' Player of the Year award, thus becoming the first man to win it on both sides of the border. The success story continued in 1991/92, Gordon Strachan leading Leeds United to the last-ever English First Division championship crown at the age of 35, the Yorkshire side, perhaps ironically, finishing four points clear of Alex Ferguson's Red Devils. He also enjoyed an Indian Summer with his international career, the veteran of the 1982 and 1986 World Cups making the last of his 50 appearances for Scotland against Finland at Hampden, in March 1992.

Ferguson would have his revenge at the end of the next season, Manchester United winning the new, rebranded FA Premier League in 1992/93, a first English title for Old Trafford since the Best, Law and Charlton era of 1967, whilst Leeds plummeted to 17th in the table, just two points ahead of relegated Crystal Palace, having sold Eric Cantona to their bitter rivals in the decade's most bizarre transfer.

Europe was also a disappointment for Gordon that season. Leeds United's return to the continent's premier competition, 17 years since losing the 1975 final to Bayern Munich in Paris, saw them pitched with the current German champions, VfB Stuttgart. A 4-1 Elland Road win saw them eliminated on away goals, only to be reinstated after it was discovered that the Bundesliga side had fielded a fourth (and therefore ineligible) foreign player as a substitute. That game was then awarded as a 3-0 Leeds win, thus equalling the first-leg victory of the hosts in Bavaria and meaning a deciding match would be required. It was played in the Camp Nou, in front of only 7,000 spectators, Strachan scoring the third and decisive goal of the game in the surreal atmosphere of the giant, empty bowl. In the next round, they would face Rangers, and despite an early Gary McAllister strike at Ibrox, Leeds contrived to lose both games to miss out on the inaugural Champions League group stage. This time there would be no reprieve. That would prove to be Gordon's last involvement as a player in continental competition.

There was one last hurrah for Strachan in Yorkshire, as he led his side back up the table to finish fifth in 1993/94. However, he then fell out of the first team picture the following season, accepting an offer from old boss Ron Atkinson to become his assistant and eventual successor at Coventry City in March 1995. With Gordon also remaining in a playing role, his new club would finish just above the relegation slots a few weeks later and would again cling onto their Premier status the following year, albeit only just, seven goals better off than - almost unbelievable to consider today - Manchester City. With Coventry back in the drop-zone again in November 1996, the planned succession kicked in a few months early, Strachan taking the hotseat whilst Atkinson moved upstairs to a Director of Football role. Recently-sacked Hibernian boss Alex Miller came in as assistant manager, whilst skipper Gary McAllister had followed his new manager's path earlier in the season, moving to Coventry from Leeds.

The Scottish duo would lead the Sky Blues to yet another great escape in May 1997, finishing a single point ahead of relegated Sunderland, after an incredible late winning run which included unlikely victories at Anfield, White Hart Lane and at home to Chelsea, whilst their closest rivals faltered. Even with those results, Coventry only survived due to a three-point deduction imposed on Middlesbrough for a late fixture cancellation. Future Celtic striker Dion Dublin scored in all three of those games, including an injury-time winner in Liverpool, whilst his manager made history against a Stamford Bridge side featuring another soon-to-be Celt, Craig Burley, and current Scotland manager, Steve Clarke. At 40 years and 59 days, Gordon Strachan became the oldest outfield player to start an English Premier League match. His renowned 'bananas and yoghurt' diet had enabled him to play well beyond the normal career expectancy of his fellow top-flight footballers. He had come a long way from the naïve teenager caught having had one too many with Jimmy Johnstone all those years ago, whilst the pair were team-mates under Tommy Gemmell at Dundee.

In addition to Dublin, Strachan's spell at Coventry saw him play with or manage several other players who would later join him at Celtic. Steven Pressley left Highfield Road for Dundee United in July 1995, whilst Jonathan Gould, the back-up keeper to Steve Ogrizovic, joined Bradford City on a free transfer at the end of that campaign and midfielder Paul Telfer, signed from Luton Town for £1.15m at the start of the 1995/96 season, linked up with Gordon as he would at several other clubs in the future. Telfer would gain his only full international cap whilst under the Scot's regime at Coventry, appearing against France at Hampden in March 2000. Four years earlier, on 8 April 1996, he had been replaced by former Aberdeen striker Eoin Jess, a recent £2m signing, at Old Trafford, on the day that Sky Blues' defender Dave Busst suffered the worst leg injury I have ever seen. Some three years later, I watched in Lyon as Henrik Larsson suffered what appeared to be a similar break on the wet turf of the Stade Gerland. Fate would treat both differently. Whilst Celtic's King of Kings made a full recovery, and would actually go on to even greater things, sadly the unfortunate Busst would never play football again.

Alex Miller was influential in bringing his former Hibernian star Michael O'Neill to Highfield Road in the close season of 1996. The Portadown man would spend two years there, making only a handful of appearances. Twenty years later, he and Strachan would be colleagues as international managers on opposite sides of the Irish Sea. O'Neill was heavily tipped to succeed Gordon as Scotland manager in 2018, however, he chose to stay in Ireland. Strachan's former Pittodrie team-mate Alex McLeish was then appointed to the Hampden post, for what would prove to be a brief and rather cruel tenure. Miller himself only remained in the Number

2 role at Coventry for 12 months, replacing former Celtic captain Roy Aitken as the manager of Aberdeen in November 1997. Following an unsuccessful year at Pittodrie, rather bizarrely he re-appeared at Anfield in 1999 as Director of Scouting, enjoying triple cup success under Gerard Houllier in 2001 - having linked up again there with Gary McAllister - before sampling Champions League and FA Cup glory on the coaching staff under Rafael Benitez.

Alex Miller's departure from Coventry would see the start of Gordon Strachan's working partnership with former Birmingham City and West Bromwich Albion defender Garry Pendrey. Whilst the two men share a birthday - Pendrey the elder by eight years - the origins of the friendship are less clear. Pendrey was certainly moving in West Midlands coaching circles in the late 1980's, working at Walsall and Wolverhampton Wanderers before returning to his former St Andrew's stomping ground as manager. He would be Strachan's new right-hand man at Highfield Road, a relationship which would continue all the way to the East End of Glasgow and beyond.

Swedish international goalkeeper Magnus Hedman joined Coventry City on a free transfer from AIK Solna in July 1997, as Eoin Jess headed back to Aberdeen for one third of his original purchase fee. Hedman spent five seasons at the club, before joining Martin O'Neill's Scandinavian colony at Celtic in August 2002. One of Gordon Strachan's youth prospects at Highfield Road had also, inadvertently, played his way into the Celtic story. Craig Faulconbridge spent much of 1998 on loan to Dunfermline Athletic, scoring only one goal in his two spells at the Fife club. It was a significant goal though. His looping header for the Pars in the 83rd minute at East End Park on Sunday, 3 May 1998 meant that Simon Donnelly's first-half strike would not clinch Celtic's first League title in a decade as Wim Jansen's exciting side sought to preserve Jock Stein's precious legacy. It also ruined the family party we were enjoying on my godson's 15th birthday. Instead, we would have to endure another five days of torture then Pampers Saturday, before Henrik and Harald scored against St Johnstone to stop the dreaded 10.

Donnelly's fellow Hoops striker Darren Jackson had been dropped by Jansen for the Dunfermline clash, following a goalless draw with his former side Hibernian at Celtic Park the previous week. He would be literally 'sent to Coventry' during 1998/99, making three League appearances on loan under Gordon Strachan at Highfield Road. Jackson's days at Celtic were by this time numbered, the former Scotland internationalist eventually signing for his boyhood idols Hearts in March 1999.

Two other Coventry City youth players of the time were rather better-known to the manager, his sons Gavin and Craig. The younger, Craig, managed just a single League appearance and no goals in four seasons at Highfield Road. Gavin, the elder of the pair, would make 16 League appearances in six seasons with the Sky Blues, 11 from the bench. He scored once, in a League Cup tie against Preston North End at Deepdale in September 2000, the goal coming from the penalty spot like so many of his father's. He enjoyed his best spell of form at Coventry around 1998/99, leading to eight international appearances at Under 21 level for Scotland, and whilst he would not follow his father all the way to the senior set-up, he would emulate him by playing for Dundee. Gavin commenced a four-month loan spell at his dad's old Dens Park haunt in January 1999, featuring nine times, although he remained on the bench throughout Dundee's visit to Celtic Park on Saturday, 3 April 1999, as the Hoops supporters enjoyed watching the early fruits of a promising Henrik Larsson /Mark Viduka strike partnership, both on target in a 5-0 win.

There was a brief one-month spell at Motherwell under his dad's former Aberdeen colleague Eric Black in February 2002, before Gavin met up with Peterborough United manager Barry Fry for the first time, the Posh securing his services in March 2003 on loan until the end of the season. He would return to London Road in January 2007, following a successful spell at Hartlepool United, teaming up this time with the current Peterborough manager, Darren Ferguson, son of Alex, his dad's old Aberdeen and Manchester United boss! On Friday, 13 July 2007,

Gavin was a second-half substitute as a Celtic side featuring Italians Massimo Donati and Andrea Capone beat Peterborough United 2-1 at London Road in a pre-season friendly. In the opposite dugout to Ferguson junior was Strachan senior, Gavin's dad Gordon, now the Parkhead club's manager. Such is the small and crazy world of professional football.

The junior Strachan and Ferguson would pair up again after Gavin's playing career had ended, the former commencing his coaching career with the youths at Peterborough then working his way up to a first-team role under Darren before following him to Doncaster Rovers as his assistant manager in October 2015. The duo left the Keepmoat Stadium in June 2018 before returning yet again to Peterborough in January of the following year, with Barry Fry now director of football at London Road. In June 2020, Gavin Strachan left the Posh to join yet another of his father's former clubs, as first team coach under Neil Lennon at Celtic Park, following the departure of Damian Duff for family reasons.

Back at Coventry City, Gordon Strachan had broken the club's transfer record to bring teenager Robbie Keane in from Wolves for £6m in August 1999. The Irish striker had a successful season at Coventry, before moving to Inter Milan for a mouth-watering £13m the following July. The cash windfall allowed Strachan to secure the services of two Welsh hitmen who would also light up Parkhead in years to come, Craig Bellamy arriving from Norwich for £6.5m in August then John Hartson moving from Wimbledon on a 'pay for play' deal in February 2001, having lost out on moves to a number of other clubs due to concerns about his fitness. Hartson would prove the doubters wrong, scoring six goals in 12 League games there before moving to Celtic for £6m in August 2001, where he would hit more than a century of goals in five trophy-laden years in Paradise. Six weeks earlier, Bellamy had moved from Coventry to Newcastle United for the same fee.

Despite such attacking firepower, and after numerous close shaves, Coventry City finally succumbed to relegation in May 2001. It was the end of a reign in the English top-flight going back to the summer of Lisbon 1967, and a first demotion of any kind for the Sky Blues since 1958. The writing would be on the wall for the Scottish redhead, in his first managerial role. In September 2001, five games into the new season, having achieved only a solitary win and with the West Midlands club hovering just above the relegation slots in the second-tier, Gordon Strachan was sacked as Coventry City manager.

He would not be unemployed for long. On 1 October 2001, Gordon was appointed as the new manager of Southampton, replacing Stuart Gray who had only been in the role himself for six months. The south-coast club, like Celtic, had their roots in the parish of St Mary's and had recently moved from The Dell into a beautiful new stadium in that area of the city, the first game taking place there on 1 August 2001. They were struggling badly in the Premier League drop-zone when the Scot took over.

Legendary skipper Matt Le Tissier was in the final season of a glorious one-club, 16-year career. At the other end of the age spectrum, an 18-year-old striker from Melbourne was trying to make his way in the game. Scott McDonald would make just one first-team start before heading out to Huddersfield Town then Bournemouth on loan. After a brief spell at Wimbledon in 2003, he joined Motherwell in January of the following year. Fate would then place him in the Celtic penalty-box at Fir Park on Black Sunday, 22 May 2005. My stomach still sinks at the very thought of that dreadful day.

Gordon Strachan's first two signings for Southampton were both from his previous club. Paul Telfer followed his boss on a free transfer from Coventry City in October 2001, within weeks of the manager's appointment. Midfielder Telfer would spend the next four seasons at St Mary's, re-inventing himself as a right-back. Defender Paul Williams had been at Highfield Road for the full six-year Strachan tenure. He arrived in the same month, initially on loan, before signing up for the next two campaigns. Both would reach the 30-appearance mark as the Saints finished a mid-table 11th, Telfer scoring the final goal of the season in a 3-1 home win over Newcastle United.

Gordon would inspire Southampton to an eighth-place finish in 2002/03, their highest-ever in the Premier League. This was complemented by a run all the way to the FA Cup Final, as the little Scot's current stock soared. Arsene Wenger's Arsenal would edge the final in Cardiff's Millennium Stadium, the first to be played 'indoors' as the rain came down, with a Robert Pires goal late in the first half, after a shot from future-Celt Freddie Ljungberg had been blocked. Another player who would later arrive in Glasgow's east end, Kolo Toure, watched the action unfold from the Gunners' bench. As Arsenal had already qualified for European football through their second-place Premier League finish, FA Cup runners-up Southampton would book a place in the 2003/04 UEFA Cup, just four days before Celtic would agonisingly lose out to Jose Mourinho's Porto in Seville in the current season's finale. It would mean a first continental appearance for the south-coast club since 3 October 1984, when they exited the same competition in the first round at the hands of SV Hamburg. On the same evening that Celtic were disposing of Belgians KAA Gent by 3-0 at Celtic Park to set up their ill-fated clashes with Rapid Vienna, the Bundesliga side's new striker, a certain Mark McGhee, scored the last-minute goal in the Volksparkstadion which would end Saints' participation in Europe for the next two decades.

Strachan's initial taste of European football as a manager coincided with the first such game to be played in Southampton's St Mary's Stadium, on 24 September 2003. Their opponents were former European Cup winners Steaua Bucharest, English goal-machine Kevin Phillips equalising for Saints after Claudiu Raducanu's early strike had given the Romanians the lead. Three weeks later, Radacanu notched the only goal of the game in Bucharest to confirm Steaua's progress to the next round, where they would lose out to Gerard Houllier's Liverpool. It would be another 12 years before Southampton players would have the opportunity to compete at this level again, although their manager would be testing himself against Europe's elite within two seasons elsewhere.

The 2003/04 domestic season had also been a disappointing one for Southampton, the club slipping four places to finish 12th in the Premier League, with early exits in both cup competitions. Stephen Crainey had joined the Saints from Celtic on 6 February 2004, although he would move on to Leeds United at the end of the campaign, having made just five League starts. The Kirkintilloch-born left-sided defender was briefly reacquainted with two familiar faces from the Scottish game, former Hearts and Rangers pair Antti Niemi and Neil McCann, who were both on the books at St Mary's at that time. There was also some fantastic potential in the Southampton youth squad, with emerging talents such as Nathan Dyer, Adam Lallana, Theo Walcott and Gareth Bale all looking to make inroads to the club's first team set-up. The big news came just seven days after Crainey's arrival, on 13 February 2004, as Gordon Strachan resigned as the manager of Southampton. The change had been brewing for a few weeks, after the club had issued the following statement on 9 January 2004;

"In keeping with our philosophy of open and transparent management of our club, it is with some sadness that Southampton Football Club has decided not to extend [Gordon Strachan's] contract with us beyond the end of this season. A new contract has been under discussion for some time now, but Gordon has decided that, for medical and other personal reasons, he needs a break from the demands and pressures that are associated with being a Premier League football manager."

There was praise forthcoming from the top, as the Saints' chairman Rupert Lowe added;

"Gordon's enthusiasm and commitment have inspired everybody, and the club has moved forward during a crucial period after leaving The Dell and moving to St Mary's Stadium. He has assured me that he will give 110% for the balance of this season, in order to capitalise on our current position in the League. Our fans will be sad to see a man, whose passion matched theirs, taking time out of the game."

Whilst those internal conversations had agreed on a parting at the end of the current season, the 'official leaking' of the news by the club brought about the change much earlier. There was much speculation that Glenn Hoddle would be invited to return to the post he had vacated in March 2001. However, his departure had been acrimonious, the former England star having 'upped and left' to join his boyhood favourites Tottenham

Hotspur. The situation quickly became untenable for all concerned and, perhaps ironically, on Friday, 13 February 2004, Gordon Strachan said goodbye to his players at St Mary's and left the club for the last time.

The official Southampton statement read as follows;

"Gordon Strachan has today parted company with Southampton Football Club after two and a half years at the helm. The Scottish manager was a hugely popular figure on the south coast and will be dearly missed by the players, everyone at the club and fans alike. After news of his intentions to resign at the end of the season was leaked to the press in January, the situation has become increasingly difficult and a decision was reached yesterday that it would be in the best interests of all parties for Gordon to step down with immediate effect."

Strachan himself continued that narrative.

"This is a truly great club with a truly great squad of professionals. It is with regret that I am leaving for my own reasons. Steve Wigley will do a first-class job until the end of the season and I fully support that appointment."

Gordon's endorsement of Steve Wigley would come as no surprise to those 'in the know' at the club. The former Academy Director had been promoted to work with the first team by the Scot a couple of years earlier. His name would be familiar to Celtic supporters of a certain vintage, as a winger in Brian Clough's Nottingham Forest side who defeated David Hay's Hoops in the UEFA Cup back in the winter of 1983. Wigley's initial tenure at St Mary's would be much briefer than anticipated, Strachan's old Tannadice adversary and Scotland colleague Paul Sturrock replacing him after just two games. He would then have a second bite at the Saints' cherry, when Sturrock's reign ended after just five months following rumours of significant unrest amongst the Southampton players. But it would not work out. Wigley managed only one win in 14 games and was gone by Christmas, with Harry Redknapp moving along the south coast from Southampton's bitter rivals Portsmouth to take over at St Mary's.

The upheaval at the club, with four managerial changes in the calendar year 2004, would have grave repercussions for Southampton. They went into the last League game of the 2004/05 season knowing that a victory over Manchester United at St Mary's would guarantee their survival in the Premier League, however, they would then face their own Black Sunday on 15 May 2005, seven days before Celtic's visit to Motherwell. Despite taking a fortunate early lead through a John O'Shea own goal, following good work by ex-Celt Henri Camara, strikes from Darren Fletcher and Ruud van Nistelrooy either side of the interval consigned Saints to their first relegation in 27 years.

Just two weeks after seeing his old club drop out of the English top-flight, Gordon Strachan was back in football as manager of Celtic. The Scot had honoured a promise made to his family in 2002, two years before he left Southampton, to see out his contract then take a break to address a long-standing hip problem and pursue 'other things.' The rumour mill on the south coast had expedited that planned parting, allowing him to enjoy a 15-month sabbatical from managing in top-class professional football. But now he was back and what a task he had inherited. The five-year tenure of Martin O'Neill had not just delivered on the dreams of one of the world's best-supported football clubs, it had taken them to unimaginable new levels, particularly over those first four, wonderful seasons.

Rangers' owner David Murray had adopted a spending policy which to outsiders looking in bordered on reckless, the madness peaking with the £12m paid to Chelsea for Tore Andre Flo in November 2000. The Norwegian striker had moved to London for just £300,000 three years earlier, with 70 of his 163 appearances for the Stamford Bridge side coming from the bench. His 50 goals scored over that period were hardly a guarantee of the kind of success which would even begin to justify that outlay. I always suspected that the huge fee paid was more about making a statement, about backing up his infamous "for every fiver Celtic spend, we'll spend ten" remark. The £12m transfer fee for Flo remains a record amount paid by a Scottish club, more than two decades later, however, history will record Murray's approach as unaffordable, unsustainable and ultimately fatal.

In the Dutchman Dick Advocaat, who had replaced Walter Smith in the

Ibrox dugout in 1998, after 'the 10' had thankfully been stopped, Murray had a willing shopping partner. £4m-plus fees became the order of the day, as a succession of expensively-acquired players arrived in Govan over his 30-month tenure; Arthur Numan, Gabriel Amato, Henrik's pal Giovanni van Bronckhorst, Andrei Kanchelskis, Colin Hendry, Stephane Guivarc'h, Michael Mols, Bert Konterman, Fernando Ricksen, Ronald de Boer, and of course, with the stakes now raised to unprecedented levels, Tore Andre Flo.

Smith, Advocaat's predecessor, had also benefitted from the Ibrox owner's perceived benevolence, with millions shelled out for Duncan Ferguson, Paul Gascoigne, Jorg Albertz, Sebastian Rozental, Lorenzo Amoruso, Sergio Porrini and Marco Negri over the previous few seasons. It was a staggering financial outlay, the likes of which Scottish football had never witnessed. It would appear to have all been done in pursuit of Murray's stated dream, to make Rangers a force in European football, as the Govan club's greatest rivals had been for a decade from the mid-sixties, culminating in that glorious night in Lisbon on 25 May 1967. It was a dream he would fail to realise with disastrous consequences. In contrast, Martin O'Neill would quickly identify his high-profile targets, spending early then enjoying the fruits of Celtic's investment over the proceeding seasons, as the trophies rolled into Parkhead.

Advocaat's previously unassailable advantage had been brushed aside in the early part of that first season, 2000/01, the 6-2 mauling of Rangers at Celtic Park in August presenting the first signs that a new dominant force had arrived in Scottish football, as this time the Parkhead cheque book secured the talent demanded by the Irishman. In from England's top-flight came £6m men Chris Sutton and Neil Lennon and the magical left foot of Alan Thompson, to bolster the stars already in place, Henrik Larsson, Lubo Moravcik, Paul Lambert, Johan Mjallby and Stiliyan Petrov. Henrik's 53 goals jet-propelled O'Neill's Celtic to their first domestic treble since Jock Stein's wonderful summer of'69, as the crucial balance of power in Glasgow and Scotland swung dramatically to the east.

The following season saw a Celtic title successfully defended for the first time in 20 years, since Gordon Strachan's Aberdeen had looked on helplessly in May 1982 as their 4-0 defeat of Rangers at Pittodrie failed to stop George McCluskey and Tommy Burns winning the final-day battle of nerves and a second successive championship against St Mirren at Celtic Park. A third £6m Celtic signing, John Hartson, arrived from another of Strachan's old clubs, Coventry City, in August 2001, one of a trio of new recruits purchased as the Bhoys were beating Alex Ferguson's English champions Manchester United 4-3 on their own Old Trafford backyard in Ryan Giggs' testimonial, in front of 20,000 travelling Hoops fans. Midfielders Mo Sylla and Steve Guppy had committed their future to Celtic that same afternoon.

Year three of the Martin O'Neill masterplan saw the bittersweet irony of a blank domestic campaign sitting side-by-side with The Road to Seville, an incredible roller-coaster of emotions illustrated by that day at Rugby Park, when Kilmarnock goalkeeper Gordon Marshall produced a display few of us could recall from his time at Parkhead. Sadly, this would not be a one-off where Marshall was concerned, we would be shaking our collective heads again in a similar scenario in Lanarkshire just two years later. On that final day of 2003 League action, Celtic would actually be in the title driving seat well into the second half, before a missed penalty by Alan Thompson and a soft, last-gasp Mikel Arteta spot-kick for Rangers against Jimmy Calderwood's insipid Dunfermline Athletic saw the championship head for Govan, the agonising two-goal swing preventing three-in-a-row for O'Neill's Celtic. But the memories of Seville will last a lifetime and there would always be next year to reclaim our domestic silverware.

Season 2003/04 would see tears in Paradise once again, albeit this time for a different reason. After seven magnificent years, the King of Kings Larsson would be leaving Glasgow to seek a new challenge. The double was comfortably regained, with only a controversial decision in the League Cup Final against Rangers - a valid John Hartson goal inexplicably ruled offside - preventing progress towards a second treble for Martin O'Neill. Henrik would strike twice in his last competitive game, the Scottish Cup

Final at Hampden against Dunfermline Athletic, to yet again turn a critical match Celtic's way. A few nights later, amidst a sea of emotion, 60,000 disciples packed into Parkhead to say goodbye to a modern-day Hoops icon, for a benefit game with, rather cruelly in the circumstances, Spain's Sevilla.

Martin O'Neill's final season at Celtic would be defined by two critical and, on the face of it, unrelated events, which both took place in May 2005. Whilst he still possessed two superb strikers in Chris Sutton and John Hartson, attempts were made to fill the vacuum left by the Swedish superstar in the summer of 2004. Senegalese international Henri Camara seemed a strange choice for that particular challenge. He had arrived from relegated Wolverhampton Wanderers in a season-long deal, reputedly costing Celtic £1.5m. Camara had no real track record as a prolific goalscorer, however, he vowed to replace Henrik Larsson, requesting the legendary Swede's iconic number seven shirt, wearing which he promised to deliver. He was given the number 27 jersey to wear and, perhaps predictably, the talk exceeded his performance, the African striker managing just eight goals in 26 forgettable appearances before being shipped out to Southampton in January for another loan spell. As mentioned previously, at St Mary's he would face a second successive English demotion in May 2005. Camara then narrowly avoided a hat-trick of Premier League relegations in four years at his next club Wigan Athletic in 2007, having enjoyed an encouraging first season in Lancashire. Sadly, his club career would then peter out through a series of short-term contracts in England, followed by no fewer than eight spells with various Greek sides. In fairness, Henri's international record makes for much better reading, with a very respectable 29 goals in his 99 appearances for Senegal.

Whilst Camara had missed out on it, Henrik Larsson's Celtic number seven shirt was allocated in August 2004, and I have to admit that I felt that we had found the perfect fit in every sense. Brazilian playmaker Juninho Paulista arrived at Parkhead that month, having established a tremendous reputation at Middlesbrough, where he would later be voted their greatest-ever player, our 'Jinky' if you like. He had won both the

Copa Libertadores and World Club Championship with Sao Paolo in his native country before heading for the riches of the English Premier League with unfashionable Boro in 1995. An immediate hit with the fans on Teesside, following Middlesbrough's relegation two years later he moved to Atletico Madrid for £13m, in an attempt to secure a spot in Brazil's World Cup squad for France '98. Sadly, he suffered a devastating leg-break in a challenge with Celta Vigo's Michel Salgado in February 1998, a subsequent six-month spell on the sidelines putting paid to that ambition.

Having enjoyed a loan spell back at Middlesbrough during his five-year stint at the Vicente Calderon, Juninho signed up again permanently at the Riverside Stadium in the summer of 2002, just weeks after winning the World Cup with Brazil in Japan. This time around, the transfer fee involved was £6m. His third period at Boro saw the club lift its only major silverware to date, the 2003/04 League Cup, with a 2-1 victory over Bolton Wanderers in Cardiff, having earlier knocked out Tottenham Hotspur then English Double-winners Arsenal in the last four, with Juninho on target at Highbury. He would later memorably describe that League Cup victory as being better than winning the World Cup.

Six months after the Cardiff triumph, Juninho was heading to Glasgow to join the Martin O'Neill revolution at Celtic. On the face of it he was an ideal signing, an exciting Brazilian World Cup-winner on the back of an excellent season in the English top-flight, where he had won silverware and top-scored for his club. His Celtic Park debut against Rangers on 29 August 2004 did nothing to dispel that feeling, the little South American excelling on the right of midfield. The game was settled in Celtic's favour with just five minutes remaining, Juninho's left-wing colleague Alan Thompson hitting an unbelievable shot, the ball swerving and dipping past Stefan Klos to explode in his net for an incredible winner. It was a goal any one of those magical Brazilian players over the years would have been proud to have claimed as his own.

There was a poignant evening on the same ground the following month, when both old and new Celtic number seven's lined up against one another, as Henrik arrived in town with his new club Barcelona for a Champions League Group Stage clash, his first European game for the Catalans. Well, strictly speaking, they did not face each other that evening on the pitch. Juninho was replaced by Chris Sutton with Celts one goal-down at the interval, the big Englishman transforming the attacking performance and grabbing an equaliser, whilst his old sparring partner Larsson came off the bench later in the half to replace another Brazilian, the incredible Ronaldinho, before breaking our hearts again by scoring Barcelona's third in a 3-1 win following a mistake by Alan Thompson, meaning that Celtic had lost a Champions League tie at home for the first time. That goal also created a rather unusual pub quiz question, as the great Swede ensured that both his first and last goals at Celtic Park would be against the same opposition – Celtic! He had scored an own goal against Tirol Innsbruck back in August 1997.

Juninho's arrival at Celtic also saw the addition of a new term to the Scottish football vocabulary, Employee Benefit Trust, normally shortened to EBT. The Celtic chairman in 2004 was Brian Quinn, a former Deputy Governor with the Bank of England. On being made aware of the existence of an EBT element in Juninho's contract, where part of his income was paid into a trust fund rather than directly through his salary, Quinn sought guidance from HMRC to ensure that Celtic remained within both tax and football governance rules. The response prompted Quinn and Celtic to pay the amount due in full, thus avoiding any potential issue at a later date. It would prove to be a prudent move by the chairman.

Both Juninho and Henri Camara were on the scoresheet at Celtic Park in October 2004, as a Hearts side featuring the infamous 'Riccarton Three' of Steven Pressley, Craig Gordon and Paul Hartley, all of whom would later sign for the Hoops, were defeated 3-0. It would prove to be the Brazilian's only Celtic goal. After just 14 starts, he left Glasgow in April 2005, heading back to Sao Paulo and Palmeiras on a Bosman transfer. Almost 20 years down the line, it remains a huge source of both mystery and disappointment to me as to why that particular transfer did not work out.

60

Martin O'Neill then made a third attempt at signing a new Celtic hero to replace Henrik Larsson, when he brought in Craig Bellamy on loan from Newcastle United on 31 January 2005. Like Juninho, Bellamy made his debut against Rangers at Celtic Park, on 20 February, a blunder from Hoops keeper Robert Douglas allowing Frenchman Gregory Vignal to put the Ibrox side ahead. Spaniard Nacho Novo would add a late second goal as Celts lost this fixture for the first time in 11 meetings. It would prove to be an extremely costly three points to have conceded, when the tally was done at the end of the season.

Despite that disappointing start, the fiery Welshman was a huge hit at Celtic, tearing up the opposition with his lightning pace and finishing technique. Bellamy hit a stunning hat-trick at Tannadice in a 3-2 win in March 2005 to send the Hoops back to the top of the League, then the following month he curled in a glorious second goal at Ibrox as Celts won 2-1 to virtually ensure the title would remain in the east end of Glasgow. With just four games now remaining, Celtic were a healthy five points clear. It was surely all over bar the shouting.

Craig Bellamy had limped off early in the second half at Ibrox, holding his problem hamstring, and he was still missing from the line-up the following Saturday when Hibernian visited Celtic Park. As more than 58,000 expectant supporters turned up to cheer the Hoops on towards another championship, the Leith club decided to rewrite the script. Home substitute Craig Beattie had equalised an early Garry O'Connor goal before Ivan Sproule fired Hibs ahead with just 11 minutes to play. Nineteen-year-old Scott Brown then introduced himself to the Celtic fans by lobbing David Marshall for a late third. The euphoria from the previous week was suddenly replaced by anxiety, as our one lifeline was conceded.

Natural order was restored by two successive wins against Aberdeen and Hearts, as Celtic recovered from the Hibs hiccup to put themselves one victory from the flag. Two goals from top-scorer John Hartson saw off the Dons, with just under 60,000 packed into Celtic Park, then Craig Bellamy returned at Tynecastle, a late Craig Beattie strike sealing a crucial 2-1 Hoops win. I remember letting out a huge roar of relief as I listened to that goal being scored on the BBC Radio commentary. I really felt that was the goal which would seal the title. O'Neill's Celtic now led by two points going into the final game.

Now comes the hard part.

The events of Sunday, 22 May 2005 will haunt me forever.

I have never felt so low as a Celtic supporter.

Not watching the dream of 10 disappear as a 14-year-old schoolboy back in 1975.

Or even witnessing Jock Stein's horrendous final season in 1977/78, as we lost our Kenny...then Pat Stanton...then the previously indestructible Danny...then the plot, to finish out of the European slots.

Or the pain of watching us toil against English Second Division side Burnley in the Anglo-Scottish Cup the following season, then seeing our hard-won reputation smeared following events at Turf Moor.

Not even the Bob Valentine League Cup Final of March 1984 or the injustice of Rapid Vienna later the same year. Hell, not even the pain of enduring *that* nine-in-a row in Govan felt like this.

Desperate stuff.

I had been struggling badly for away tickets that season and Fir Park, Motherwell was no exception. My local, the Cross Keys in Milngavie, a 'mixed' shop, had been turned over to the Rangers regulars for the day, as the local publicans sensibly put their heads together to achieve a compromise. Ticketless Celtic supporters like myself would be accommodated in the nearby Talbot Arms, a pub I had never been in. For a ridiculously superstitious guy like me, this was not a good omen. But there were no better offers, so the Talbot it was, propped up against the bar with a Guinness and a prayer.

The position was straightforward. Match Rangers' result and the title was ours. Win the game and the flag would be flying at Paradise again next season regardless of their score. There was no doubt we were the much better placed of the two contenders, unlike that final day in Ayrshire in 2003.

Even in the bar, you could feel the tension oozing from the Lanarkshire stadium, the noise deafening. Grounds like Fir Park and Rugby Park are transformed on such days, when the nonsense of empty seats and ticketless fans gives way to packed stadia. Kilmarnock 2012, anyone?

Apart from the new pub, there were other omens, few of them good.

Unusually, albeit looking back, appropriately, the Steelmen were wearing black, in their goal the ghost of Celtic past Gordon Marshall, just as he had been at Kilmarnock two years earlier, when he had played out of his skin to restrict us to just the four goals, agonisingly one short of what we needed.

Former Ibrox skipper Terry Butcher was in the home dugout, so it would be reasonable to assume that his Motherwell team, with nothing tangible to play for, would not be going through the motions.

"No Celtic party on my watch."

My heart sank when I realised the referee would be Hugh Dallas. I'll just leave that one there, in the interests of diplomacy.

On the plus side, the Hoops fans were making a tremendous racket and our multi-million-pound strike force of Craig Bellamy and John Hartson, backed up by the three Chris Suttons, were all starting the match. Despite all the signs, maybe, just maybe, this would be okay.

"Another Guinness, please!"

Dallas confirmed my worst suspicions early on, allowing a last-man rugby-tackle on the lightning Bellamy to go unpunished, as the Welshman leaves a defender for dead.

Not even a foul. Incredible.

Then it happened.

Alan Thompson and John Hartson combine wonderfully down the left wing, on the main stand side. The Englishman's low cross is fumbled by

Gordon Marshall and the attacking Chris Sutton slides in to give the Hoops a vital lead. It's bedlam in Fir Park...and the Talbot.

The precious lead is maintained at the interval, allowing us to pause for air and recharge our glasses. Then early in the second half, there is a moment of panic, Stephen Craigan's header from a Motherwell corner is blocked on the line by the face of Didier Agathe before being scrambled to safety.

Pampers time.

We need a second.

John Hartson heads high over, where one hundred times before he buries it. Then the chance of the match, as Craig Bellamy sprints clear, one-on-one with Marshall but this time the keeper stretches out a hand to divert his shot wide. Minutes later, he is at it again, Chris Sutton brilliantly dummies a defender to bear down on goal, the big stopper blocking his effort. Moments later, the cameras scan into the away end. Novo has scored at Easter Road. We will have to win. The tension is unbearable.

It is one-way traffic here, as Celtic go for the clincher which will ensure the title, no matter what happens in Leith. Marshall is now playing the game of his life, blocking twice again from Hartson when he seemed certain to score. That sinking feeling starts to creep back into your stomach. *"What if?"*

We are into the last minute of play and my stomach is heaving when former Celtic General Manager, Jock Brown, commentating live from Fir Park, utters the immortal words;

"They know that one false move will cost them the title."

He has hardly finished speaking before a long ball into the Celtic box is partially cleared by Stan Varga, the danger only temporarily averted as a mishit return shot finds Motherwell striker Scott McDonald with his back to goal. One touch on his barrel-chest and an acrobatic hitch-kick sends the ball flying high past Rab Douglas into the Celtic net.

And at that moment, we just know.

64

David Faulds also knew. The Celtic Star editor was in the family section of the main stand that day. He recalls the final stages vividly.

"Moments before the first goal, Stan Petrov was urging the Celtic players to come out. They were getting deeper and deeper. It's the only time that I can ever say this but in those minutes, in front of my eyes, I saw a team die. Their collective legs had gone. It was awful. The supporters were shocked leaving there. A horrible, horrible day."

But there's still time. For a Celtic winner or a Hibs equaliser.

One goal will change a game, a season and a legacy.

And this is football, so it does. But for all the wrong reasons.

Every Celt except Varga and Douglas has pushed forward to chase that second Hoops goal which will bring the destiny of the flag back into our hands, as the ball is frantically cleared from the Motherwell box towards the Celtic corner flag. McDonald is chasing it ahead of Varga and he gets there first. The Australian hitman has turned and is facing our goal, and now he has shuffled to the side and attempted a shot, as a second defender arrives to support the big Slovakian. McDonald's effort takes a nick off a Celtic boot and spins high into the air. Douglas is leaping, his fingers grasping, but in that split-second we know. There is only one place that ball will land, and our dreams will be shattered within seconds. I recall the barman next to me shouting for joy then, realising the situation, quickly withdrawing to the back of the pub, no doubt punching the air, out of sight.

I am totally numb.

Five minutes earlier the pub was vibrant. Now there is a strange silence, other than doors slamming as a few thousand summers are ruined in Milngavie together with millions more across the world.

A half-hour or so later, I see my wife and daughter approaching the pub through the large window, for the pre-arranged lift home. I see it again now. They take one look at me, still sitting traumatised at the bar, and they walk on. There is no hope in my heart. I have rarely felt so low in my entire life.

It was a defining moment in the Martin O'Neill era.

Two years earlier, I had sat with my dad watching on television in his Balornock living-room, as the title changed hands several times over 90 minutes. He was gravely ill but had hung on for Seville, a survivor of Lisbon looking for one last shot at Europe. Dad would pass away within a few months, his job done, his legacy intact and living on in the shape of his children, then our kids. Whilst Rugby Park and Seville had been sore to take, excruciatingly so, for me that defeat at Motherwell was even worse.

Two decades down the line, I can better reflect on Martin's tenure, that fine balance of objectivity and hurt having moved along the timeline sufficiently to allow that. My thoughts and views on this period are fairly clear. Despite the occasional but spectacular lows endured then, relived again in the writing of this chapter, I have no hesitation in saying that, as an overall package, I would not have swapped it for anything. If those dark days at Kilmarnock and Motherwell and the pain of watching Henrik Larsson miss out on a deserved gold medal in Seville are the price of our march with O'Neill, then so be it.

To put the Irishman's achievements in some sort of perspective, when Martin O'Neill took over at Celtic Park on 1 June 2000, Dick Advocaat's Rangers had just won the Treble, finishing 21 points ahead of the Barnes/Dalglish 'Dream Team' at Celtic. Within 12 months, the Bhoys would record their own full house of silverware, their 15-point lead in the flag race reflecting an incredible 36-point swing. The following season, that gap had been extended to 18 points, and in 2003/04, his third and final title for Celtic, there had been another 17 points between the champions and their traditional Glasgow rivals.

In contrast, the two championships lost had gone to the last minute of the season in both cases, a solitary goal the difference in May 2003 before McDonald's unwelcome intrusion in the final moments of the 2004/05 campaign turned a two-point lead into a single-point deficit. There had been a further two Scottish Cups added after the Treble of 2001, a third cruelly lost in the final seconds at Hampden in 2002 as Peter Lovenkrands had his day in the sun. And it had all been achieved with no financial sideshow and with a style and panache on the field that allowed a new generation of supporters, mine, to enjoy watching us take on the best in Europe once again as equals, playing football the Celtic way.

In my adult life, I had been thrilled by the sight of Billy McNeill's two great attacking sides, that team from his first spell in charge, which had given us 4-2 and so many memorable times, followed by his Centenary Bhoys in the fairytale season of 1987/88. There had been precious few of those types of celebrations in the 12 years or so which had elapsed since then. The arrival of Martin O'Neill in June 2000 brought a magical feeling back to supporting our team that I probably thought had gone forever.

Martin's own family were at the heart of the second defining factor that month, as the situation with his wife, who had been battling serious illness for some months, persuaded the Derry-born Celtic boss to take some time away from football. The following week's Scottish Cup final at Hampden against Dundee United would thus be his swansong. Somehow, he would have to lift the team and the support for one more challenge before heading off to deal with one of a far more personal and critical nature. He would come through the football task on a rainy day in Mount Florida, as the first part of the collective Celtic recovery from Black Sunday came in the shape of Our Cup. He would go out as a winner, at least, acknowledging the support of the crowd on a tearful post-match walkabout, something which at that time was fast becoming an annual event.

It seems a strange thing to say, having just won a major trophy, however, my over-riding emotion as we shuffled home from Hampden was still very much one of sadness. In seven seismic Celtic days we had lost a title in the most agonising of circumstances, then the most successful manager since Stein.

Black Sunday would require some major healing but heal we would, in time, to continue the quest. To reclaim our crown and re-establish Celtic as the dominant force in Scottish football. Under a new man.

Within days, the speculation became fact.

Perhaps ironically, it would be a man returning from his own personal time away from the Beautiful Game, who would be coming in to replace Martin O'Neill as the next manager of Celtic.

On Wednesday, 1 June 2005, five years to the day when O'Neill had promised to *"do everything in his power to bring success to the football club,"* and almost 30 years since his initial links to Parkhead as a promising teenager under Tommy Gemmell at Dundee, Gordon Strachan finally arrived at Paradise.

He may have felt that he had seen and done it all.

He was wrong.

The madness was just about to start.

CHAPTER 3

Out with the old and in with the new

The challenge which faced Gordon Strachan as the new manager of Celtic in the summer of 2005 was truly daunting. As if Black Sunday and the departure of the revered O'Neill were not enough, there was a major rebuilding job required in terms of the playing squad, as a number of key men moved on.

Strachan picks up the story in his autobiography, *My Life In Football.*

"When I took over, Celtic were still a club in shock, following the 2-1 defeat at Motherwell that had enabled Rangers to snatch the title from their grasp on the last day of the previous season. The psychological effect of that blow, inflicted by two 'out of the blue' Motherwell goals in the last three minutes of the game, seemed to affect the mood of people at the club for ages. On top of this, the Celtic squad needed to be rebuilt and with the club struggling to cope with their wage bill – apparently the sixth-highest in British football – and finances having fallen £20m into the red, I had to do it on a considerably smaller budget than the one with which Martin had started his Celtic career."

The day after the Scottish Cup Final, Sunday 29 May 2005, the Republic of Ireland took on Celtic at Parkhead in a testimonial game for team captain, Jackie McNamara, a reward for a decade of excellent service following his £600,000 transfer from Dunfermline Athletic in October 1995. His father, Jackie senior, had worn the Hoops under Jock Stein in the seventies, although his first-team opportunities had been limited before his move to Easter Road in September 1976 as part of the deal which brought Pat Stanton to Celtic Park. He would become a firm favourite in Leith for many years, as a solid central defender, going on to make over 200 appearances for Hibernian before moving to Morton in 1988.

The younger McNamara would prove to be every bit as popular at Celtic. Signed by Tommy Burns, he had literally hit the ground running at Parkhead, being voted PFA Young Player of the Year in his debut season and gaining senior international honours within 12 months. Following Burns' departure in May 1997, Jackie had remained a fixture in the number 4 jersey under Wim Jansen, linking up superbly with Simon Donnelly as the League Cup then our first title in a decade was secured, before adding the main PFA award to his trophy cabinet. A persistent knee injury interrupted much of his season under Dr Jo Venglos, the attacking midfielder finally making his comeback in August 1999, as the 'Dream Team' of John Barnes and Kenny Dalglish sought to reclaim domestic dominance from Dick Advocaat's Rangers.

McNamara was used at left-back at Celtic Park on Saturday, 16 October 1999, as The Magnificent Seven theme music boomed out of the stadium speakers for the first time, heralding a hat-trick from the Super Swede Henrik Larsson, a feat matched by his strike partner Mark Viduka, as Ebbe Skovdahl's Aberdeen were on the receiving end of a 7-0 hammering. Five days later, Jackie suffered an ankle injury in Lyon, an event which went almost unnoticed as tragically Henrik was stretchered from the Stade de Gerland in agony, his club season over after a double leg-fracture, a major factor in the subsequent unravelling of the Barnes stewardship which would end in February 2000 following that infamous defeat by Inverness Caledonian Thistle in the Scottish Cup. There was then a brief glimmer of light in that dark period, as goals from Vidar Riseth and Tommy Johnson gave Jackie and Celtic a second League Cup success in three seasons, with the unfortunate Dons once again the victims.

The arrival of Martin O'Neill in the summer of 2000 would see Jackie McNamara retain his usual midfield berth before gradually being used more as a utility man, the Irishman preferring the lightning-fast Didier

Agathe as his right wing-back, ahead of a three-man central defence. Booked in the 3-1 League Cup semi-final victory over Rangers at Hampden in early February, Jackie was suspended as Celtic defended the trophy the following month. He would cut a frustrated figure in the stand as yet another Henrik Larsson hat-trick, this time against Kilmarnock - his third goal a thing of beauty as he dragged the ball away from Gordon Marshall before slotting home – kept the Celts on course for what would be a first Treble since the time of Jock Stein, back in April 1969.

Jackie McNamara came off the bench to replace goalscorer Tommy Johnson on Saturday, 7 April 2001, in front of 60,440 screaming Celtic Park supporters, as the League title was reclaimed against St Mirren, and he repeated his cameo in the Scottish Cup Final against Hibernian the following month, this time as an early substitute for the injured Slovakian 'Gift from God', Lubo Moravcik. He would make a telling contribution to the cause. Six minutes before the break, Jackie picked up a Didier Agathe pass before drilling the ball left-footed across Hibernian keeper Nick Colgan and inside the far post to put Celtic ahead. Then, early in the second half, his perfect cutback was swept high into the net by Henrik Larsson to secure the match at 2-0. Late in the game, the yellow-clad Swede made it 53 goals for an incredible season from the spot, his jersey having been tugged in the box by Gary Smith. Jackie's interventions had been timely and vital, as the coveted Treble was secured in the Hampden sunshine.

That had been a bittersweet day for McNamara senior, sitting with his Hibernian friends in the West Stand, as his son turned in a season's-best performance to swing the Scottish Cup Final Celtic's way.

"I was in the Hibs end and when he scored, I jumped up and cheered. The Hibs fans all turned around and applauded. They were quite happy for me, even though it was the Hibs he scored against. I was delighted for Jackie. It doesn't matter who he's with, I support him."

His son and namesake found the humour in the situation.

"My dad was in the Hibs end and I saw a few guys ejected from there after the goal. I hope he wasn't one of them!"

McNamara again came off the bench in the following season's showpiece final. The beaten 2001 Hibs boss, Alex McLeish, was again in the opposition dugout, this time as manager of Rangers, as Jackie replaced skipper Paul Lambert at the interval with the scores tied at 1-1. There would be no happy ending today, as a last-gasp header from Peter Lovenkrands gave the Ibrox side an unlikely cup double. Three months earlier, Bert Konterman's once-in-a-lifetime extra-time strike had beaten Celtic in the League Cup semi-final at Hampden, ensuring no back-to-back trebles for O'Neill's Hoops. The League was retained in a canter, a record 103 points on the board as the lead was increased from last season's 15 to an impressive 18. And there were memorable European nights for fans who had forgotten they had ever existed, against Ajax, Porto, Juventus and Valencia, as our first-ever Champions League campaign brought the thunder back to Glasgow's East End. It had been a disappointing season for McNamara in terms of his opportunities, the popular starting in only half of his 30 appearances in 2001/02 and failing to score at all.

Those statistics did not improve greatly in that unforgettable roller-coaster season of 2002/03, Jackie's only goal coming in the first of his 28 games for Celtic, a fabulous strike against Dundee United at Celtic Park in August. A dozen of those games would be as a substitute. He would start twice on the Road to Seville, as the Swiss knife turned in Basel so nearly led to a second continental success, the trip to Kaunas (Suduva's ground in Marijampole did not meet current UEFA standards) and the home game against VfB Stuttgart. McNamara again replaced Lambert in the final against Porto, one of five appearances from the bench on that run. He started at Ibrox on Beachball Sunday, as we clung on to hopes that our title would be retained, then looked on from the Rugby Park dugout as the dream died.

Season 2003/04 was much more productive for McNamara, all but one of his 43 appearances being in the starting eleven as he completed the full set of personal honours by winning the Football Writers' Player of the Year. In one of those strange quirks that football throws up, he again scored a solitary goal, a tremendous finish in the 5-0 home defeat of Dundee United, almost exactly a year to the day when that same chain of events had played out! It was the icing on the cake on the day he captained Celtic in the absence of the injured Paul Lambert. Injury caused Jackie to miss the December exits from the Champions League in Lyon and the League Cup in Leith, however, he was back for the UEFA Cup triumphs over Barcelona in March 2004, skippering the side again in the Camp Nou as David Marshall broke the hearts of Ronaldinho et al, the Glasgow Celts overcoming La Liga opposition over two legs for the second season running, following the victory over our Vigo brothers in the winter of 2002.

The Yellow Submarine of Villarreal would torpedo Celtic's hopes of a Grand Gothenburg finale for the departing Larsson. Ironically, as well as future Liverpool goalkeeper Pepe Reina, and the wonderful Joan Roman Riquelme, the latter enjoying a two-year loan spell from Barcelona, the Spanish side featured attacking full-back Juliano Belletti. Two years later, the two men would be teammates in the Stade de France, as substitute Henrik set up the Brazilian Belletti for a Champions League-winning goal against Arsenal, his only strike for the club. Two years after the agony of Seville, perhaps his greatest-ever Celtic performance, Henrik Larsson would finally receive the medal his fabulous career deserved.

Celtic had been missing two key men for the critical second-leg tie against Villarreal in El Madrigal, Chris Sutton through injury and Alan Thompson to suspension. However, man-of-the-match Jackie McNamara was philosophical at the end of the game, the skipper for the night commenting;

"It is a big loss not having Thommo and Sutty but I still thought we could win here. We lost two bad goals, from our point of view but we had a spell when I thought we could come back into it. We knew it was going to be hard, as they are a very good side. But they are not better than Barcelona and I thought we could have won here."

For now, Henrik Larsson and Jackie McNamara would have to content themselves with another League and Cup Double, the second for Martin O'Neill's men in four seasons. Celtic's 39th title was clinched four days after the 2-0 defeat at El Madrigal with a Stiliyan Petrov goal, almost unbelievably at the same Rugby Park which had witnessed the final day tears the previous May. It was secured in record-breaking style, with no defeats whatsoever until the championship had been decided, including a 25-game winning run from a home victory over Dundee United in August to the 1-1 draw with Motherwell at the same venue in March, a new British landmark. There was a first-ever four-game League whitewash over Rangers, with a 1-0 Scottish Cup quarter-final victory over them thrown in for good measure. Late home defeats to Aberdeen and Dunfermline Athletic saw the long unbeaten record finally go and the gap at the top reduced to a more merciful 17 points by the time the great Larsson marked his farewell League appearance at Celtic Park by scoring two goals in the last seven minutes to beat Dundee United, taking the Bhoys to an unprecedented 105 points for the season. The Celtic Invincibles of 2016/17 remain the only team to beat that tally to this day, Brendan Rodgers' side creating a new Scottish record with 106. And the following week the fairy-tale ending was complete, Jackie leading the Celts out at Hampden for the King of King's final competitive game in the Hoops, the Scottish Cup final. Henrik scored two trademark goals, numbers 241 and 242 of a magnificent seven-year career in Glasgow's east end, to transform the match against Jimmy Calderwood's Pars, before he and Jackie raised the famous old trophy together in triumph in front of a tearful mass of green and white who knew they were witnessing the end of something really special.

Life after Larsson commenced with McNamara installed as new team captain, as Paul Lambert's focus turned to a career in coaching and management, the Champions League-winning midfielder making only seven appearances in what would be his final season at the club. In contrast, Jackie would lead the team out on more than 40 occasions and would also skipper his country. His by-now customary single goal would again come at Celtic Park in August, opening the Hoops League account for the season against Motherwell in a 2-0 victory, as Celtic fans cheered the raising of the flag whilst mourning the loss of one of our own, Bertie Peacock, who had passed away a few weeks earlier. The Irishman was Celtic's captain when I came into this world in March 1961, Peacock leaving Glasgow to join his home-town club Coleraine as player/manager a couple of months later. Part of that immortal half-back line of 'Evans, Stein and Peacock,' Bertie had enjoyed a tremendous 12-year career at Celtic Park, playing in some truly iconic victories under Jimmy McGrory. His first winner's medal was earned in the Scottish Cup win over, ironically, Motherwell, in April 1951, and he added the Coronation Cup two years later, Bertie taking a pass from fellow Irishman Charlie Tully to open the scoring in the semi-final against Manchester United. The following year saw the first League and Cup double for Celtic since the time of Willie Maley, 40 years earlier. Peacock then lined up beside skipper Bobby Evans as Celts lifted their first-ever League Cup at Hampden in 1956 against Partick Thistle, and he had replaced Evans as captain by the following October, when Celtic created a record score for a major UK cup final, 7-1 against bookmakers' favourites Rangers at Hampden in the Sun, to retain the trophy, the last major honour of the 20-year Jimmy McGrory era.

Bertie Peacock's present-day successor, Jackie McNamara, would also have an eventful time wearing the armband, albeit for 12 short months. Celtic's European hopes would end in the group stage of the Champions League, a brutal draw against Henrik Larsson's Barcelona, plus that season's beaten finalist AC Milan and perennial Ukrainian champions Shakhtar Donetsk producing just a single victory and a bottom place as the heroic wins of the previous two campaigns left with Henrik. Ironically, the Swede's first game in the competition for his new employers began on the bench at Celtic Park, his goal that night an absolute dream for the headline-makers but merely adding to the pain felt by his still-adoring and hurting Hoops followers. Sweden would also feature that Autumn in the only occasion Jackie was handed the captain's armband for Scotland, in what was Tommy Burns' solitary game in charge of his country. The Swedes won 4-1 at Easter Road in a friendly played in mid-

November 2004, between the tenures of Bertie Vogts and Walter Smith in the Scotland hotseat.

The 2004/05 League Cup campaign ended at Ibrox the same month, Celts just five minutes from the last four thanks to a John Hartson header before Dado Prso's late equaliser and Shota Arveladze's extra-time winner turned the tie around. The League was lost on Black Sunday and the Scottish Cup won the next week to salvage a crumb of comfort from a devastating last month.

On Sunday, 29 May 2005, the day after the Scottish Cup final at Hampden, Martin O'Neill said goodbye to 50,000 supporters as Ireland arrived at Parkhead for Jackie McNamara's testimonial game. It would not be the only farewell that day. Contract talks with McNamara had been dragging on for some time but most still expected the Celtic captain to sign on again, particularly when he received a ringing endorsement from incoming boss Gordon Strachan. However, Jackie eventually opened up talks with other clubs, notably Wolverhampton Wanderers, who made him an offer, and despite a last-minute attempt by Celtic to secure his services, he signed for the Midlands club on Tuesday, 14 June 2005. Just two weeks into his new job, Gordon Strachan had lost his skipper.

Jackie McNamara's predecessor as Celtic captain, Paul Lambert, would also wear a Celtic jersey for the last time at the Ireland game. He had been signed in November 1997 from European champions Borussia Dortmund, his family reputedly homesick following a year in Germany which saw him reach the pinnacle of club football in Munich, as Juventus were defeated by Dortmund in the Champions League Final of May 1997. Having won the Scottish Cup as a 17-year-old with St Mirren in the 'McLean brothers' final' a decade earlier, he had backed himself to succeed in Dortmund by leaving Motherwell to go there on trial. It was a brave and ultimately life-changing decision.

His family's pain was Celtic's gain, as he enjoyed a tremendous eight-season career at Parkhead under a succession of managers. Paul scored a fabulous goal against Rangers in the Ne'erday derby of 1998, a crucial strike as Wim Jansen's men stopped the dreaded 10 against all the odds, and the 5-1 victory over the Ibrox side in November of the same year - the first such Celtic win since Stevie Chalmers' hat-trick in the fog of January 1966 - was the highlight of the season under Jo Venglos. The same opposition were again involved 12 months later, as Lambert suffered a horrendous facial injury in a challenge with Jorg Albertz at Ibrox, referee Kenny Clarke then incredibly awarding a penalty-kick from which the hosts equalised before going on the win the game 4-2, as the John Barnes era continued to unravel following the recent heartbreak of Henrik Larsson's double leg-break in Lyon.

Paul would miss much of the Dream Team's remaining tenure through injury, including the Scottish Cup debacle against Inverness Caledonian Thistle in February 2000 then the relative high of the League Cup Final win over Aberdeen under Kenny Dalglish soon afterwards. Lambert then paired up with Neil Lennon to form the midfield anchor underpinning Martin O'Neill's greatest sides, the Treble of 2001 followed by another championship and the Football Writers' Player of the Year award in May 2002. Paul replaced Tom Boyd as Celtic team captain for the Road to Seville, scoring in the home victories over Suduva and Stuttgart to play in his second major European final in six years. He also notched a memorable midweek double on his old Fir Park stomping ground in May 2003, as Celts roared to the top of the League with a 4-0 victory and just three games remaining. And in the stands that evening, we started to believe that a title and UEFA Cup double was on. Sadly, Celtic would fall just short in both competitions, the footballing gods, just for once, frowning on the fairytale club.

With just shy of 50 games in the Hoops that season, this would be Paul's last as a first-team regular. Injuries curtailed him to just 22 appearances in 2003/04, Martin O'Neill's men bouncing back from the disappointments of Seville and Kilmarnock to win a League and Cup double in stunning style, before Lambert waved goodbye to his pool-playing partner Larsson at the end of that campaign. The following season brought his move into the coaching world, described previously, with Lambert making his final competitive appearance from the bench at Broadwood, replacing Neil Lennon as Celts knocked Clyde out of the Scottish Cup on Sunday, 27 February 2005. He saw out the season as an unused substitute, taking a final Hoops bow in Jackie McNamara's testimonial game before making the leap into a new career as the player-manager of Premier League outfit Livingston, following the resignation of Richard Gough. Paul Lambert was appointed at Almondvale on the same day that Gordon Strachan took over at Celtic Park. He would be another extremely difficult act for the new Parkhead boss to replace.

A third member of the Seville team also wore the Celtic jersey for the final time against Ireland, whilst a couple of returning heroes rolled back the years. Henrik Larsson and Lubomir Moravick thrilled the crowd with second-half cameos, as did future Celts Roy and Robbie Keane, the latter netting the only goal in the dying seconds. By the time they all joined the fray, goalkeeper Robert Douglas' five-year Hoops career was over, ironically replaced by David Marshall on the half-hour. An interval fracas in the UEFA Cup first-leg tie with Barcelona at Celtic Park in March 2004 had seen the Lanark-born keeper unjustly red-carded, together with Thiago Motta, presenting 19-year-old back-up Marshall with the opportunity of a lifetime. The youngster literally grabbed it with both hands, keeping Ronaldinho at bay for the second-half before turning in the performance of his career two weeks later in the Camp Nou, Celtic heroically defending their 1-0 first-leg lead to knock the favourites out of the tournament.

Whilst David Marshall would not look back, the young keeper making his Scotland debut against Hungary at Hampden in August of that year, it was the beginning of the end for Rab Douglas at Celtic. He had been brought in from Dundee by Martin O'Neill in a £1.5m deal in November 2000 to challenge first-choice keeper Jonathan Gould, as the Irishman continued to build up his squad. Whilst the cup-tied Douglas missed the League Cup final win over Kilmarnock, he was immediately restored to the side the following week, clearly now viewed as the number one choice at Celtic. A virtual ever-present in 2001/02, that season would also see his finest hour in the opinion of many supporters. I watched enthralled from my perch high up in the imposing Mestalla, as he single-handedly defied Valencia until the closing stages of the UEFA Cup match, before finally being beaten by Vicente. And just to complete the Spanish set of defining moments in his Celtic career, his performance in Seville is one which divides opinion. My own take on this is of a not fully-fit goalkeeper putting his body on the line for such an important game in the absence of a better option for O'Neill. Magnus Hedman was also injured and Javier Sanchez Broto had been cup-tied with Livingston, prior to his move to Celtic. You may recall that Sanchez Broto was between the sticks four days later for the ill-fated title decider at Kilmarnock. In any case, Douglas played in the cauldron of Seville and was subsequently criticised from some quarters for his handling at both the first and third goals. Such are the swings in the fortunes of the goalie.

I had the pleasure of chatting with Rab briefly, at a fundraising dinner for the Beatsons Cancer charity in May 2019, where the big stopper, then a coach at Arbroath, had raised an incredible £250k through a variety of events. No longer at Celtic Park but still very much embracing the principles of Brother Walfrid in his attempts to help others. I had my two sons with me and mentioned that we had all been in Seville on that hot, bittersweet evening 16 years earlier. He looked at us and smiled apologetically, before uttering a quiet "sorry!" He spent some time with the fans and came across as a lovely big guy.

As Coventry City boss, Gordon Strachan had sold Magnus Hedman to Martin O'Neill and Celtic for £1m in August 2002, surely a serious rival for the goalkeeper's jersey for Rab Douglas. The missing piece of the jigsaw. However, the big Scot would see off the Swede over the following seasons and only fate and the emergence of young David Marshall against Barcelona would bring about the demise of his Hoops career. Rab headed south to join Leicester City in June 2005, quickly followed out the exit door by Magnus Hedman, released the next month after just 26 appearances. So, in addition to his team captain and a Champions League-winner, new Celtic manager Gordon Strachan now had to replace two international goalkeepers!

The revolving Celtic Park door continued to spin in the same direction. Another Seville veteran, Joos Valgaeren, had played his last game for the Hoops in the Scottish Cup Final, replacing John Hartson for the closing 15 minutes of his Celtic career. Martin O'Neill had defied the conventional 'moneyball' theory or wisdom, by signing the big defender largely on the basis of his performances for hosts Belgium in Euro2000, a tournament the Irishman was covering in his role of BBC analyst. He paid Dutch Cup-winners Roda JC £3.8m for the services of Valgaeren in July 2000, the 5-year deal expiring in sync with the manager's own tenure at Celtic Park. He was a key part of O'Neill's three-man central defence in early Celtic successes before injuries progressively curtailed his appearances in the latter seasons. As well as inspiring the popular chant, *"Who let the dogs out?"* the highs and lows for Joos in the Hoops would occur in European games at Celtic Park in 2001, his headed goal against Juventus in the Hallowe'en 4-3 victory then his twice-missed penalty-kick as Valencia knocked Celts out a few weeks later. His contract now up, he left on a free transfer to return to his native Belgium with Club Brugge.

Also returning home as a free agent was another defender who had featured in the UEFA Cup Final in Seville. Ulrik Laursen had impressed Martin O'Neill during his spell at Hibernian, the tall Dane playing well at Hampden in the 2001 Scottish Cup Final as Celtic clinched a first domestic treble in 32 years. By August 2002, Ulrik was wearing the Hoops, following his £1.3m transfer from Leith. An impressive first season saw him make 36 appearances but ended in disappointment, Laursen trying in vain to stop Derlei's deflected shot hitting the net for Porto's bizarre and cruel winner. He had replaced the booked and bruised Joos Valgaeren after an hour in the Estadio Olimpico but would be missing from the squad at Kilmarnock the following weekend then the entire next season, a combination of injury, loss of form and the omni-present Stan Varga restricting him to a solitary 12-minute cameo from the bench in a League Cup tie at Firhill. Ulrik did feature 21 times in his third and final season at Celtic Park, before re-joining Odense in July 2005.

Two other Seville substitutes joined the Parkhead exodus in that summer of change. The versatile Mo Sylla had signed from St Johnstone in August 2001, part of a triple announcement - with John Hartson and Steve Guppy - made as Celts were winning a thrilling testimonial match for Ryan Giggs by 4-3 at a packed Old Trafford. The Guinean winger's Hoops highlight would undoubtedly be his stunning volley in a vital Champions League qualifier against Basel in August 2002, the third goal in a 3-1 win which would ultimately prove insufficient, as the Yakin brothers set about Celtic in Switzerland. Sylla would remain very much a squad player during his four seasons at Celtic, making more than half of his 79 appearances from the bench, that being no disgrace in such exalted company. He headed south to join Rab Douglas at Craig Levein's Leicester City in June 2005.

Spanish striker David Fernandez had been a revelation in Livingston's debut Premier League season, the West Lothian side finishing third in 2001/02. Martin O'Neill signed a £1m cheque to bring him to Celtic Park in June 2002, however, if Mo Sylla's task was difficult, then the challenge facing Fernandez was even more daunting, to be selected ahead of Henrik Larsson, Chris Sutton and John Hartson. No pressure there then. David made just four starts in the Hoops, with a further dozen appearances as a substitute, his only goal coming in the second leg UEFA Cup tie with FK Suduva, a brave strike which saw him hurt by the goalkeeper as Celts took the first step on the Road to Seville. He was released at the end of his contract in July 2005, the talented Spaniard joining Dundee United the following month.

It is incredible now to look back at the turnover of the Seville squad between that night in May 2003 and the arrival of Gordon Strachan just two years later. Of the 18 players available to Martin O'Neill, the two Swedes, Henrik Larsson and Johan Mjallby, would depart at the end of the following season, bound for Spain with Barcelona and Levante respectively, whilst unused substitute winger Jamie Smith left for Dutch club Den Haag at the same time. Eight of the remaining 15 men would leave Celtic Park in the summer of 2005, whilst a further two, Chris

Sutton and Didier Agathe, would be away by January. Only five Celts – Bobo Balde, Alan Thompson, Neil Lennon, Stiliyan Petrov and Shaun Maloney – would survive to contest the honours at the end of season 2005/06. A quite remarkable turnaround by any standards.

Stephane Henchoz left Celtic in July, the Swiss defender returning to Liverpool after a disappointing four-month loan spell at the club. Half of his eight appearances had come from the bench as the anticipated impact failed to materialise. But for all the upheaval over the period, perhaps the greatest loss to Gordon Strachan over that summer was another player who did not actually belong to Celtic. Fiery Welsh striker Craig Bellamy had been a record £6.5m signing for Strachan at Coventry City in August 2000, as the Scot sought to replace Milan-bound Robbie Keane. Bellamy paired up with international partner John Hartson at Highfield Road in February 2001, their few months together sadly ending in relegation from the top-flight. As Hartson talked terms with Celtic, Bellamy joined Newcastle United in July of that year for another £6.5m cheque, this time Geordie boss Bobby Robson the man with the pen. Always a shrewd judge of character, Robson was typically on the money with his assessment of Bellamy as *"a great player wrapped around an unusual and volatile character."* The Welshman's first two seasons on Tyneside saw him in sensational form, linking up with England captain Alan Shearer to devastating effect, picking up the 2001/02 PFA Young Player of the Year award and appearing in the Champions League. In years three and four, however, despite a run to the last four of the UEFA Cup, the other less-appealing side of the Bellamy package emerged. A combination of injuries and internal confrontations, most notably with Robson's successor Graeme Souness, following his appointment at St James' Park in August 2004, severely restricted his performances for Newcastle United and led to a very bitter and public parting of the ways in January 2005.

Craig Bellamy's next destination would be Glasgow and Celtic, teaming up with John Hartson again as Martin O'Neill sought the spark which would propel his post-Larsson Hoops to the Double in what would turn out to be his own final season at the club. Neither Henri Camara or Juninho had fulfilled on their promise or potential to fill the boots of the great Swede or, indeed, the gap in Celtic hearts since Henrik's move to Barcelona. O'Neill turned to the electric but unpredictable Welshman to deliver the goods and but for that Black Sunday minute of madness at Motherwell, he would have done so. I recall being genuinely excited upon hearing of his imminent arrival. There was no doubt that there was an element of gamble in his signing. Thanks to the blanket coverage of the English game up here, his various outbursts and conflicts were shown in all their glory for public consumption. But he was definitely a 'bums off seats' player and, properly-managed, could light up a stadium. I had watched, enthralled, as he inspired Newcastle United to qualify from a Champions League group despite losing their opening three games, one performance in Rotterdam sticking out in particular, as he terrorised Feyenoord before scoring a late winner to send the Geordies through.

His four months in Scotland were the highlight of that season for me and I have already covered his hat-trick at Tannadice and superb winning strike at Ibrox in the previous chapter. Like Henrik Larsson, Craig Bellamy for me always appeared to be operating at a level above any of the other players on the park, faster, sharper, more inventive and with more than a touch of arrogance. A genuine match-winner. He continued to make all the right noises about his stay at Celtic, in particular his respect for and appreciation of Martin O'Neill, with comments such as, *"I would play for that man for the rest of my career."* But 'that man' left and Bellamy quickly followed, just after the McNamara testimonial, this time heading for Blackburn Rovers and another Welsh reunion with manager Mark Hughes. Craig Bellamy would be yet another huge loss for the incoming Gordon Strachan, as he sought to pull together a team in the most trying of circumstances, something he alluded to in his autobiography.

"I did not have a transfer kitty when I started. I could only spend what I brought in on outgoing transfer deals. One example of the financial guidelines under which I had to operate was our inability to hold onto Craig Bellamy, on loan from Newcastle. He did an excellent job for Martin in the 2004/05

season, and his partnership up front with John Hartson – which, of course, I had previously initiated at Coventry – was one I was keen to maintain. Newcastle, though, were not prepared to let us have him on loan again; and because of the £5m fee they wanted for him, and what we would have to pay him, buying him would have put me in the position of not being able to afford anybody else."

So, who *did* the new Celtic manager have to work with?

He had been joined from the outset by trusted lieutenant Garry Pendrey, having worked with him both at Coventry City and Southampton, Strachan's comments suggesting an open mind on others.

"Garry Pendrey will come along with me. He's been with me the past eight years and he will be my assistant. For the rest of my backroom team, it's not a problem. I don't have to take a whole lot of people around with me. I've got good belief in my own ideas. I am quite secure in that as well, but I am quite happy to meet new people and they might give me some ideas as well."

He was as good as his word. Only Jim Blyth came in as goalkeeping coach, having carried out the same role for Gordon at Coventry, where he had given a decade of service as a player, earning his only two international caps for Scotland - against Bulgaria then Wales at Hampden - whilst at Highfield Road in 1978. Although he travelled to Argentina as back-up keeper to Alan Rough for that ill-fated adventure, Jim will have more cause to remember his last three minutes of Scotland action, in May against Wales. Firstly, he looked on relieved as Brian Flynn's 87th minute spot kick crashed off his post to safety to preserve Scotland's 1-0 lead, then, two minutes later, he played a part in perhaps the most bizarre own goal ever scored at Hampden, Blyth rolling the ball to Willie Donnachie, to use up a few more precious seconds, then watching in disbelief as the full-back hit it back beyond him into the empty net.

Tommy Burns, Strachan's former adversary and contender for a spot in Scotland's midfield of the early 80's, was the fourth member of the new Celtic management team, stepping up as first-team coach whilst retaining his existing role as Head of the Youth Academy. Burns would also continue as assistant to Scotland manager Walter Smith, so would bring first-hand knowledge of the current domestic and international scenes, as well as precious insight to the internal workings of his beloved football club.

Despite the significant exodus post-O'Neill, there was still some decent playing talent remaining at Celtic Park as Gordon Strachan's new team took stock and made plans for their first season in charge. The 'Seville Seven,' mentioned previously, were still available for selection, albeit the case could be made that the best years of most of those were perhaps behind them. And there was John Hartson, the current Scottish Player of the Year. The big Welshman had missed the UEFA Cup Final through a troublesome back problem but had bounced back to hit 30 goals the following season, Hartson bursting into the gap vacated by the departed Henrik Larsson and the hugely versatile if less-prolific Chris Sutton to become the main striker at Celtic Park. Youngsters Craig Beattie, David Marshall, Stephen Pearson and, in particular, Aiden McGeady, had been developing well under Martin O'Neill, whilst there was still hope that another tremendous prospect, central defender John Kennedy, would make a full recovery from the horrendous injury suffered on his international debut for Scotland the previous March against Romania at Hampden. Kennedy had come to prominence with Marshall just the week before that brutal tackle, the 20-year-old stopper an absolute rock at the heart of the Celtic defence in the stunning qualification over Ronaldinho's Barcelona in the Camp Nou. It would prove a cruel and ultimately fatal blow in terms of his top-class career, the classy centre-half, grandson of the legendary Jimmy Delaney, literally cut off in his prime. In John's absence, there would be a different name filling that pivotal position beside Bobo Balde for the next couple of years. The low-key signing of Slovakian international defender Stanislav Varga, a free agent after his release by Sunderland in January 2003, had proved to be an outstanding success.

Good players all, however, there was no doubt that new manager

Gordon Strachan would need quality reinforcements - plenty of them - and quickly.

There was little excitement in the ranks when news of his first signing came through. Guinean left-back Mo Camara had spent five years in English football with Wolverhampton Wanderers then Burnley, joining Celtic on a 'Bosman' transfer on Wednesday, 22 June 2005, just three days short of his 30th birthday. Mo had apparently been on Martin O'Neill's radar before the Irishman's personal situation altered his immediate focus and both Ipswich Town and his current side, Burnley, had been keen to tie him up at the season's end. It was still fairly uninspiring stuff from a Celtic supporters' perspective but the player himself was overwhelmed.

"Celtic is an absolutely massive club for me. I know I am not from a big club and I am not a big-name player and that's why I'm desperate for the season to start, so fans can see I deserve this shot. When I heard about Celtic's interest, I was willing to wait for a long time because coming here is like a dream come true. My life is unbelievable at the moment. I just want to come in now and prove myself and fight for my place."

The Celtic manager also spoke passionately and positively about his new recruit.

"He's got pace, he's got enthusiasm and he's got experience now. If we can sign someone of this quality on a Bosman, we have to take it."

There was a second new face at Parkhead the following week, as Jeremie Aliadiere joined the Hoops on a season-long loan from Arsenal. A graduate of the renowned Clairefontaine academy, there were high hopes for the young French striker in North London as a future replacement for countryman Thierry Henry or Dutch magician Dennis Bergkamp. Aliadiere had recently signed a new contract at Highbury and headed to Glasgow for valuable game time, an exciting young talent with the potential to bring something different to Celtic.

"My ambition is to score a lot of goals and play in the Champions League. I knew straight away this would be the best opportunity for me. It is a big club

with big ambitions. To play in front of 60,000 people is really exciting and is a big factor."

His new manager Gordon Strachan was equally excited at the move.

"If the fans are screaming for him to stay and he has scored lots of goals, I would love it. I'm not disappointed I have got him for just a year. It makes me happy because it is a bonus. It just was not possible to have him for longer. A lot of people in England would have liked him for a year so I can't be too greedy. When I spoke to Arsene Wenger, he told me he has a future at Arsenal, they just want him to prepare for that future with us. At the moment, probably the world's top striker, Thierry Henry, is keeping him out of the team and Bergkamp has been a genius for the last ten years. So, it has been hard for him. He needs now to play first-team games. He is at an age now where reserve team football is no good to him. He needs to find out how good he can be."

The manager's third move into the market was also met with general approval, as Polish international captain Maciej Zurawski joined the Hoops from reigning champions Wisla Krakow for £2.2m on Thursday, 7 July 2005. The 28-year-old striker had fired Wisla to four domestic titles in five seasons, notching over a century of League goals in the process. He was also in fine scoring form for the national team as they sought qualification for the 2006 World Cup Finals in Germany, netting in wins in Belfast and Cardiff plus the 2-1 defeat by England in Chorzow. He would go on to score the winners in Poland's return fixtures with the Welsh, the Irish and Austria, a seventh goal in Baku making the man known as 'Majic' the top marksman in the qualifying group, as the Poles finished just one point behind England to reach Germany. The significance of Zurawski's signing was then emphasised with his allocation of the revered number seven Celtic squad number.

The deal had required some effort and patience to proceed, with the proposed payment structure at the crux of the issue between the clubs. Celtic chief executive Peter Lawwell eventually travelled to Krakow to finalise the agreement. He later commented;

"Although the process took a little longer than we had hoped, we had to

ensure that this was the right deal for the club. We are delighted now to have concluded Maciej's signing and welcome him to Celtic Park. Having secured Mo Camara, Jeremie Aladiere and Zurawski, we are hoping to make a few more additions to Gordon's squad over the coming weeks."

Gordon Strachan himself was, if you pardon the pun, short and to the point.

"We are delighted Maciej has signed. His goalscoring record is exceptional."

And the new Hoops striker Zurawski seemed equally excited.

"I am very happy to sign for a club of Celtic's stature. It has a great history and wonderful fans."

Poland was again the destination for Celtic's next addition, this time the capital city of Warsaw. Having failed to sign the Finnish international goalkeeper Antii Niemi, who had been outstanding in Scottish football with Hearts and was currently starring for Gordon's old club, Southampton, Strachan secured a year-long loan deal, with an option to extend, for Poland's back-up keeper Artur Boruc of Legia Warsaw, to challenge David Marshall for the gloves at Parkhead. On Wednesday, 13 July 2005, the 'Holy Goalie' arrived in Glasgow to start a love affair with the Celtic support which exists to this day. Boruc was quite clear in his objectives, despite his rival's recent Champions League success in Istanbul.

"I want to be number one with Celtic and Poland and win myself a longer contract here. If I play well over here, then Jerzy Dudek will have a little problem in Liverpool. This is a big club, a great club and maybe we are going to be in the Champions League. I remember seeing one Celtic game on television – in Seville against Porto – and the one thing I remember was that there were so many supporters."

He also acknowledged the presence of his international skipper as a positive factor in his decision to move to Glasgow, having had offers to go to Turkey with Trabzonspor, or to London and Crystal Palace.

"For me, the acclimatisation should be a bit easier at a new club because I

can speak English a bit. But I will have a Polish colleague too, which is very important."

Life would never be quite the same for the eccentric Artur or for Celtic. We just hadn't realised it yet.

Three days later, Saturday, 16 July 2005, all four new signings were involved as the Gordon Strachan era at Celtic commenced with a friendly against Fulham at Craven Cottage. It was a day of firsts, as Celts sported their brand-new Nike-sponsored away kit, all emerald green with white trims, in front of 17,000 in the quaint West London ground, the majority of them supporting the visitors. The 3-5-2 formation, beloved by Martin O'Neill, was replaced by the more common 4-4-2 model, as life under the new manager began. Mo Camara started at left-back, with young Gary Irvine on the right, the established pairing of Bobo Balde and Stan Varga in central defence ahead of David Marshall. Stan Petrov, Neil Lennon, Chris Sutton and Aiden McGeady made up a strong midfield quartet, whilst John Hartson and Jeremie Aliadiere formed an interesting twin-pronged attack. Poles Artur Boruc and Maciej Zurawski both started on the bench, with the striker's second-half debut spoiled when his late penalty was saved by Fulham keeper Mark Crossley, after he had fouled fellow substitute Shaun Maloney in the box. The game finished goalless.

There was a touch of deja-vu the following Tuesday, as Gordon Strachan took his new side to the East Midlands for a second pre-season challenge match, this time with Leicester City. The Foxes had Rab Douglas and Mo Sylla making debuts just weeks after switching clubs, whilst Artur Boruc started for Celtic. The Polish goalkeeper made an excellent impression, saving a spot-kick in the opening minutes from Strachan's former Coventry City striker Dion Dublin, before making a succession of fine saves as the game again ended 0-0. The only other change in the starting line-up was Maciej Zurawski for Jeremie Aliadiere, the Polish striker getting a good 90 minutes under his belt but no opening goal. Gary Irvine suffered a bad foot injury early on and was replaced by Craig Beattie. Sadly, for the youngster, his second Hoops appearance in three days would also prove to be his last for the foreseeable future.

The next morning, Strachan dived back into the English market, and again his target was relatively unknown in Scotland. Adam Virgo had performed well for hometown club Brighton & Hove Albion in his initial two seasons in senior football, the big defender voted Player of the Year in 2004/05 as Mark McGhee's promoted side retained their Championship status. Virgo had suffered significant personal tragedy just six months earlier, his father dying in January 2005 as a result of injuries sustained during a burglary at this home. It was another dreadful blow for the player who had lost his mother to a heart attack when he was just 13 years old. The timing of the Celtic offer was, therefore, far from ideal, however, the lure of playing for the giant Scottish club and Champions League football won the day. On Wednesday, 20 July 2005, Adam Virgo became Gordon Strachan's latest Celtic signing, joining for a fee of around £1.5m. The player admitted that we would have to wait to see him wearing the Hoops.

"I have not had a pre-season, as I broke down with Brighton. But the Celtic physios are happy, and I will be working with them to get my general fitness back and hope to be back ready for the first team in about three to four weeks. Although, last season I played the majority of games up front, I see my best position in central defence, but the manager has made it clear he wants me in the right-back spot at the moment and that is fine by me. It's a dream come true. No disrespect to Brighton, they have given me some great years down there but the offer from Celtic was too good to turn down. It's every boy's ambition to play for a massive team and Celtic are one of the top teams in the UK."

Selling manager Mark McGhee, Strachan's old teammate, was glowing in his assessment of the player.

"He is a great athlete, has a fantastic attitude and can play in the heart of defence, right-back, midfield or up front. But I think his best position is in defence and that is where he will make his name with Celtic. When I arrived at the club, he was on loan at Exeter, but I quickly realised his abilities and he has been in my team since then. He has the ability to succeed at Celtic and the fact that they have offered £1.5m for him shows the faith they have in him too."

The day after Adam Virgo's signing, Gordon Strachan's Celtic took their home bow in the friendly game against Sporting Lisbon in front of

35,000 curious supporters, the bizarre fielding of striker Craig Beattie at right-back highlighting the scarcity of cover in that position. A third successive appearance in the green away kit - for once the team wearing the Hoops were the visitors - saw the now-familiar outcome of a draw, although this time at least there were four goals shared. Aiden McGeady had the honour of scoring Celtic's first goal of the new era, his strike on the half-hour cancelling Douala's early opener for the Portuguese. John Hartson then took a Chris Sutton pass to give Celts the lead just before the interval, a lead they held until the dying seconds when Sporting's Cameroonian striker Douala spoilt the plan by scoring a late equaliser, his second goal of the game.

The problem full-back slot was addressed the following morning, Gordon Strachan going back to his former club Southampton for veteran defender Paul Telfer. The once-capped Scot had also played under him at Coventry City and although now aged 33, his proven versatility was seen as key as the European transfer deadline approached. The Edinburgh-born Telfer signed a two-year deal to become the sixth Celtic signing of the close-season.

Gordon Strachan was relatively philosophical about the challenging situation.

"It's too late now to get anybody in for the first European games but I hope that we can do a bit more before the season starts. We have tried to bring in young players, but they cost money and like Adam [Virgo], he [Telfer] brings many options. They can both play in many positions and that's what we need. This is a small squad and we need more quality, but those players can play in various positions."

The new Celt himself was thrilled with his somewhat unexpected move.

"I am delighted to sign with a club like Celtic at this stage in my career. I look forward to working with Gordon and Garry [Pendrey] again and hope to be part of a team which brings much success to Celtic and its supporters."

Paul Telfer got an immediate opportunity to impress his new fan-base as Celtic took on Leeds United the following day, a final home friendly before the commencement of the European campaign in midweek. Youngsters Stephen McManus, Michael Gardyne, Paul Lawson, Ross Wallace and Craig Beattie all started, as Gordon Strachan gave some of his senior players a rest before the imminent journey to the continent. The visiting Leeds support took the opportunity to show some love and respect to their title-winning captain from 1992, now sitting in the home dugout. Despite a spirited showing by his young team, the match ended goalless, as Strachan's Celtic rang up a fourth successive draw and third blank in front of goal, not the ideal preparation for Europe.

It had been a hectic re-introduction to Scottish football for Gordon Strachan, as he reshaped his squad, formulated plans and tested formations ahead of the competitive season. The events of Black Sunday the previous May would have further repercussions, as Celtic entered at the second qualifying round to begin their campaign two crucial weeks earlier than the Scottish champions and without the safety net of UEFA Cup football, should the inconceivable happen. Their opponents would be the Slovakian title holders, who had fought back from a 2-0 first-leg defeat by Kazakhstan's Kairat Almaty in the first round of qualifiers to win 4-1 after extra-time in Bratislava and squeeze through on a 4-3 aggregate. They were an unknown quantity to most observers in Scotland, by the name of Artmedia Bratislava.

But that's another story.

CHAPTER 4

A nightmare in Bratislava

On Wednesday, 27 July 2005, just over two months from the day of his appointment, Gordon Strachan made his competitive debut as Celtic manager in Bratislava in a Champions League second qualifying round tie against Slovakian title-holders Artmedia. The club from Petrzalka, a southern district of Bratislava on the banks of the River Danube, just a stone's throw from the Austrian border, had evolved from FC Petrzalka and then through a series of name changes to emerge in 2004 as Artmedia Bratislava, the latest branding reflecting both their advertising agency sponsor and the recently-integrated Rapid Bratislava. Artmedia had won their first-ever Slovak Superliga in 2004/05, thanks largely to 22 goals from star striker Filip Sebo, who would move to Austria Vienna in the close-season and so would miss the imminent ties with Celtic. However, in the remarkably small world that is European football, Sebo would face the Hoops in the colours of Rangers within a year, his name thereafter becoming a byword for wayward shooting at Celtic Park which persists to this day.

With Artmedia's Stadion Petrzalka failing to meet UEFA standards, the game would be played at Slovan Bratislava's Tehelne Pole home in the north of the city. This should have been a good omen for Celtic. In March 1964, the 11 men immortalised in the famous old song, "Celtic, Celtic, that's the team for me," had played Slovan there in the quarter-final of the European Cup-Winners' Cup, defending the slender lead given to them by a late Bobby Murdoch penalty at Parkhead. Minus key midfielder Jozef Venglos but roared on by a partisan 30,000-strong support, the Slovaks laid siege on the Celtic goal. However, a fine defensive performance by the Bhoys was rewarded with just five minutes remaining, John 'Yogi' Hughes picking the ball up at the halfway-line and outstripping several Slovan defenders before slotting the ball past Viliam Schroif in the home goal, to seal a tremendous Celtic victory.

More than 40 years later, in front of just 17,000 spectators, the man facing Gordon Strachan in the home dugout was Vladimir Weiss. Son of a Czech international of the same name from the early 1960s, Weiss had also represented his country, notably as a teammate of Lubo Moravcik as Czechoslovakia progressed to the last eight of Italia '90 under that same Jozef Venglos. Weiss had come off the bench for the opening two games in Florence, replacing Lubo for the last few minutes against the USA with the Czechs 4-1 up, before making another late cameo in the single-goal defeat of neighbours Austria. He then started the final group game, against the hosts in Rome's Stadio Olimpico, making way on the hour mark as a header from Toto Schillaci and a wonderful solo effort from the Devine Ponytail, Roberto Baggio, confirmed that the Italians would qualify as section winners ahead of Czechoslovakia.

Vladimir Weiss was an unused substitute as the Czechs comfortably beat Costa Rica in Bari in the Last 16, Scotland's Central American conquerors losing by 4-1 with Moravcik again completing the full 90-minutes in the white '11' shirt. The midfielder had just agreed a transfer from his hometown club FC Nitra to St Etienne in France, and it would be the best part of a decade before Lubo, once infamously described by a well-known Scottish journalist as *"a Slovakian has-been,"* would light up Celtic Park, having been brought there aged 33 from MSV Duisburg by - yes, you guessed it - Jozef Venglos. A two-footed footballing genius, the Slovakian 'gift from God' Moravcik remains an iconic figure for those of us fortunate enough to have witnessed that particular four-year spell towards the end of his career.

Inter Bratislava midfielder Weiss remained on the bench as the Czech's brave journey ended in the San Siro, a first-half penalty from Lothar Matthaus - the German skipper at that time plying his trade with Inter Milan, so playing in his home stadium - enough to take the favourites through to a tear-filled semi-final with England in Turin and eventual World Cup glory in Rome. Having started every game in Italy, Lubo Moravcik's tournament then ended 20 minutes early, the playmaker dismissed when a second yellow card was brandished by the Austrian referee for alleged simulation following a heavy tackle on him in the German box, the little Czech playmaker having picked up a caution in the opening quarter of the match. Lubo left the pitch clutching his left boot and a strong sense of injustice. At 25, it would be his farewell appearance at a major international tournament.

Having returned to Bratislava in 1996 to see out his playing career with the then FC Petrzalka, Vladimir Weiss had remained to cut his coaching teeth with the club, teaming up with one of Lubo Moravcik's former Nitra colleagues Michal Hipp to steer a rebranded Artmedia to the Slovak Cup in 2004 then the national title the following season. Their opening tie in the qualifying phase of the 2005/06 Champions League had gone surprisingly well. Seeded second for that round behind cup-holders Liverpool - the Merseyside club having been given special dispensation by UEFA to defend their trophy, despite finishing fifth in the English League - Artmedia drew the lowest-ranked side in the competition, Kairat Almaty of Kazakhstan. A 2-0 defeat in the first leg in Almaty's Central Stadium left them with much to do in the return, played at the Slovakian Football Association's National Training Centre at Senec, 25 kilometres north-east of Bratislava for reasons mentioned above. However, the Slovaks fought back well to level the tie after 90 minutes before falling behind again in the opening minute of extra-time. An immediate response from the penalty spot, courtesy of Slovak international midfielder Jan Kozak, took the tie to the brink of a shootout for the right to face Celtic in the second round, but Pavol Stano struck in the dying seconds to ensure Artmedia would porogress as 4-1 winners on the night. As a brief aside, Kozak signed for West Bromwich Albion six months later and would later skipper his country.

Artmedia's next challenge would be much more daunting, at least on paper anyway. Former European Cup winners Celtic were second seeds behind Liverpool for the second qualifying stage, a tournament co-efficient of 63.5 dwarfing the Slovakians' 4.850, UEFA Cup runners-up in 2003 and quarter-finalists in the same competition the following year, having knocked out favourites Barcelona. It was true that the Scottish giants had lost the inspirational Henrik Larsson since then and had struggled in a 'Group of Death' in last season's Champions League, finishing fourth behind AC Milan, Barcelona and Shakhtar Donetsk, however, only a last-minute collapse in Motherwell had forced Celtic to enter at this early stage, having gone directly into the Group phase in 2004/05. It was the proverbial 'no-contest.'

The Slovakians' main opportunity to progress would perhaps lie in the timing of the tie, in relation to the massive changes currently taking place at Celtic Park. New Hoops manager Gordon Strachan had worked tirelessly in his initial two months in the role, in trying to pull together and blend a squad comprising the remnants of the Martin O'Neill era with some new recruits. With only a short pre-season and four friendly games to do so, ahead of the most important phase of the season, Strachan's task was still very much a work-in-progress. With the dark clouds still hanging over the club following Black Sunday, the departure of a beloved manager and several key top-class players, as I look back at it now, Bratislava was an accident waiting to happen.

Nevertheless, Gordon Strachan was still able to field a side which to most Celtic observers looked well capable of handling the Slovakian champions. Resisting the urge to start his new Polish goalkeeper, Artur Boruc, it would be David Marshall, the hero of the Camp Nou, between the sticks. The vastly experienced central defensive pairing of Stan Varga and Bobo Balde were both in there, behind a powerful midfield quartet of Stan Petrov, Neil Lennon, Chris Sutton and Alan Thompson. New signing Maciej Zurawski was partnered up front with John Hartson. If there was a Celtic concern, it was at full-back, where the absence of the departed Jackie McNamara and the injured Didier Agathe meant competitive debuts for Paul Telfer and Mo Camara. This enforced choice would prove critical.

On a hot, balmy Bratislava evening, Gordon Strachan's green-shirted Celts had made a reasonable start to the match before being dealt the first crushing blow, Chris Sutton coming off worse in a collision with Neil

Lennon, a broken cheekbone ending the big Englishman's participation in proceedings within 15 minutes. Aiden McGeady came off the bench, with Stan Petrov pushed inside, as the Celtic manager shuffled his pack. His side had not played particularly well but were approaching the interval with the game still goalless before the first Slovakian incision, a pass from the halfway line catching Mo Camara sleeping, Blazej Vascak sliding the ball across the box for new striker Juraj Halenar to tap home, with Paul Telfer nowhere to be seen. It was schoolboy defending.

Twelve minutes into the second half, the roles were reversed as Artmedia Bratislava scored a second. This time it was Telfer caught out by Halenar's run, the tall Slovakian striker then repaying the earlier favour by laying it on a plate for Vascak to pounce at the far post with Camara stranded and helpless, the Guinean full-back on the wrong side of play. Gordon Strachan's immediate response was to ring the changes, Shaun Maloney and Jeremie Aliadiere replacing Maciej Zurawski and Alan Thompson. Celtic's best spell of the match then followed, Maloney going desperately close before setting up McGeady perfectly for 2-1, the precociously talented youngster somehow contriving to hit the Artmedia crossbar from a few yards out. An away goal at that point would have changed the course of the tie and modern Celtic history, however, things were about to get much, much worse.

With 15 minutes left to play, there was a genuine moment of magic, as Halendar drifted out of the box to meet a corner kick on the volley, his vicious shot rasping past David Marshall into the corner of the net for 3-0. Still Celts refused to shut up shop, continuing to chase a vital away score but the next goal came at the other end, just three minutes later, this time Martin Mikulic turning away from Stan Varga and the wayward Camara to fire the ball home. Celtic's misery was complete in the dying seconds, as yet another simple through ball beat the entire Hoops defence, Halendar racing past Bobo Balde before shooting through Marshall to complete his hat-trick, sealing an abject European night and a 5-0 trouncing. This was only Juraj Halendar's second match for Artmedia, having signed from Inter Bratislava a few days earlier and after scoring twice for Inter on the opening day of the season against MFK Ruzomberok. MFK would succeed

The most bittersweet of days. Martin O'Neill deep in thought amidst the celebrations then bidding farewell to the Celtic supporters at Hampden as a winner, following the Scottish Cup final victory over Dundee United on 28 May 2005.
(Photos by Laurence Griffiths/Getty Images)

Gordon Strachan is introduced as the new manager of Celtic on 31 May 2005.
(Photos by Getty Images)

The Strachan era begins at Craven Cottage as Celtic take on Fulham in a friendly on 16 July 2005.
Top: Celtic manager Gordon Strachan is surrounded by the media ahead of kick-off.
Bottom: New captain Neil Lennon showing his tenacity in this challenge with Steed Malbranque.
(Photos by Jamie McDonald/Getty Images)

In with the new Bhoys.
Top left: Jeremy Aliadiere *(Photo by IMAGO/Colorsport)*
Top right: Mo Camara *(Photo by IMAGO/Allstar)*
Above: Paul Telfer *(Photo by IMAGO/Allstar)*

Top: Polish international duo Maciej 'Majic' Zurawski and Artur Boruc sign for Celtic.
(Photos by IMAGO/East News)
Above: Shunsuke Nakamura arrives in Glasgow on 28 July 2005.
(Photo by Ian Stewart/AFP via Getty Images)

The strangest rollercoaster of weeks to start Celtic's competitive season.
Top: A shell-shocked Shaun Maloney in Bratislava on 27 July 2005.
(Photo by Petr David Josek/Associated Press)
Bottom: John Hartson celebrates his first-half hat-trick in the 4-4 draw at Motherwell on 30 July 2005.
(Photo by Ian Stewart/AFP via Getty Images)

So near yet…
Alan Thompson, John Hartson and Craig Beattie all on target against Artmedia Bratislava at Celtic Park on 2 August 2005, as was Stephen McManus in a 4-0 win, but Celts fell one goal short to exit Europe.
(Photos by Christopher Furlong/Getty Images)

Shunsuke Nakamura's sensational Celtic debut against Dundee United at Celtic Park on 6 August 2005.
Top: Tommy Burns watches Shunsuke and Maciej Zurawski going through their paces before the game.
Above: Celtic's new Japanese star takes in the stadium he would soon light up.
(Photos by IMAGO/Colorsport)

A new star is born in the east…end of Glasgow.
Top & centre: Shunsuke Nakamura in debut action against Dundee United on 6 August 2005.
Bottom: John Hartson is congratulated by teammates after opening the scoring in a 2-0 win.
(Photos by IMAGO/Colorsport)

A controversial defeat at Ibrox on 20 August 2005.
Top: Shaun Maloney scores Celtic's goal from the penalty spot.
Bottom: Neil Lennon is shown a red card by referee Stuart Dougal after the full-time whistle.
(Photos by Ian Stewart/AFP via Getty Images)

"We've got Majic and Stan…

…and the King of Japan!"

Top: Artur Boruc saves a penalty kick from ex-Celt Mark Burchill at East End Park, Dunfermline on 28 August 2005. Both Maciej Zurawski and Shunsuke Nakamura scored their first Celtic goals that day.
(Photo by Steve Welsh/PA Images)
Bottom: Poetry in motion. Shunsuke Nakamura on the ball at Easter Road on 18 September 2005.
(Photo by Glenn Campbell/AFP via Getty Images)

Images from Celtic's top of the table clash with Hearts at Celtic Park on 15 October 2005.
Top: Chris Sutton is cautioned by referee Dougie McDonald.
Above: Craig Beattie, who opened the scoring in a 1-1 draw, and Didier Agathe.
(Photos by IMAGO/Allstar)

Top: Stan Petrov scores the only goal of the game at Rugby Park, Kilmarnock on 23 October 2005.
(Photo by Danny Lawson/PA Images)
Bottom: John Hartson celebrates his 100th goal for Celtic at Falkirk on 6 November 2005.
(Photo by Stuart Franklin/Getty Images)

Two November victories over Rangers at Celtic Park within 10 days set down a marker for the season.
Top: Shunsuke Nakamura in action in the 2-0 League Cup quarter-final win played on 9 November 2005.
(Photo by Ian Stewart/AFP via Getty Images)
Bottom: John Hartson opens the scoring for Celtic in the 3-0 League rout of Rangers on 19 November.
(Photo by Chris Lee/Getty Images)

Top: Aiden McGeady celebrates scoring Celtic's third goal in the League victory at Celtic Park.
(Photo by IMAGO/Allstar)
Bottom: The season is turning out very differently for old pals Alex McLeish and Gordon Strachan.
(Photo by Chris Lee/Getty Images)

A Cork Bhoy signs for Celtic on 15 December 2005.
(Photos by Alan Peebles/Getty Images)

Artmedia as Slovakian champions the following May.

That final 15 minutes in Bratislava will remain long in my mind, as I sat shell-shocked in front of the television. I recalled a similar evening, some 14 years earlier, as Liam Brady faced his second European tie as Celtic manager, a comfortable looking match-up with mid-table Swiss outfit Neuchatel Xamax in the UEFA Cup, the Hoops having disposed of Belgian side Germinal Ekeren in the previous round. That night, an Egyptian striker called Hossam Hassan had helped himself to four of the best as the Celts lost 5-1, our worst-ever result in Europe. Somehow, Gordon Strachan's team had managed to outdo even that calamity and had done so in his first real game as manager. It was undoubtedly Gordon's worst nightmare and it was difficult to see even at that early stage how he could possibly recover from such a horrific start. The new Celtic boss himself was badly shaken by the scale of the defeat, Strachan recollecting the events surrounding that traumatic night in his autobiography, *My Life In Football.*

"For some strange reason, disappointing starts have been par for the course for me over my managerial career. But the one I made at Celtic was by far the most traumatic. Throughout all my time in professional football, no one result or performance has shocked me more, and put a darker cloud over my club, than the 5-0 European Cup defeat by Artmedia Bratislava in my first competitive Celtic match in July 2005 – the heaviest European defeat in the club's history and their biggest in any competition for some 42 years. It is still horrible to have to acknowledge those facts."

The significance and enormity of this defeat is perhaps best illustrated by the game he refers to in the above statement, a 6-0 defeat by Kilmarnock at Rugby Park in March 1963. That night, a Hoops side decimated by injuries had been forced to make no fewer than eight changes to the weekend line-up against Willie Waddell's high-flying Killie, with no fewer than three youngsters making their debuts. Goalkeeper Dick Madden played two games for Celtic that evening, his first and his last. Third-choice stopper behind Frank Haffey and John Fallon, the unfortunate Madden would later be the butt of the Hoops supporters' joke as *"the only thing Haffey ever kept out."*

Centre-half John Cushley made the first of what would be 41 appearances for Celtic in the thankless role of understudy to Billy McNeill. A fluent Spanish speaker, he had accompanied manager Jimmy McGrory in the bold but ultimately unsuccessful attempt to lure Alfredo Di Stefano to Celtic Park in 1964, John playing in a losing League Cup final team later that year before winning a Championship medal in 1966, as Celtic won the first of nine-in-a-row. Cushley played his last game for Celtic in May 1967, then joined West Ham United in the aftermath of Lisbon, swapping one legendary captain for another as he teamed up with England hero Bobby Moore. He returned to Scotland with Dunfermline Athletic in 1970, before finishing his playing career at Dumbarton six years later. John did come back to his beloved Celtic Park as a coach then, latterly, as Education & Welfare Officer before sadly passing away from Motor Neurone Disease in March 2008.

Exactly two years earlier, that same horrific illness had taken the life of the third Rugby Park debutant from March 1963, the incomparable Jimmy Johnstone. Unlike the others, the heavy defeat that night would still lead to a long and glorious career in the Hoops for the incredible Jinky, voted by the club's supporters as the 'Greatest-Ever Celt' in 2002, the ultimate accolade amongst a litany of fabulous players who graced the Celtic Park turf, spanning well over a century, even at that time.

The Celtic manager for that Kilmarnock defeat had been Jimmy McGrory, in the closing years of a two-decade spell in the Parkhead dugout and back at the ground where he had commenced his managerial career in December 1937. Ironically, his first match in charge of Kilmarnock had been a Christmas Day 8-0 humiliation at Celtic Park, just five days after his appointment, on the field where he had broken so many goalscoring records from his own Hoops debut in January 1923 until retiring just a few weeks previously. Despite facing some of the greatest attacking sides on the planet, none of McGrory's predecessors - from trophy-winning managers Jock Stein, Billy McNeill, David Hay, Tommy Burns, Wim Jansen and Martin O'Neill to the less successful tenures of Liam Brady, Lou Macari, Jozef Venglos and John Barnes - had faced such an indignity as that

Bratislava defeat during their spells in charge. At least Brady's sorry bunch had managed to get on the scoresheet in Neuchatel. That unwelcome fact and unwanted record would not be lost on the proud Strachan. Not now and I suspect not ever.

There would be an opportunity to salvage both the tie and damaged reputation the following Tuesday, as Artmedia Bratislava visited Celtic Park for the return leg. A crowd of 50,063 turned out to see if the new manager and his team could make a different kind of European history, by becoming the first side to overturn a five-goal Champions League defeat and thus progress to the next round.

Gordon Strachan made three changes to his Bratislava starting line-up. The 'Holy Goalie' Artur Boruc made his competitive debut between the sticks, whilst young Stephen McManus replaced Stan Varga to partner Bobo Balde at centre-half, the Slovakian defender's groin injury not healing in time for him to face his countrymen. Another youngster, Ross Wallace, came into the side on the left side of midfield, replacing broken-cheek victim Chris Sutton. Making their European debuts, both McManus and Wallace would play a key role in that evening's events, as Celtic lined up as follows.

Artur Boruc: Paul Telfer, Bobo Balde, Stephen McManus & Mo Camara: Alan Thompson, Stan Petrov, Neil Lennon & Ross Wallace: John Hartson & Maciej Zurawski.

The game kicked off to a deafening roar, the Celtic support looking to rattle Slovakian confidence from the off. In their previous attempt to recover from a four-goal loss, against Neuchatel back in 1991, Celtic had been awarded an early penalty, a godsend. On that occasion, Charlie Nicholas had missed, and the tie was gone long before Joe Miller's solitary response. Midway through the first half against Artmedia, history would repeat itself, a softish decision as Maciej Zurawski turned his opponent in the box. The magic wand that is the left-foot of Alan Thompson made no mistake this time, drilling the ball to his right as keeper Juraj Cobej went the other way. *"That's one of the four back. Come on Celtic!"*

100

With seconds remaining before the break, Parkhead erupted as Celtic notched a crucial second goal, keeping them on course for an implausible recovery. Ross Wallace was as brave as his legendary Scottish namesake William as he won an aerial challenge in midfield, the winger flicking the ball on before feeling the sickening impact of a defender's head on his. John Hartson provided the class finish such raw courage deserved. 2-0. Game on.

Early in the second half, the Celtic manager introduced Shaun Maloney to the fray, young Wallace having played his part heroically for the cause by setting up the second goal. Within seconds, the little substitute had teed up the shaven-headed Stephen McManus for a close-range header, following a vicious Thompson corner on the right, a fortunate deflection taking the ball through Cobej's legs for 3-0. *"We couldn't, could we?"*

A quick fourth goal then would surely have swung the tie in Celtic's favour. Crucially, though, we were into the final 10 minutes before Mo Camara, in his one productive input to the tie, swung over a delicious left-foot cross which Craig Beattie, who had replaced the tiring Zurawski on the hour mark, headed cleanly past Cobej for 4-0. Cue absolute bedlam around the stadium, with the dream back on.

I have to say that, at this point, my normally pessimistic outlook had been replaced by the strongest feeling that we would actually get a fifth, to take the match to extra-time and certain Celtic victory. There is a last throw of the dice from Gordon Strachan, as Jeremie Aliadiere comes on for Thompson for what would prove to be the final three minutes of his fledgling Celtic career. Agonisingly, however, the clock ticks down furiously as the chances are passed up, one following another as the tension becomes unbearable. It had been close enough to touch but suddenly there is a blast on the Spanish referee's whistle, and we are cruelly, so cruelly, out of the Champions League and, indeed, Europe altogether for this season. In fairness, it had been a tremendous effort by the team on the night to repair the desperate damage from Bratislava, however, ultimately, we had fallen just short of creating history. Celtic captain Neil Lennon summed up his feelings after an incredible roller-coaster of a night.

"I think everyone could see tonight that the boys are right behind the manager and we're all pleased for him. We only have ourselves to blame after letting ourselves down last week but tonight there was quality, passion and everything you'd want from a Celtic team. We can take a lot from the performance and the fact we never gave up. The dressing-room is a bit subdued, but we wanted to give it everything tonight and we certainly did that."

Artmedia Bratislava manager Vladimir Weiss was a much happier and also a mightily relieved man.

"I have never seen such an atmosphere in all my years in football. It was a difficult job to convince the players that miracles couldn't happen coming into this game. Thank God there was no miracle but there almost was! I am very proud of my team."

He would have further cause to feel that sense of pride. As Gordon Strachan's men licked their wounds and the Hoops support put their European dreams on hold for another season, the Slovakian side went on to prove that they were perhaps a better side than their reputation and co-efficient had suggested. Adopting Celtic's seeded status in the final qualifying round of the Champions League, Artmedia went into the draw alongside Liverpool, Inter Milan and Villarreal, thus avoiding the big guns. Nevertheless, they were still paired with the dangerous Serbians, Partizan Belgrade, who would start favourites. Two goalless draws meant that the tie would be settled on penalty kicks, Artmedia eventually winning 4-3.

By doing so, they became the first team to naturally progress all the way from the first qualifying round to the group stage of the Champions League. Holders Liverpool could technically claim the same distinction that season, albeit their circumstances and seeded status made this materially different.

The football gods were obviously having a chuckle as they paired the conquerors of Celtic - Artmedia Bratislava, the lowest-ranked team remaining in the competition - with our old foes, Inter Milan, Porto and Rangers. The Slovakian makeweights were about to prove that they were anything but. A narrow home defeat by Inter, embarking on what would be the first of five successive seasons as Italian champions under Roberto

Mancini and Jose Mourinho, was followed by an incredible fightback in Oporto's Estadio do Dragao, from 2-0 down to triumph 3-2 against the side who had been champions of Europe just 16 months earlier, giving Artmedia a rather unique 'Seville Double.' Back-to-back draws with Rangers and a 4-0 defeat in the San Siro against the runaway group-winners Inter Milan meant that victory at home to Porto in the final game would take the Slovakians through to the Round of 16. Agonisingly, a late missed chance against the Portuguese saw the match in Bratislava finish goalless, allowing Rangers to creep through with a paltry seven points, just one ahead of Artmedia. It had been a tremendous effort by Weiss' side. By finishing third in the group, Artmedia dropped into the UEFA Cup Round of 32, and a tie with Levski Spartak. There the great run would finally come to an end, after 1-0 and 2-0 defeats by the Bulgarians.

The European form did not extend to domestic competition, Artmedia failing to defend their title as they finished second in 2005/06, six points behind new champions MFK Ruzomberok. Much more worrying was the situation with their goalkeeper Juraj Cobej, who had to undergo surgery in December 2005 to remove a brain tumour, just a few short months after keeping Celtic's tally down to four in Glasgow. Thankfully, Cobej would make a full recovery and, indeed, would gain his first and only international cap for Slovakia with a brief appearance in a friendly against Belgium in Trnava in May 2006. Manager Vladimir Weiss had moved to Russia in mid-season to take charge at Saturn Moscow Oblast, the Slovak taking several of his players along with him before returning to Bratislava in June 2007, to the club by now renamed once again as Artmedia Petrzalska. In his final season there, Weiss would win a second Slovak Cup, repeating the success of four years earlier.

At the end of 2007/08, Vladimir Weiss left Artmedia to manage the Slovakian national team, his side making history by qualifying for the 2010 World Cup finals in South Africa, its first appearance in a major tournament since securing independence from Czechoslovakia. That had involved finishing top of a tricky World Cup qualifying group which included neighbours Poland and the Czech Republic, as well as Slovenia and Northern Ireland. Weiss' squad for the finals would include his son, also called Vladimir, surely a unique situation where a grandfather, son and grandson, each bearing the same name, have represented their international team. Weiss III would feature in three of the four games in South Africa, missing the victory over Italy in Johannesburg which took Slovakia through to a Last 16 defeat by eventual runners-up Netherlands. He would also feature in the next qualifying campaign, for Euro2012, scoring in the 3-1 defeat in Yerevan as the Slovakians trailed in a disappointing fourth behind Armenia, play-off contenders Republic of Ireland and group winners Russia.

At the time of the 2010 World Cup finals, the youngest Vladimir Weiss was on the books of Manchester City but on loan at Bolton Wanderers. He would spend time under Walter Smith at Ibrox on a further loan deal the following season, having been linked with a move to Celtic, picking up League Cup and Premier League medals, the final trophies for Rangers before their liquidation in 2012. Although Weiss would win 66 international caps, his club career would fail to get off the ground, spells in Spain, Italy, Greece and Qatar creating more headlines for a series of off-the-field incidents than for anything he ever achieved on it. Now aged 33, at the time of writing, Weiss is currently plying his trade back in Slovakia with champions Slovan Bratislava, having returned to his homeland from Qataris Al-Gharafa in February 2020.

Failure to qualify for Euro2012 would see Weiss' father resign as Slovakia manager in February 2012. He had combined his international duties in the 2011/12 campaign with a club role in charge of Slovan Bratislava, whom he led to the Group Stage of the Europa League following a Play-Off victory over Roma. A tough draw against Paris Saint Germain, Red Bull Salzburg and Athletic Bilbao saw the Slovakians struggle and finish bottom of the section. Weiss left in August 2012, his next challenge being in Kazakhstan, perhaps ironically to manage Artmedia Bratislava's Champions League victims from 2005, Kairat Almaty. In his second season there, Weiss won the Kazakhstan Cup, repeating that feat in 2014/15. Kairat then narrowly missed out on a double and the solitary Champions League slot, finishing one point behind the wealthy champions FC Astana. In March 2016, he became the manager of the Georgian national team, spending more than four years in there before resigning in November 2020. He returned to Slovan Bratislava for a second spell in May 2021 and led them to the Slovak Super Liga in both his first and second seasons. Weiss remains there at the time of writing, August 2023.

I'll leave the last word on the Artmedia Bratislava episode to the man Weiss faced that week in the early part of the 2005/06 season, new Celtic manager Gordon Strachan, writing the following year.

"As for that first leg against Artmedia, the argument that the game came too early for us was best illustrated by the upheaval to our defence in the full-back slots. The regular incumbents under Martin had been Didier Agathe and Jackie McNamara, Celtic's captain. But with the former unavailable through injury and the latter having left for Wolves – much to my regret, following a contractual dispute, which I am convinced would have been settled to the satisfaction of both parties had Jackie and his agent adopted a more patient negotiating stance - we were forced to give debuts to both Paul Telfer and Mo Camara. The other back four headache concerned Bobo Balde's contract situation. Bobo had a clause in his agreement stipulating that, at that particular time, he could leave Celtic for any club prepared to match or better his terms with us. He had every right to explore this possibility but in the build-up to a game as important as the one in Bratislava, his meetings and telephone conversations with other clubs were a distraction that we – not to mention Bobo – could have done without."

"For all this, there is little doubt that we should have done better against the Slovakian champions. I had the impression that their coach was as shocked about the scoreline as I was. Celtic did not play well but up to Artmedia's young striker Juraj Halenar getting the first of his three goals, two minutes before half-time, I was thinking that the likeliest outcome would be a 0-0 draw. Even when Artmedia made it 2-0 early in the second half, I really could not see us taking the hammering we did. Hence the fact that, while some managers might have tried to bolster their defence and opted for a damage-limitation

approach, I went the other way. My substitutions after Artmedia's second goal – Shaun Maloney for Maciej Zurawski, who had struggled to make an impact on his Celtic debut, and then Jeremie Aliadiere for Alan Thompson, who had not been fully match-fit – were later described by some pundits as naïve. However, because of the importance of away goals in European matches, and my belief that Artmedia would prove as vulnerable at the back as we had been if we could put greater pressure on them, I felt that the gamble was justified. I still do. It could easily have paid off for us. Shaun Maloney missed one excellent chance and Aiden McGeady, who had come on in the first half for the injured Chris Sutton, failed to convert an even better one. The roof then fell on us again but bearing in mind that we beat Artmedia 4-0 in the return leg at Parkhead, we would still have gone through had one of those opportunities been taken."

"When I die, I reckon the inscription on my headstone should read:

"This is much better than Bratislava."

CHAPTER 5

Enter the Dragons…and the lion's den… well, minus any real lions obviously!

The SFL fixture computer had definitely been a bit naughty.

Sandwiched between the two European legs with Artmedia Bratislava, it decided in its emotion-free wisdom that Gordon Strachan's first League match in charge of Celtic would involve a return visit to Fir Park, Motherwell, just two short, pain-filled months after the horrific events of Black Sunday.

There were 10,000 fans packed into the compact Lanarkshire ground on Saturday, 30 July 2005, most wearing the green and white colours of Celtic, to see how the new Hoops manager would fare in his first competitive domestic challenge, just three days after the disaster of Bratislava. Strachan had made three changes from the midweek line-up, the first two enforced as Maciej Zurawski failed to recover from the ankle injury sustained in Slovakia, Shaun Maloney partnering John Hartson in his absence, with Aiden McGeady retaining his slot in midfield due to Chris Sutton's broken cheek, despite the youngster's glaring and costly miss in Bratislava. The last change caused a few raised eyebrows, Bobo Balde dropped to the bench amidst speculation of an imminent move to Olympique Marseille, with young Stephen McManus stepping into central defence beside Stan Varga in the following team.

David Marshall: Paul Telfer, Stan Varga, Stephen McManus & Mo Camara:
Aiden McGeady, Neil Lennon, Stan Petrov & Alan Thompson: John Hartson & Shaun Maloney.

The Celtic supporters would be feeling a bit better about life within 15 minutes, as Alan Thompson did superbly well to swing over a cross from the left for John Hartson to do what he does best, outmuscle a defender to power home a header at the far post. There was a setback for the Hoops six minutes later, as Mo Camara was left exposed by a slick Motherwell passing movement before Jim Hamilton fired a fine equaliser past David Marshall for 1-1. On the half-hour, Hartson again put Celts in front, this time the big Welshman stretching those powerful neck muscles to meet Aiden McGeady's cross and flick the ball into the corner past the despairing dive of Gordon Marshall. And just seconds before the interval, he appeared to have given Gordon Strachan a first Celtic victory, ramming home a spot-kick for an excellent first-half hat-trick, after the veteran Motherwell keeper, now 41 years old, had brought Bulgarian midfielder Stan Petrov's strong attacking run to an illegal and premature halt.

For the first time in a couple of months it felt good to be a Celt, as the first shoots of optimism appeared post-O'Neill. However, two goals just either side of the hour changed all that. First Hamilton nodded home from close-range, with the defence posted missing, then, incredibly, Scott McDonald, the Black Sunday pantomime villain and one of the smallest men on the field, outjumped his marker to glance a header past David Marshall for 3-3. Both centre-halves missed glorious opportunities to win the match for their respective teams, first the Slovakian Stan Varga then the Irishman Stephen Craigan heading over when it looked easier to score.

Then, just when we were thinking that the Celtic manager's introduction to his new role couldn't possibly get any worse, it did. There were just six minutes remaining when John Hartson, defending a set-piece, badly mistimed his jump, then appeared to wait for a free-kick which was not forthcoming. Instead, the ball was flashed across the Celtic box by Jim Hamilton for yet another headed Motherwell goal, this time Willie Kinniburgh the grateful recipient. On the ropes and staring a second consecutive, alarming defeat in the face, Gordon Strachan's Celtic somehow found the courage to strike back. In the dying seconds, Hartson won an aerial duel to play in the onrushing Craig Beattie, a second-half replacement for Aiden McGeady, the young striker claiming the vital touch as he beat his marker for pace to nudge the ball past Gordon Marshall for a face-saving equaliser, the match ending 4-4.

Whilst the fightback to salvage a point was commendable, there was alarm at the number of goals conceded in 180 minutes of football against opposition who could be deemed no better than average. The nine balls deposited past David Marshall reflected Celtic's poorest defensive performance since October 1991, when a brief period of success and hope under new manager Liam Brady was blasted away, following a shock 4-3 defeat at Brockville then the 5-1 collapse in Neuchatel, three nights later.

Strachan's team had worryingly conspired to match that feat in his opening two games as Celtic boss, the manager not having his worries to seek ahead of the midweek return with Artmedia Bratislava.

"I don't think anyone thought we would lose that many goals. To concede as easily as that is hard to take. It's obvious where we need to sort things out, but it must happen quickly. I can ask the fans to be patient, but I'll just have to put up with any reaction from them. Defensively, today it didn't work, so we will have to think of something else for Tuesday. In an attacking sense, it gives us a bit of hope for Tuesday after we scored four goals. What we don't want to do is panic. That would be the worst thing to do. Our defending is not at its best and needs to be sorted one way or another."

Whilst the team as a whole had defended badly, Stephen McManus had shown enough to remain in the manager's plans moving forward, although there were fears that the young stopper, booked by referee Mike McCurry for one challenge too many, would not even see out those opening 90 minutes! The Celtic manager later recalled that afternoon in Motherwell.

"I remember Stephen McManus's first match of the season in that 4-4 draw with Motherwell. Stephen, a long way down in the first-team centre-back pecking order the previous season, was as hyped up as any player I have ever seen in the first ten minutes of that game. He gave the impression of looking upon it as a trial game that would decide his entire career. We had to shout at

him to calm down – had he not done so, he would have blown up in a cloud of smoke or got sent off. Being kept in the team inevitably did wonders for his confidence. One of the great things about him, apart from his willingness to learn and his technical ability, was his communication."

As one local player staked his claim for a place in Gordon Strachan's Parkhead revolution, another footballer from the other side of the world watched that Motherwell game from the stands, whilst a third man was en route from the Far East to Glasgow's East End. Celtic's scouting network had taken the Orient Express to land Japanese playmaker Shunsuke Nakamura and Chinese national captain Du Wei, a central defender. They would go on to have vastly different careers at Celtic.

Former Asian Young Player of the Year Du Wei had made his name in the World Youth Cup of 2001, China progressing from a group which included Ukraine, USA and Chile before narrowly losing to hosts and eventual winners Argentina - inspired by top-scorer Javier Saviola - in the Last 16, a game refereed by our old friend Mike McCurry. Future Celts Andreas Hinkel, Glen Loovens and Scott McDonald would also represent their respective countries in this tournament, the German playing with VfB Stuttgart at the time, some 18 months before his club's meetings with Martin O'Neill's Celtic on the Road to Seville, whilst 17-year-olds Loovens and McDonald, two of the youngest players out there, were working with Bert van Marwijk at Feyenoord and under Gordon Strachan at Southampton, respectively. A number of future international stars also featured in Argentina, most notably Brazil's Kaka, Michael Essien of runners-up Ghana, and the Dutch trio of Klaas-Jan Huntelaar, Rafael van der Vaart and Arjen Robben.

Notwithstanding such exalted company, Du Wei's performance in South America, as goals from Maxi Rodriguez and Alejandro Dominguez brought the brave Chinese run to an end, drew praise from none other than Argentine superstar Diego Maradona, who said that the big stopper had *"the perfect sense of how defending should be played, his speed is unparalleled."* That last phrase always draws a smile!

The following year, Du Wei was part of the Chinese squad which qualified for the World Cup finals for the first time, not featuring in the opening 2-0 defeat by Costa Rica but playing against winners-elect Brazil and surprise semi-finalists Turkey, as China lost all three group games in South Korea to face an early trip home. The Chinese team was coached by Bora Milutinovic, leading his fifth different nation in successive World Cup Finals. The legendary Serb had actually managed group rivals Costa Rica in Italia '90, infamously beating Scotland in Genoa before losing to Lubo's Czechoslovakia in the Last 16.

Du Wei's World Cup Finals debut was the proverbial baptism of fire, facing a Brazilian side which I felt never truly received the praise such a devastating attacking line-up deserved. Roberto Carlos' stunning free-kick in the opening quarter set the tone, with Cafu and Ronaldinho setting up a second for Rivaldo shortly afterwards. On the stroke of half-time, Ronaldinho made it 3-0 from the spot, after Ronaldo had been pulled back in the box, with Ronaldo picking up his goal early in the second half from another Cafu assist. It was a masterclass from the exciting samba superstars against the inexperienced Chinese. Another future Celt, Juninho, about to return for a third spell at Middlesbrough from Atlético Madrid, played the first 70 minutes of the match, behind Luis Felipe Scolari's fantastic 'Triple R' strike force.

China's third and final game also failed to produce a goal and ended in a 3-0 defeat by surprise package Turkey in Seoul. Like the previous game, the damage was done early, Galatasaray pair, Hassan Sas and Bulent scoring within the first 10 minutes. The woodwork denied Yang Chen his place in history before Shao Jiayi saw red for a dreadful challenge. A late third by another Gala man, the Mohawk-brandishing Umit Davala, on loan from Inter Milan, hammered the final nail in the Chinese World Cup 2002 coffin.

Back on home soil, Du Wei's performances for Shanghai Shenhua saw him become the national team captain and attracted interest from German clubs Borussia Monchengladbach and Kaiserslautern, a 2004 trial there failing to produce a deal. Twelve months later, he was heading to Glasgow and Celtic.

His arrival at Parkhead in early August was reported as the commencement of a six-month loan deal from Chinese Super League side Shanghai Shenhua, with the option of Celtic signing him permanently for an agreed fee of £700,000. Within a fortnight, however, the player was back in China, the clubs having failed to successfully negotiate the terms during his brief stay in Scotland. In the best Glasgow tradition, Shenhua's spokesman got his retaliation in first.

"We don't want to lose our captain but if the move is in the best interests of Chinese football and a price can be agreed, the player will move to Scotland. There is a difference at present in the two clubs' valuations, but we think this will be overcome."

Celtic chief executive Peter Lawwell also remained optimistic, dismissing claims that the delay was related to the collapse of a proposed move to Marseilles for Bob Balde.

"Although it is a complicated deal, the talks with Du Wei are progressing well. In no way is the deal dependant on Bobo Balde moving on."

And Gordon Strachan was upbeat, albeit taking a pragmatic view of any transfer.

"He's been here just a couple of days and played in a closed-door game. There's something there but I can't commit myself after two days. I spoke to the player and he loved it here and we will try to make an arrangement to keep it ongoing."

Shunsuke Nakamura had also cut his international teeth in a World Youth Cup, this time the Malaysian finals of 1997. He scored an early goal as the Japanese beat Costa Rica 6-2, securing his team's passage from a group also containing Spain and Paraguay. Japan would go on to beat Australia in the Last 16, before succumbing to an extra-time defeat by Ghana. At that same quarter-final stage, Uruguay would beat a French side boasting Thierry Henry, David Trezeguet and Nicolás Anelka, 7-6 on penalty kicks. Former Celtic coach Damien Duff had scored an extra-time winner for the Republic of Ireland in their Last 16 tie against Morocco, the Irish then memorably beating Spain before losing 1-0 to an Argentina side including the wonderful Joan Roman Riquelme and Pablo Aimar in the semi-final.

The Argentines would beat neighbours Uruguay in the final, a rematch of the first World Cup Final, whilst Duff would again produce a winner in the Play-off with Ghana, to secure an excellent bronze medal for Ireland.

On his return from Malaysia, Shunsuke signed for Yokohama F Marinos, a club from his birthplace, owned by Nissan Motors and where he had commenced his early career as a youth. In February 2000, he was given his international debut by Philippe Troussier, later being named Most Valuable Player in the J-League. Nakamura was an ever-present as Japan won the Asian Cup in Lebanon that October, before falling out of favour with the Frenchman Troussier after a crushing 5-0 defeat from the coach's home country. Despite regaining his place shortly before the 2002 World Cup, to be held in his native Japan and South Korea, a combination of injury and competition for places saw Shunsuke miss out on a dream appearance on home soil.

A disillusioned Nakamura then decided to ply his trade abroad and, despite interest from Real Madrid, his next destination was Italy's Serie A, with newly-promoted Reggina. A productive first season there, where his goals and assists were vital in *'gli amaranto'* retaining its top-flight status, was capped by a strong performance in the 2003 Confederations Cup, held in France. Nakamura's double in the Stade de France helped the Japanese to a 3-0 first-game victory over New Zealand, the playmaker on target again in his side's 2-1 defeat by the hosts in St Etienne. Injury caused him to miss the single-goal defeat to Columbia, which marked the end of Japan's participation, however, his three goals were enough to earn him the Bronze Boot behind Thierry Henry and Turkey's Tuncay, missing out on the Silver award by a solitary assist. The tournament will be remembered for the saddest of reasons, as Olympique Lyonnais star Marc-Vivien Foe, at that time on loan to Manchester City, collapsed and died on his home pitch during Cameroon's semi-final victory over Colombia, the same Stade de Gerland in Lyon where Henrik Larson had suffered a horrific double leg-break four years earlier. In a lovely tribute, Foe would posthumously be awarded the Bronze Ball, Henry and Tuncay again filling the top two places.

An injury-plagued domestic 2003/04 season concluded on a high, Nakamura voted the Most Valuable Player as Japan retained the Asian Cup in China, beating their hosts and fierce rivals 3-1 in the final. Nakamura now sported the famous No.10 jersey once worn by his new national coach, the Brazilian superstar Zico. Lining up against him in Beijing was future Celt, Zheng Zhi. He would succeed Du Wei as national captain and become the second Chinese player to sign for Celtic, making his debut at Ibrox under Tony Mowbray in a 2-1 defeat in October 2009. Incredibly, the then 38-year-old Zhi was still the captain of China and earning his 108th cap in the 2019 Asian Cup, held in the United Arab Emirates whilst I was over there preparing for the Tokyo Marathon and sharing a Dubai hotel with a Celtic squad enjoying their own winter training camp in what would prove to be the final weeks of the first Brendan Rodgers regime.

Zheng Zhi opened his country's 2004 account from the spot in the opening 2-2 draw with Bahrain, whilst Shunsuke Nakamura did likewise, with the only goal against Oman, the Japanese playmaker then scoring the equaliser in their second game, a 4-1 win over Thailand. Zheng went one better with a late penalty double in China's 3-0 quarter-final victory over Iraq, whilst Nakamura surprisingly missed the first shootout spot-kick then heaved a sigh of relief as Japan edged past Jordan by 4-3. Zheng converted the opening penalty as China won their semi-final by the same margin against Iran, however, the Final say went to Nakamura, a man-of-the-match performance securing a third Asian title for Japan. A third future Celtic star was also on the scoresheet in this competition, stocky Eintracht Frankfurt defender Cha Du-ri plying his trade with his hometown team, thus becoming the first player to represent South Korea having not been born in the country. His moment of glory came in first-half stoppage time in the final group game against Kuwait, the third in a 4-0 victory to secure qualification.

Shunsuke Nakamura began his third season on Italy's 'big toe' under a fifth coach, Walter Mazzarri, the Japanese midfielder's only two goals of 2004/05 both securing vital 1-0 wins as Reggina escaped relegation by just two points. Frustrated by constant managerial change and annual survival dogfights, Nakamura sought a move elsewhere.

First though, there was the small matter of the 2005 Confederations Cup, to be held in Germany in the second fortnight of June, Japan again representing Asia in their role as continental champions. The hosts featured future Celt Andreas Hinkel, plus a young defender who had a trial at Celtic Park under Martin O'Neill in July 2000, before joining Aston Villa from Bayern Munich's youth academy, Thomas Hitzlsperger. 'Der Hammer' would go on to have a fine career in the Midlands then with VfB Stuttgart, winning the Bundesliga and the majority of his 52 senior caps with the latter. Hitzlsperger appeared in the home World Cup of 2006, where the Germans took bronze, then Euro 2008, when they lost to Spain in the final in Vienna, but he then missed the final cut for the 2010 squad bound for South Africa. Following less productive spells at Lazio, West Ham, Wolfsburg and Everton, Thomas retired in 2013, later becoming the highest-profile professional footballer yet to 'come out' as gay.

In the Germans' group back in 2005 was Australia, featuring former Celtic striker Mark Viduka, by then approaching his 30th birthday and playing at Middlesbrough. His tournament would comprise just the second half of the Socceroos' 4-2 defeat by Argentina in Nuremberg, then the first half of a 2-0 loss to Tunisia in Leipzig.

Japan were paired with World Champions Brazil in Group B, and they got off to the worst possible start as Mexico recovered from a goal down to win 2-1 in Hanover, Shunsuke Nakamura having been substituted after an hour with the sides locked at 1-1. However, they bounced back immediately with a single-goal victory over Greece in Frankfurt, Nakamura turning in a man-of-the-match performance before leaving the field in the last minute. He took the star man honours again in the final group game, against the Brazilians in Cologne, Nakamura scoring the first equaliser as the Japanese fought back twice for a 2-2 draw, the Samurai Blue losing out on qualification to the brilliant South American stars and eventual winners only on goal difference.

With Japan's interest in the Confederations Cup over, Shunsuke weighed up his options. New Celtic manager Gordon Strachan had been impressed with the performances of the Japanese playmaker in Germany and, despite interest from the Bundesliga, Spain, Italy and England, Strachan would win the prized signature, and for less than half the reported £2.5m fee. Over the next few seasons, that would be up there with the Henrik Larsson deal in terms of value for money. It also raised the profile of Celtic in his native Japan beyond all expectations, as I observed first-hand on a visit there in 2019. Then 41 years of age, Nakamura was still playing in the Japanese top-flight with Jubilo Iwata and he would then spend a further three seasons with hometown club Yokohama FC, before retiring in October 2022. A truly wonderful footballer, respected, revered and adored by supporters from Tokyo to Tollcross.

Whilst Du Wei would be an observer from the stand as Gordon Strachan's Celtic played their first game after the European elimination by Artmedia Bratislava - a home League fixture with Dundee United on Saturday, 6 August 2005 - and would remain on the first-team sidelines for some time, Shunsuke Nakamura would hit the ground running… and then some. His debut that sunny day is a JFK moment for me, the Japanese midfielder quite scintillating, a joy to watch for myself and the other 56,000-plus supporters in the ground. His sublime touches enabled Celtic to dominate a United side featuring future Bhoys Mark Wilson and Barry Robson, Parkhead striker John Hartson powering through on the half-hour to score his fourth League goal in two games and send the Hoops in 1-0 at the interval. The crossbar then prevented Celtic's Welsh Dragon from making it two successive hat-tricks, twice United keeper Derek Stillie was stranded as Hartson headers bounced back into play from his goalframe. The debutant Nakamura saved his own piece de resistance until later on, a stunning free-kick which was screaming into the 'wrong' corner before Stillie stretched out a fingertip to touch it around the post. With six minutes remaining, the Japanese genius left the field to a well-deserved standing ovation. He was replaced by Craig Beattie, the young striker then firing in a superb volley from fellow-substitute Shaun Maloney's flighted cross to clinch the match at 2-0 with just two minutes remaining. This would prove to be a turning point in Gordon Strachan's first season at Celtic Park.

The following weekend, there was another huge crowd inside the stadium to see former Celtic defender John Hughes bring his newly-promoted Falkirk side to Glasgow. The Hoops were unchanged, whilst the Bairns' midfield included Steven Thomson, not to be confused with the present-day BBC Sportscene summariser Steven Thompson, who turned out for Dundee United, Rangers, Cardiff City, Burnley and St Mirren. Falkirk's Steven Thomson had begun his senior career at Crystal Palace, his first goal there being against Gordon Strachan's predecessor at Celtic, Martin O'Neill, Thomson's strike not enough to prevent the Irishman taking Leicester City all the way to League Cup glory at Wembley against Tranmere Rovers in February 2000, just months before moving to Celtic. As an aside, O'Neill's team had included future Celts Neil Lennon and Steve Guppy, whilst Clint Hill was sent off for the Birkenhead outfit some 17 years before equalising for Rangers at Parkhead. A decade after his Crystal Palace debut and now at St Mirren, that same Steven Thomson would score twice against a side managed by Tony Mowbray, Strachan's successor at Celtic. That fateful night in Paisley, on Wednesday, 24 March 2010, would not end well for Mowbray, a disastrous 4-0 defeat ending his disappointing tenure at Parkhead.

It was the visitors Falkirk who drew first blood at Celtic Park on Saturday, 13 August 2005, former Ibrox youngster Darryl Duffy converting a spot-kick as the interval approached, having been taken out by Mo Camara when through one-on-one with Artur Boruc. In the opening minutes of the second period, Shunsuke Nakamura swung over a delightful cross from the left for John Hartson to maintain his fine scoring run with another trademark header at the far post. With 15 minutes remaining, the big striker turned provider, Hartson's chested lay-off setting up Alan Thompson to show that Nakamura was not the only Celt to possess magic in his feet, his ferocious left-foot drive from outside the box rocketing high past Matt Glennon in the Falkirk goal. In stoppage time, the gifted Geordie struck another goal of rare quality, this time his free-kick from the right finding that same top corner for 3-1.

With seven points gained from a possible nine, Celtic travelled to Ibrox the following Saturday with a single-point advantage over the defending champions, who had lost 3-2 at Pittodrie six days earlier. Whilst not quite meeting the Steven Gerrard definition of a visit to the lions' den, due mainly to the absence of real lions, this would undoubtedly prove to be a challenging and intimidating atmosphere to test some of the new Bhoys. Gordon Strachan's first taste of the Glasgow derby had also produced an interesting sideshow, a personal duel with old friend and former Aberdeen and Scotland teammate Alex McLeish, now Rangers manager. Strachan made one change from the two recent home victories, Craig Beattie partnering John Hartson up front in place of Maciej Zurawski, who dropped to the bench. Hartson had captained Wales for the first time in the midweek goalless draw with Slovenia, played in his native Swansea, whilst the Polish striker had featured in both of his country's matches as they won the Valeriy Lobanovskyi Memorial Tournament in Kiev. Zurawski's international teammate Artur Boruc had missed the victory over Serbia & Montenegro but had started the second match against Israel, although Artur being Artur, he had lasted all of 34 minutes before being sent off! The Unholy Goalie was back between the sticks at Ibrox, Celtic lining up as follows.

Artur Boruc: Paul Telfer, Bobo Balde, Stephen McManus & Mo Camara: Stan Petrov, Neil Lennon, Alan Thompson & Shunsuke Nakamura: John Hartson & Craig Beattie.

Celtic started the game well in front of 50,000 spectators, Mo Camara foraging down the left flank to force a corner, which was expertly swung over by Shunsuke Nakamura to pick out the unmarked Bobo Balde. Incredibly, the big Guinean mistimed his header, before watching it bounce up and over the empty goal. This crucial miss would be exacerbated just minutes later, Alan Thompson clattering into Nacho Novo on the halfway line, and as we waited for referee Stuart Dougal to produce a yellow card, he flashed red, Thompson heading down the Ibrox tunnel early for the third time in five years. To compound matters, within 10 minutes Celts were a goal down, Paul Telfer's hesitation allowing Dado Prso to meet Marvin Andrews' speculative floated cross to hook the ball past the helpless Artur Boruc. Being behind was harsh on a 10-man Celtic team who had been by far the more accomplished side.

Early in the second half, there was another crucial decision which went against Celtic, Dougal choosing to ignore Barry Ferguson's blatant kick out at Neil Lennon, the ball then played forward for Belgian midfielder Thomas Buffel to chest it between two defenders before poking the ball through the legs of Boruc for 2-0. With the game slipping away from Celtic, Gordon Strachan brought on Shaun Maloney and Maciej Zurawski for Nakamura and John Hartson, the little Scottish wide man producing hope for the Bhoys with just four minutes remaining, drawing a clumsy challenge from Ian Murray before wrong-footing Ronald Waterreus with a perfect penalty-kick. With Adam Virgo introduced for a late debut, the former Brighton defender replacing Camara as Celts desperately chased an equaliser, that hope was extinguished immediately, the Hoops defence allowing a hopeful ball to bounce in the box, Prso taking full advantage by knocking it past Stan Petrov before collapsing in a heap. Stuart Dougal pointed to the spot for the second time, Novo's poor penalty-kick pretty much summing up the day, the ball agonisingly squirming under Boruc to creep over the line as the big keeper stretched for the post. There would be some final drama played out in the poisonous cauldron of Ibrox as the teams left the field, Celtic captain Neil Lennon, booked earlier, remonstrating angrily with referee Dougal before becoming the second visiting player to be 'red-carded' on this most forgettable of days.

Hoops manager Gordon Strachan later commented on the two dismissals and overall performance.

"He [Lennon] *told the ref he wasn't very enamoured with his performance, but he never swore at him directly. It was industrial language. Thommo put the ref in a position where he had to think about it. When Shaun's penalty went in, I thought, "we'll get something out of the game," but they scored again within two minutes. I was really happy with the way we settled in at the start of the match and when we went down to 10 men in the first half, we were OK.*

I thought there was nothing to be scared of."

The first domestic defeat also gave Gordon a first-hand insight into the less-savoury side of Scotland's most explosive fixture. He recalls the incident in his autobiography, My life in football;

"My most unpleasant experience came after the 3-1 defeat by Rangers, when I stopped at a garage for some petrol. [My wife] Lesley was also in the car with her mother, who had come down from Dundee to stay with us for a few days, and, as I got out, a lad in a vehicle being filled up by a middle-aged guy at the neighbouring pump to mine wound down his window and started taunting me."

"3-1, 3-1, 3-1," he sang."

"It was not having much effect on me, but I could sense the discomfort in Lesley and her mother. The lad, who must have been 14 or 15, appeared to sense it as well. No doubt encouraged by getting some kind of reaction, he kept going."

"3-1, 3-1, 3-1,"

"He went on and on, and as he did so, the middle-aged guy, whom I took to be his father, started laughing. Eventually, when I'd finished at the pump and was ready to pay – with "3-1, 3-1, 3-1," still ringing in my ears – I went over to the lad."

"What's all that about, son?" I said."

"It's just a laugh, Strachan," the guy replied, smirking."

"Well, you might think it is a laugh," I said, "but I have my wife and mother-in-law in the car, and we are all feeling low enough [about the Rangers result] without you trying to make it worse."

"With that, they went through the "3-1, 3-1, 3-1," routine together."

"By this time, I knew full well that Lesley and her mother were upset. What really got to me was that the guy still seemed to think his son's conduct was funny. I turned to the lad again."

"Look son, I don't blame you for being a moron, I blame the moron who brought

you up to be a moron."

"What are you talking about?" the middle-aged man said."

"It's not the kid's fault," I replied. "Someone had to show him how to conduct himself and as you are his dad, it must have been you."

"The guy erupted. He called me every name under the sun. I was "an effing this, an effing that."

*"You are a cocky little ****," he said. The language was something else."*

"Once more, I addressed myself to the lad."

"Hear that, son? Your dad has some new words for you – or have you heard them from him before?"

'It was back to "3-1, 3-1, 3-1," as we went into the garage shop."

"The father of the lad was in front of me in the queue. When it was my turn to pay, the lady at the counter, clearly on my side, said to me, "Sorry about that."

"It's not your fault that he's a moron," I told her."

"As the guy and his son were driving off, they gave me the finger. Lesley and her mum did not say a word."

"What a world we live in, eh?" I said."

Back on the field, Gordon Strachan's Bhoys bounced back from the painful Ibrox defeat with five successive victories. Jim Leishman's Dunfermline Athletic were dismantled 4-0 at East End Park eight days later, with Adam Virgo getting a first Celtic start, playing a holding role in front of the defence. Maciej Zurawski was the other change as Celts were forced to replace the suspended duo of Neil Lennon and Alan Thompson. The Polish striker would be the outstanding performer on the day in front of 9,000 fans. In the fifth minute, he cut in from the left to fire a low drive past Bryn Halliwell in the Pars goal for his first Celtic strike. Just before the hour, Maciej beat his man superbly on the touchline before setting up Shunsuke Nakamura perfectly for his first Hoops goal, Celtic's third. Zurawski then had a fine headed goal disallowed, a dreadful offside decision, before running on to a John Hartson flick-on to finish the scoring at 4-0 with 15 minutes remaining. Earlier, on 10 minutes, Hartson had benefitted from a goalkeeping error to notch yet another League goal, Halliwell's miscued clearance falling at the feet of the big Welshman for a tap-in. The Fifers did have a chance to reduce the deficit just before the half-hour, Virgo's clumsy challenge on Mark Burchill allowing the former Hoops striker an opportunity to beat Artur Boruc from 12 yards. Although, Burchill struck his shot well, the Celtic keeper produced a fabulous save, diving low to his left to parry the ball to safety. At 3-0, young midfielder Paul Lawson had replaced Virgo for his own first team debut. It had been a satisfactory afternoon all round for Celtic in the ancient kingdom.

The three points kept the Hoops tucked in five points behind runaway leaders Hearts, the Tynecastle men enjoying a 100% record under George Burley. Over at Ibrox, a second-half Ivan Sproule hat-trick gave Tony Mowbray's Hibernian an unexpected 3-0 victory. This result, combined with their earlier defeat at Pittodrie, meant that Alex McLeish's Rangers now trailed his old friend's team by a point, despite their rather flattering and fortunate derby win.

The Du Wei saga finally came to an end – well for the time being anyway - as September dawned, with the clubs agreeing a fee for a four-year deal with, crucially as it turned out, a break clause inserted in January. Peter Lawwell saw opportunities off the field as well as on it, given the recent captures of players from Japan and China, as he commented on Du Wei's acquisition.

"First and foremost, he's a footballer and we have a very high regard for him as a footballer. People talk about Celtic as a global brand but in Scotland we don't get the exposure we could get abroad. But with Shunsuke Nakamura and Du Wei here, they could open up different markets and, hopefully, through those two transfers we are able to benefit and take us worldwide, which will increase our revenue. For too long, Scotland and Ireland have been our mainstays and the fans have been fantastic but there's a limit to that. We can't keep coming back to that and we have to look at different markets. He came here on trial three or four weeks ago and he impressed everybody at the club, particularly Gordon Strachan. He is a fantastic footballer, fantastic individual and a very

strong character. He has signed a four-year deal but there is a break in January to see if Du Wei settles, coming from China to a different lifestyle and culture. I am confident he will. The club and the Chinese nation have great hopes and I am sure he will be here for the four years and beyond."

For his part, Du Wei seemed relieved that he could finally focus on his football.

"I'm very happy to be in Glasgow again and I'm ready to take the next step in my career with Celtic. I hope to be ready for the first team very soon. That's why I'm here. The things that have been happening over the last few weeks are now in the past for me. I'm just so grateful for Celtic making such a strong commitment to me and putting so much effort into pushing this transfer through. I'll now be doing everything in my power to prove I'm worth the trust Celtic have placed in me. I'll fight to get my chance at Celtic and I'm confident that this can be a success."

Time would tell if that confidence would be misplaced.

CHAPTER 6

Back-to-back wins over old pal McLeish as Strachan's Bhoys go top

The first week in September was reserved for international fixtures across the globe as the race to reach the 2006 World Cup finals tournament in Germany approached its final stretch. Scotland's vital qualifying clash with Italy at Hampden on Saturday, 3 September 2005 saw Craig Beattie make his first appearance at that level, the young Celt replacing goalscorer Kenny Miller with 15 minutes remaining, just seconds after Fabio Grosso had equalised for the star-studded Italians, who would win Group 5 then the trophy itself the following summer in Berlin. Wolverhampton Wanderers' striker Miller would add a double in midweek as the Scots beat Norway 2-1 in Oslo, Beattie again a late substitute, this time for Everton's James McFadden. The Norwegians included former Celtic defender Vidar Riseth, now enjoying a second spell with Rosenborg after three years spent in Germany with 1860 Munich.

John Hartson went close several times in Wales' qualifying tie against England at Cardiff's Millennium Stadium on the Saturday, a deflected Joe Cole shot giving the English victory. He was then suspended for the midweek trip to Warsaw, his Celtic teammate Maciej Zurawski scoring the only goal from the penalty spot early in the second half as the Welsh failed to gain revenge for the 3-2 defeat in their previous clash in Cardiff 11 months earlier, when both Hartson and Zurawski had been on target. Poland thus continued their excellent form in Group 6, Artur Boruc enjoying a second successive clean sheet in a match which saw the first international appearance of Joe Ledley. The Cardiff City youngster came on as a late substitute for Hartson's replacement, Robert Earnshaw. Boruc and

Zurawski had also played in a 3-0 win over Austria in Chorzow four days earlier, the striker claiming Poland's third.

There was another Celtic reunion of sorts in Stockholm that same afternoon, as Sweden faced Stan Petrov's Bulgaria in a Group 8 qualifier. The home front three comprised Stan's old teammate Henrik Larsson plus Zlatan Ibrahimovic and Freddie Ljungberg, the latter on target in a 3-0 win. Hristo Stoichkov's men did taste victory in midweek, Bayer Leverkusen star Dimitar Berbatov with Bulgaria's first goal as they fought back from two goals down to beat Iceland 3-2 in Sofia, Stan Petrov playing the full 90 minutes. Elsewhere, Stan Varga came on for the final five minutes of Slovakia's 1-1 draw with Latvia in Riga, whilst his defensive partner Bobo Balde put in a full shift as Guinea beat Malawi 3-1 in Conakry but the furthest travelled international Celt that week was Shunsuke Nakamura, who scored with a penalty kick 10 minutes into the second half in already-qualified Japan's 5-4 friendly win over Honduras in Miyagi on the Wednesday night before commencing the long flight back to Glasgow.

The international stars were all to the fore at the weekend. Aberdeen were the visitors to Celtic Park on Saturday, 10 September 2005, the 20th anniversary of the great Jock Stein's death, just as they had been back in 1985, four days after the tragedy in Cardiff. The visiting supporters displayed a banner with the words, 'RIP Jock Stein,' a nice touch appreciated by the home crowd. With Neil Lennon and Alan Thompson restored to the starting line-up, Maciej Zurawski followed up his Dunfermline and Poland goals with another fine performance, the Polish striker scoring the opener in 13 minutes then setting up Stan Petrov to beat Pittodrie keeper Ryan Esson with a low drive for the decisive second on the hour, as Jimmy Calderwood's Dons were sent packing in front of just under 60,000 spectators. At the Falkirk Stadium the same afternoon, Rangers followed up their home defeat to Hibernian two weeks earlier by dropping another point in a 1-1 draw.

A tricky trip to Easter Road the following Sunday was settled by a moment of magic in the first five minutes, Shunsuke Nakamura's delightfully threaded pass allowing Stan Petrov to beat Hibernian's goalkeeper Zbigniew

Malkowski and future Hoops defender Gary Caldwell to slide home his second goal in consecutive games. The Japanese midfielder was inches away from a second after the interval, his long-range free-kick beating the 'other Polish keeper' all ends up but thumping back off the post to safety. There were a couple of late scares for Celtic, as first Steven Whittaker then Steven Fletcher threatened to grab an undeserved equaliser, but Artur Boruc and his defenders stood firm and the black-clad Celts returned along the M8 with another three precious points in the bag.

There was another fright for Celtic in midweek as Falkirk returned to Parkhead for their second visit in a month, this time in the League Cup in front of the regular 25,000 hardy 'Home Cup Ticket Scheme' souls. The Bairns had been on the end of an 8-1 mauling from Martin O'Neill's Celtic at the same stage of the competition the previous season, the Irishman choosing to make eight changes that night on the back of, strangely enough, a tough game at Easter Road and ahead of the Champions League trip to Milan. Ross Wallace had scored a hat-trick that evening, however, the young winger did not even make the bench here, Gordon Strachan making only three tweaks to Sunday's winning team. Those saw Shaun Maloney and fit-again Chris Sutton coming in for suspended midfield duo Neil Lennon and Alan Thompson, whilst John Hartson had earned a welcome breather in the back seat of the home dugout, Craig Beattie getting an opportunity to partner Maciej Zurawski up front.

There would be no danger of any repeat of that 8-1 humiliation as Falkirk traded blows with Celtic, Bairns veteran playmaker Russell Latapy a particular delight on the eye. Having opened the scoring in the recent League match in Glasgow, the visitors managed to do so again, this time through Alan Gow, 10 minutes into the second half, the big striker robbing the rusty Sutton to fire home. Strachan was concerned enough to call up his prize hitman Hartson from the bench to replace Beattie on the hour, his introduction paying immediate dividends as the big Welshman combined brilliantly with Maloney to set Zurawski up for a curling equaliser just two minutes later. Artur Boruc then made an excellent fingertip save to prevent Gow winning the tie in the dying seconds, Falkirk having cause to rue that miss just four minutes into extra-time as Hartson rose yet again to become Celtic's saviour, his header taking Celtic into the draw for the last eight of the competition. It had been a bit too close for comfort.

Gordon Strachan was brief but balanced in his assessment afterwards.

"If you create four times as many chances as your opponents, you have to be impressed with that. We made changes from Sunday but should have had the game finished before extra-time. Chris Sutton returned to the side after injury and did very well before tiring."

At least Celtic had progressed. Across at Almondvale, Paul Lambert's Livingston faced Hearts, 10 days after a 4-1 mauling at the same venue from the League leaders. The Lions had managed just a solitary point from their opening six matches but turned the form book upside down to win 1-0 and send the Gorgie men tumbling out of the competition. Another struggling side, Dunfermline Athletic, edged a seven-goal thriller with Kilmarnock at Rugby Park whilst at Ibrox, Rangers were just 17 minutes from elimination at the hands of First Division Clyde, co-managed by their former player Graham Roberts and ex-Celtic winger Joe Miller – before they won through after extra-time.

The club guaranteed to bring shivers into the heart of every Celtic fan of a certain vintage was the next visitor to Celtic Park, as Inverness Caledonian Thistle player-manager Craig Brewster brought his side to Glasgow's east end on Saturday, 24 September 2005. Craig Beattie retained his starting place, partnering John Hartson as the injured Maciej Zurawski missed out, and he repaid his manager's faith in some style, beating future Hoops goalkeeper Mark Brown twice in 10 minutes either side of the hour as Celts recovered from the loss of an early second-half Dennis Wyness strike to win by the odd goal in three. Brown's performance that day would have pleasant repercussions for the Caley keeper but that 'r' word must have figured in the thoughts of Rangers manager Alex McLeish, whose side lost 1-0 to Hearts at Tynecastle the same day, a third defeat in the opening eight games of his title defence.

Hearts boss George Burley was in the Almondvale stand on the first day of October, as Celtic faced a Livingston side who had followed up their League Cup win over Hearts with a creditable point at Pittodrie. Burley's side were due to visit Celtic Park in the next fixture, a top-of-the-table encounter, and the former Ipswich Town and Scotland full-back looked on as Celts turned on the style for the packed crowd basking in the autumn sunshine. Stephen McManus headed the first goal on 36 minutes from a knocked-on corner, Shaun Maloney then swivelling in the box to double the visitors' lead seconds before the break. A near-post header early in the second half from Maciej Zurawski – in for John Hartson - put Celtic 3-0 ahead, before Chris Sutton made it four on the hour, the big Englishman volleying home after a free-kick had been diverted into his path. Celtic-daft Robert Snodgrass had replaced Paul Dalglish, the Son of the King, for the Lions before Craig Beattie tapped home at the far post to seal a 5-0 victory, Celtic's biggest winning margin since Gordon Strachan had taken charge. The following day, along the M9 at Grangemouth, Hearts would finally drop points in a 2-2 draw at the Falkirk Stadium. That would prove to be a bizarre day for another future Celt, Steven Pressley, who put through his own net to give Falkirk a 2-0 lead with just 20 minutes remaining, before performing his own one-man rescue act, the big defender pulling a goal back then equalising in the dying seconds to preserve the League leaders' long unbeaten record.

Another frustrating international break kicked in before Celts played again, a feeling no doubt shared by the Tartan Army as Scotland went down by a solitary early goal to Belarus at a packed Hampden on Saturday, 8 October 2005 to end any hopes of reaching a second finals tournament in Germany, more than three decades after the memorable events of summer 1974. Once again, Celtic players were conspicuous by their absence in the starting line-up, albeit Shaun Maloney became the second of Gordon Strachan's young stars to make his international debut that autumn, the Malaysian-born midfielder replacing Ian Murray of Rangers at half-time. With the pressure off, and Scotland being Scotland, they then proceeded to beat Slovenia 3-0 in Celje in midweek, with no Celts involved.

John Hartson returned for Wales the same afternoon in the 3-2 qualifying win over the Six Counties in Belfast, whilst Artur Boruc and Maciej Zurawski also played the full 90 minutes in Poland's 3-2 friendly win over Iceland in Warsaw 24 hours earlier. All three Celts were involved in midweek, a Ryan Giggs' double enough for Wales to see off Azerbaijan in Cardiff but Zurawski's involvement in the 2-1 defeat by England at Old Trafford was curtailed by injury just before half-time. Ironically, his replacement, former Wisla Krakow star Tomasz Frankowski, now plying his trade in Spain with Elche, scored the Polish equaliser that evening to finish level with Maciej on seven goals as the top scorer in Group 6. Both England as group winners and Poland as best-placed runners-up could look forward to the finals in Germany at the end of the season, whilst Wales finished a disappointing fifth of the six nations.

Stan Petrov also failed to appear in the second half of Bulgaria's 2-0 win over Hungary in Sofia in Group 8 and he was missing as the Balkan nation completed their schedule with a 1-1 draw with Malta in Ta'Qali in midweek. Croatia and Sweden were the qualifiers there with Bulgaria in third place. And Stan Varga was an unused substitute as Slovakia and Russia played out a goalless draw in that same Tehelne pole stadium in Bratislava where the Artmedia nightmare had occurred three months earlier. That result was enough to edge out the Russians from second spot in Group 3 on goal difference, Portugal progressing directly whilst the Slovakians would now face a knock-out play-off with Spain to reach the finals in Germany.

Shunsuke Nakamura was also playing in Europe in that international break, the Japanese star putting his side 2-0 up from the penalty spot early in the second half in Riga before making way for Alex Santos. The Latvians would fight back to claim a last-gasp draw in their friendly match. Nakamura would again start but not finish in Japan's 1-0 defeat by Ukraine in Kiev four days later, the hosts also scoring in the final minute from a penalty. The final Celt involved was Bobo Balde, who played the full 90 minutes as Guinea beat Botswana 2-1 in Gaborone to secure a place in the 2006 Africa Cup of Nations but miss out on World Cup qualification to Group 5 winners Tunisia.

Back with domestic football, there was an incredible 60,100 crowd inside Celtic Park three days later, Saturday, 15 October 2005, most hoping that the Bhoys could reduce the three-point lead currently enjoyed by visitors Hearts. Alan Thompson and Neil Lennon returned in midfield, with Shaun Maloney dropping to the bench and Chris Sutton moving up front to partner Craig Beattie in the absence of injured Maciej Zurawski, Celtic lining up as follows.

Artur Boruc: Paul Telfer, Bobo Balde, Stephen McManus & Mo Camara: Stan Petrov, Neil Lennon, Alan Thompson & Shunsuke Nakamura: Chris Sutton & Craig Beattie.

It was Beattie who opened the scoring early on, his shot deflecting high past Hearts keeper Steve Banks, making his debut between the posts in place of the suspended Craig Gordon. Banks was then a relieved man seconds later, as he watched a header from Bobo Balde strike the face of his post. The Hoops lead was short-lived, however, a moment of fatal hesitation between Artur Boruc and Paul Telfer being punished by Rudi Skacel just three minutes later, the Czech striker thus continuing his excellent scoring run. Banks then did his best to emulate his famous namesake, the late, great Gordon, as he pulled off a string of saves from Balde, Telfer and twice from Thompson before his best moment, the Hearts goalkeeper producing a stunning fingertip save from substitute Maloney's curling thunderbolt. Banks was the key man as the Gorgie side left Glasgow's east end with their lead and unbeaten record intact, and a glorious opportunity was missed by Celtic, particularly as word came through that Rangers had dropped yet another point on their travels, this time in a goalless draw with Dundee United at Tannadice.

There was good news two days later though, as Celts ended the ongoing speculation surrounding on-loan goalkeeper Artur Boruc by tying the 25-year-old Pole up on a three-and-a-half-year contract. Initially signed on a year-long loan deal from Legia Warsaw, the Holy Goalie's recent form in the Celtic goals had been drawing admiring glances from a number of clubs, most notably Arsenal. Parkhead manager Gordon Strachan expressed his delight that Boruc had been signed permanently, with a perhaps unwitting but nevertheless classic pun thrown in for good measure.

"It doesn't make a difference whether it was Arsenal or Juventus who were interested in him, we were blinkered and wanted Artur here. We were in pole position. We brought Artur to the club and, once he was here, we knew he would like it. Everybody at the club – the players, coaching staff and people behind the scenes – are delighted."

The big keeper was in his usual place the following Sunday, up against a young and hirsute partnership of Kris Boyd and Steven Naismith as Celtic travelled to face Jim Jeffries' Kilmarnock. Shaun Maloney replaced Alan Thompson, whilst top goalscorer John Hartson once again had to be content with a spot on the bench, Gordon Strachan sticking with Craig Beattie and Chris Sutton up top. The English striker was involved in the only goal of the game, midway through the first half, Sutton holding the play up perfectly for the marauding Stan Petrov to dash between two defenders and dink the ball over Graeme Smith in the home goal. Just as it had been that title-winning day back in April 2004, the midfielder's goal would be enough to clinch the three points at Rugby Park.

The Bulgarian powerhouse was on fire in midweek, as an unchanged Hoops line-up began the second round of League fixtures against Terry Butcher's Motherwell at Celtic Park, Petrov opening the scoring within 15 minutes after a delightful through ball from Shaun Maloney. The new Scottish international midfielder made it 2-0 soon afterwards, Maloney bringing a crossed ball down on his chest before firing home at the far post. Just before the interval, a tremendous Petrov drive from the edge of the box crashed into the net off the post for a glorious third, but the highlight of the evening was Celtic's fourth goal, a wonderful free-kick from Shunsuke Nakamura which flew into the postage stamp corner with former Rangers keeper Graeme Smith a helpless onlooker. As an aside, it can't be too often that you face two different goalkeepers in successive matches with identical names! The biggest cheer of the night was then nipped in the bud by a linesman's flag, after Neil Lennon had scored what appeared to be his first goal in five years, but a fifth Celtic goal would soon be forthcoming, Petrov completing his hat-trick with another trademark run and finish, after Sutton had delightfully dummied a through ball on the right of the Motherwell penalty area. This was the first night I recall Parkhead reverberating to the chant of *"One Gordon Strachan,"* after a really weird introductory three months, his side on the up whilst Alex McLeish's Rangers appeared to be in freefall. The title-holders lost a two-goal lead in the second half to draw at Almondvale, Hoops-daft Robert Snodgrass with a double for Livingston. The Celtic manager was fulsome in his praise of his own Bulgarian scoring star in his post-match comments.

"[Stiliyan] *has got everything, and he showed us his range of skills from the middle of the park. I was delighted to get five goals and the manner in which we got them was very pleasing. We started slowly but our imagination and variation of play was excellent. Everyone played their part."*

The Celtic supporters were singing again at Tannadice the following Sunday, 30 October 2005, as Gordon Strachan's side claimed top spot in the League. Hearts' long unbeaten run had finally ended just where they would most have wished it not to, with a 2-0 defeat by Hibernian at Easter Road, meaning that Celts could leapfrog them on goal difference with a win in Dundee the next day, and Rangers continued to throw away points with a 2-2 home draw with Inverness Caledonian Thistle. It didn't start well for the Hoops, and Chris Sutton in particular, his near-post header from Barry Robson's corner flashing past Artur Boruc to give Dundee United the lead within four minutes. The big Englishman would make amends for that error, and how. First, for the second successive match his clever dummy led to a Celtic goal, the restored John Hartson – in for Craig Beattie - finishing clinically for 1-1. Next, Sutton instinctively stuck out a boot as Shaun Maloney's low shot came into the box, the change of direction wrong-footing Derek Stillie in the United goal to put Celts ahead. Back came the home side to equalise within two minutes, Collin Samuel turning smartly on Mark Wilson's pass to beat Boruc at the post. An incredible five minutes of play continued as Sutton put pressure on the United defence at a corner, Alan Archibald getting the final touch to become the latest member of the Tannadice Own Goal club. It was no surprise that things calmed down significantly after that, the game's sixth and final goal coming in the 88th minute, substitute Stephen Pearson winning the race at the far post to meet Stan Petrov's tantalising low cross, 4-2 enough to seal top spot for the Bhoys.

There was a poignant moment in Celtic's modern history the following Saturday, 5 November 2005, on the eve of the club's 118th birthday, as Kate Robinson's stunning statue of Brother Walfrid was unveiled by Hoops chairman Brian Quinn, Walfrid's great-niece and nephew, his fellow Sligoman Sean Fallon and two refugees. This was the first such artwork to be installed at the main entrance to Celtic Park and it would later be joined by three others, acknowledging Parkhead legend, Jock Stein, Jimmy Johnstone and Billy McNeill over the coming years. The four plaques on the base of Walfrid's statue are quite beautifully presented, retelling the story of the origins of Celtic, our greatest moment in Lisbon and the present, using the quotes of Willie Maley and Stein and the Marist motto, *'Ignoti et quasi occulti in hoc mundo'*, translating to 'unknown and hidden in the world.' That phrase would probably have sounded like a decent option for Alex McLeish, as his Rangers side stuttered to a third successive League draw, this time a goalless match with his old club Aberdeen at Ibrox. They had also shared the points twice in their head-to-head Champions League clashes with our old friends Artmedia Bratislava in the same period.

The next day, the men currently wearing the Hoops were in action in Falkirk, where title rivals Hearts and Rangers had both recently stumbled. There would be no such problem for Gordon Strachan's men, Celts going ahead for the first time in three games against the Bairns when Shaun Maloney tapped home Mo Camara's perfect cross from the left just before the break. Within a minute, the Celtic lead was doubled, Aiden McGeady - in for the injured Chris Sutton for his first start since the opening day at Motherwell, with Maloney pushed forward to partner John Hartson - dancing in from the left to beat Matt Glennon at his near post. On the hour, Celts got a third, another piece of history as Camara again did well on the left to set up Maloney, whose fierce drive was brilliantly parried by the keeper, only for the big Celtic Dragon John Hartson to fire home to reach his century of goals for the Bhoys. The game finished 3-0, allowing

Celtic to regain the top spot. A beaming Hartson explained afterwards how it felt to achieve that particular milestone.

"Some great players have reached 100 goals for Celtic, and to be in that sort of company makes me very proud. Hopefully, there will be a few more to come."

And his manager, Gordon Strachan, took time out to acknowledge his striker's contribution, in the midst of stories surrounding his personal life.

"I'm delighted for John. He's had a rough time over the last couple of months. Being on the football field is the one place he can relax. I was really pleased with the performance. We kept our concentration really well and did not allow the crowd to get excited."

In midweek, there was a chance for Strachan's Celtic to seek revenge for the August League defeat at Ibrox, the sides drawn together at this stage of the League Cup for the second successive season, as with Falkirk in the previous round. The Hoops manager went with the following team.

Artur Boruc: Paul Telfer, Bobo Balde, Stephen McManus & Mo Camara: Shunsuke Nakamura, Stan Petrov, Neil Lennon & Aiden McGeady: John Hartson & Shaun Maloney.

The fixture at Ibrox 12 months earlier had seen Celts lose 2-1, Martin O'Neill's fourth and final attempt to win a second League Cup ending in failure, despite his side leading as the game entered its closing stages. This year, the Hoops would have home advantage, and they took it, Shaun Maloney's incredible 30-yard drive on the half-hour ripping past a badly-positioned Stefan Klos to put Celtic 1-0 up. The German keeper had been a teammate of Paul Lambert as their Borussia Dortmund side beat holders Juventus to win a first Champions League in Munich, back in 1997. However, this would be a night for him to forget. After Greek defender Sotirios Kyrgiakos had been shown a second yellow card then a red, for sarcastically applauding referee Kenny Clark, Klos seemed more intent on watching the fearsome Bobo Balde charging towards him than dealing with Shunsuke Nakamura's teasing cross, the ball hitting the distracted keeper before rolling over the line to finish the game as a contest with eight minutes remaining. The final whistle blew shortly afterwards, with the old ground shaking to the sound of "You'll never walk alone", and Celtic in the last four of the League Cup. Strachan revealed after the match that he had spoken with Maloney at the interval.

"He wasn't at his best in the first half. He told me at half time that he could play better than this and I said, "you're right." His goal was fantastic, but I am expecting a bit more and he gave it."

And the Celtic manager's overall impressions following his first victory over Rangers?

"We had to work incredibly hard at times to win the ball out there. We stayed above the often-scary atmosphere, in terms of how you expect an Old Firm tie to be played. The result is first and foremost but to play like that is an added bonus and we're feeling good about ourselves."

His old friend Alex McLeish was coming under increasing pressure, as the results continued to be poor.

"I don't quit easily. It's not easy at the moment but we'll keep soldiering on. Our discipline has been good, so I was disappointed to lose Sotorios Kyrgiakos. It made it difficult for us. I need to have an explanation. I understand he was sent off for dissent, but we will deal with that internally because you can't afford to lose guys like Sotorios. They are dropping like flies at the moment and we also lost Julien Rodriguez to injury out there. It could be damage to his calf, or a bone injury. Once we see the scans in the morning, I'll be able to tell you further."

Whilst Celtic's win had been widely predicted, the other three quarter-final ties went against the form book. Livingston and Dunfermline Athletic were struggling at the foot of the table, but they upset the odds by defeating Inverness Caledonian Thistle and Hibernian respectively at home, whilst Motherwell also defeated a team above them in the League, Jimmy Calderwood's Aberdeen, by 1-0 at Fir Park. The Steelmen would be Celtic's semi-final opponents at Hampden in the new year.

Shaun Maloney received a second Scottish cap in a 1-1 draw with the USA in a Hampden friendly on Saturday, 12 November 2005, the diminutive Celt joining the fray in the 73rd minute at the same time as young Hibernian midfielder Scott Brown received his international baptism. Maloney was the only Celtic player to feature, whilst Hearts boasted four of the starting line-up, three of whom like Brown would later move to Parkhead, Craig Gordon, Steven Pressley and Paul Hartley.

The main focus for the final international break of 2005 was the World Cup qualification play-offs. The only Celt involved was Stan Varga, albeit he could only look on from the bench as Spain hammered his Slovakia 5-1 in Madrid's Vicente Calderon to render the second leg in Bratislava a dead rubber. Artur Boruc was also on Spanish soil as Poland beat Ecuador 3-0 in Barcelona's Montjuic Stadium, whilst John Hartson endured a frustrating night in Limassol as Cyprus beat Wales 1-0 in another friendly match. Stan Petrov played 50 minutes of Bulgaria's 6-2 win over Georgia in Sofia then the vast majority of his country's 3-0 victory over Mexico in Houston, Texas, but perhaps the strangest pairing of the break involved Shunsuke Nakamura, who featured as Japan beat Angola 1-0 in Tokyo.

With international football cast to the sidings until the new year, the focus could once again return to the domestic scene. Rangers goalkeeper Stefan Klos paid for his poor performance in the recent defeat at Celtic Park, the German replaced by a Dutchman, Ronald Waterreus, as the teams clashed again at the same venue in a League game 10 days later, Saturday, 19 November 2005, Celtic going with an unchanged line-up. John Hartson wasted no time commencing work on his second century of goals, sweeping home Shaun Maloney's perfect cross in the 12th minute, after great work by Shunsuke Nakamura on the right. The Japanese magician was at it again, 10 minutes into the second half, twisting his defender this way then that, before flighting a delightful cross onto the head of Bobo Balde, who glanced it across the Rangers keeper for 2-0. Five minutes later, Wattereus had his own moment to forget, Aiden McGeady's side-footed effort from Maloney's cross somehow escaping his grasp to kill off the defending champions' bid to retain their title as early as November, Rangers now trailing Celtic by a massive 15 points. More importantly, with Hearts not due to play at Pittodrie until the following day, Gordon Strachan's men had finally put some clear daylight - and three points - between the two title-challenging sides. We would not know it at the time, but this game would mark the final appearance of another Martin O'Neill veteran, the flying Didier Agathe coming off the bench with 14 minutes remaining to replace the injured Nakamura, the man now patrolling the Frenchman's former beat, wide on the right of Celtic's midfield.

Shunsuke Nakamura was missing the following Saturday, as was Shaun Maloney, both men failing to recover from injury as the League leaders hosted bottom-dogs Dunfermline Athletic, the Pars coming off the back of seven straight defeats and manager Jim Leishman able to field only six substitutes, such was their own injury crisis. Back into the Celtic team came Chris Sutton - partnering John Hartson up front for what would be his final appearance at Parkhead - and Alan Thompson. There was a minute's applause beforehand to honour George Best, the Irish football genius who passed away the previous day, still only 59 years old, after his much-publicised battles with his own demons. Whilst I hadn't managed to witness Best at his peak in the flesh, I was present to see his first-ever match against Celtic, on Saturday, 12 January 1980. Best's cameo role that afternoon produced a goal and a point for relegation-bound Hibernian at Easter Road, Hoops keeper Peter Latchford not covering himself in glory with his attempts to keep out the Irishman's angled drive midway through the first half. Best's remaining games against Celtic would be less memorable, for him anyway, the Bhoys winning 4-0 in a League clash at Parkhead two months later before going one better in the Scottish Cup semi-final at Hampden in April, setting up a final showdown with Rangers. It seems strange to feel sympathy for a handsome, millionaire Irishman with a footballing gift from God, who counted sleeping with Miss Worlds and drinking champagne as an occupational hazard, nevertheless I was genuinely sad to see how it ended for George Best in his later, troubled years. Rest in eternal peace, George.

Still elated following successive wins over their Ibrox rivals, the mood of the home support ahead of Celtic's game with Dunfermline was brought crashing back to earth, as Greg Ross's first-half strike for the Pars proved to be the only goal of the game, keeper Allan McGregor – on loan from

Rangers, who lost yet again the same day, this time by 2-1 at Easter Road - enjoying a rare clean sheet at Parkhead. There was some relief at full-time, at least, as the news came through that Hearts had drawn 1-1 at Motherwell, future Celt Paul Hartley's stoppage-time penalty preventing an even worse result for those of a maroon persuasion. On the back of a similar score for the Gorgie men at Aberdeen six days earlier, this welcome and timely surprise allowed Celtic to maintain a single point lead at the top of the table, despite the Hoops suffering their first home defeat of the Gordon Strachan era. That didn't provide too much consolation for the Celtic boss though, as he addressed the media afterwards.

"At this time, that gives me no comfort whatsoever. We must congratulate ourselves on what we have done in the last three months. We have to expect days like this sometimes. Our style of play was not working in the first 20 minutes and we tried to get that message to the players. We switched to Plan B and that was more successful in terms of chances. If we had been better at taking our chances and got a couple of breaks, we would have been okay."

Strachan also dismissed suggestions that the absence of his main creative duo, Shunsuke Nakamura and Shaun Maloney, had been a key factor in the defeat.

"We had enough good players to do better than that."

The one-point lead was already gone by the time Celtic arrived at Pittodrie on the following Sunday, 4 December 2005, a Rudi Skacel double giving Hearts the three points at home to Livingston the day before. And when Jamie Winter fired the Dons in front with a free-kick eight minutes into the second half, Gordon Strachan may have wondered how a side featuring three changes – Mo Camara, Alan Thompson and Chris Sutton making way for Ross Wallace, Shunsuke Nakamura and Maciej Zurawski - would react. He would have his answer within 10 minutes, by which time the Hoops had scored three times. First, Aiden McGeady reacted quickest to fire a shot high past Ryan Esson, after Bobo Balde's shot had been blocked then, two minutes later, Stan Petrov did likewise, after the Aberdeen keeper had fumbled a John Hartson drive. Just after the hour, Paul Telfer picked up a short Nakamura corner on the right, evading his man like a regular winger before firing home. This would be Paul's first and, as it transpired, only goal in his Celtic career. More importantly, the crucial one-point advantage had been immediately restored. The fact that news of defending champions Rangers losing yet another two-goal lead that weekend - this time sharing the points with Falkirk at Ibrox – was greeted with something approaching apathy, showed just how much the balance of power had swung in Glasgow in a few short months. The 2005/06 title would be a two-way shoot-out between Celtic and Hearts.

There was another thrilling fightback at Celtic Park six days later, as Hibernian came to town, a young Scott Brown wearing the number seven in their starting line-up, which also featured future Celts Gary Caldwell and Derek Riordan. For the first time, Chinese defender Du Wei took a seat on the substitutes' bench, where he would remain for the duration of the game. Celtic's other two dragons were very much involved though, combining expertly for the first goal. Five minutes from the interval, John Hartson got on the end of Shunsuke Nakamura's free-kick from the left, to nod the Bhoys in front. The game then turned on its head twice in the opening 20 minutes of the second period. First, Guillaume Beuzelin forced his way in front of his marker Stan Petrov to head Hibs level from a near-post corner, then Steven Fletcher sent a tremendous left-footed volley past Artur Boruc from the edge of the box. Celts hit back immediately. As the Hibs defence prepared for another Nakamura special, Shaun Maloney stepped up to curl a beautiful dead-ball over the wall and past the stranded Zbeigniew Malkowski. The Celtic winner duly arrived on 65 minutes, Maloney's shot from a Nakamura cross beating the keeper but rebounding off the far post, only for Hartson to bundle home the fifth and decisive goal of the game. As against Dundee United back in August, the Welshman was then denied his hat-trick by the width of the crossbar. It would prove a pivotal day in the flag race, Hearts held to a goalless draw at home by Inverness Caledonian Thistle, Celtic's lead at the top thus extended to three points. Despite that, there was mixed feedback from Gordon Strachan at the post-match debrief.

"It was entertaining for people who came to watch the game, but for the coaches it

will be a restless night. We conceded from a set play, and I don't like losing goals from them, so we have to look at that, and the second. But there was some great stuff and it was a great game, as I predicted."

Next up for Strachan's Hoops was a visit to the Scottish Highlands, to face that same Caledonian Thistle on the following Sunday.

Three days before that, however, on Thursday, 15 December 2005, a very special player arrived in Glasgow as an early Christmas present for Celtic supporters.

CHAPTER 7

An Irish legend arrives at Celtic ...and discovers that a week is a long time in football

Just 24 hours before Celtic completed that November double over Rangers, events were unfolding some 200 miles south which would have direct consequences for the player involved and the Parkhead club. An official statement from Manchester United confirmed that skipper Roy Keane had left Old Trafford by mutual consent, a seemingly inevitable conclusion to a series of conflicts between player, teammates and management over recent weeks, which had culminated in an explosive interview with the club's own TV channel, deemed so contentious it was subsequently never broadcast.

I guess like many Celtic supporters, my ears pricked up at the news and the immediate possibility that he could end up in Glasgow. Roy Keane had for many years epitomised for me the identikit Celtic midfield player. The Cork-born midfielder was a world-class footballing talent with an unbelievable will to win and he had never hidden his admiration for the club. I had seen photos of him sitting in the Free Broomloan on several occasions and then at the Scottish Cup final of 2002, I had the good fortune to bump into him as I approached Hampden from Aikenhead Road with my two sons, leading to one of my most treasured photographs, Roy and my Bhoys. The highlight of that day as it transpired.

Despite the obvious tensions, both club and player made respectful noises as they parted ways, with the now former Manchester United captain Roy Keane commenting;

"It has been a great honour and privilege for me to play for Manchester United

for over 12 years. During my time at the club, I have been fortunate to play alongside some of the best players in the game and in front of the best supporters in the world. At all times, I have endeavoured to do my best for the management and the team. Whilst it is a sad day for me to leave such a great club and manager, I believe that the time has now come for me to move on. After so many years, I will miss everyone at the club. I send my best wishes for the future to the management, players, staff and supporters of the club."

That was reciprocated by Old Trafford boss, Alex Ferguson;

"Roy Keane has been a fantastic servant for Manchester United. The best midfield player in the world of his generation, he is already one of the great figures in our club's illustrious history. Roy has been central to the success of the club in the last 12-and-a-half years and everyone at Old Trafford wishes him well in the rest of his career and beyond."

Whilst the 34-year-old Keane had not played since suffering a broken foot at Anfield in September, the comments from all sides made it clear that he would be continuing his playing career elsewhere, with Celtic immediately installed as one of the favourites for his signature. Parkhead manager Gordon Strachan had previously refused to engage in discussions around the possibility of Roy Keane joining Celtic whilst the Irishman was still a contracted Manchester United player, however, that obstacle had now been removed. Even as a man in his mid-40s, this saddo was excited at the prospect of him finally wearing the Hoops, glued to the daily TV updates as the speculation mounted over the coming weeks.

With the Irishman apparently ruling out a move to another English club, despite Everton's David Moyes and Sam Allardyce at Bolton making hopeful noises, the biggest threat to Celtic securing his signature appeared to come from Real Madrid, where he would join a midfield already including his former Old Trafford teammate David Beckham, the French genius Zinedine Zidane and…er…Thomas Gravesen. At one point that deal looked sure to go ahead, Keane famously contacted by the club's vice-president Emilio Butragueno, whilst sitting on the toilet. However, on 4 December 2005, Real Madrid sacked their Brazilian coach Wanderley Luxemburgo, outspoken president Florentino Perez then announcing that any transfer decision would have to wait until the winter break on 21 December. Thankfully, that would prove to be six days too late, as to my absolute delight, on Thursday, 15 December, Roy Keane signed for his boyhood club, Celtic.

I wasn't alone. Chief executive Peter Lawwell moved quickly to welcome Keane on behalf of the club, whilst shooting down suggestions that major shareholder Dermot Desmond was funding the signing.

"We are absolutely delighted – the board, management and the players. Dermot Desmond has been a fantastic supporter of this transaction but in terms of his support, that is where it started and ended. There is no financial contribution Dermot will make towards this deal."

Celtic manager Gordon Strachan also expressed his delight.

"He has proved over the last 15 years that he is a competitor. You can't get enough competitors in your squad and this was too good a chance to miss."

As always, the doubters were quickly out in force, advising that Roy Keane was too old and/or couldn't play in the same midfield as Neil Lennon. The Celtic captain, actually six weeks the senior to his fellow Irishman and now in the final year of his own contract, dispelled that particular myth.

"We are quite similar, but that was said about Paul Lambert and myself, a few years back. I wouldn't envisage any problems with that at all. Roy has experience and will to win, and if he helps us win the title, he will be a great signing."

That same subject had cropped up in discussions involving Keane, Lawwell and Strachan at Dermot Desmond's London home to discuss and ultimately agree the deal. Gordon Strachan later provided a fascinating insight into how that transfer played out, in his autobiography, My life in football.

"The need for Celtic to tighten their purse strings even applied to the signing of Roy Keane. When Roy joined Celtic on a free transfer in December 2005, most people were left wondering how we could afford him and why he should be interested in playing in Scotland. He had been reckoned to be on something like £80,000 a week at Manchester United and it was clear that, though the Premiership clubs who were interested in him could not match that, they would

nevertheless be able to take him closer to this figure than we could. When he signed for us, a number of reports indicated that he would be on £40,000 a week at Parkhead and that the deal would be funded partly by Dermot Desmond. But neither was correct."

"The salary we agreed with him was considerably less than £40,000 a week, and even then, it was dependent on the number of first-team appearances he made. Far from being Celtic's highest earner when he joined, he was no higher than eighth on the list. Dermot was brilliant in this matter. As one of Roy's Irish admirers, he wanted Roy on board as much as anybody, but not at the expense of leaving us short of money for the group of younger players I wanted to sign."

"I had known for some time that Roy's United contract was due to expire in the summer of 2006 and that he had expressed the hope that he might be able to end his career with Celtic. Various people around the club – and especially his Irish fans like Eddie Jordan – had alerted me to this almost from the day I started at Parkhead, but it was very much a longshot as far as I was concerned. With more pressing matters to deal with, I just pushed it to the back of my mind. I was amazed when it came off."

"Coming to Celtic was some decision on Roy's part. One could argue that he already had enough money in the bank, following his brilliant 12-year career at Old Trafford, but he was only 34 and I cannot think of many people of that age in professional football who would be willing to pass up opportunities to give themselves and their families further financial security."

"Perhaps the most surprising aspect of his decision was that I could not even promise him a regular place in the team. At our meeting to discuss the move, at Dermot's house in London, I told him;

"I still see you as a central midfielder, but the problem is that Neil Lennon and Stiliyan Petrov are doing too well in that area to be left out or moved elsewhere. If I had to select a team for the next match, and the three of you were all fit, I would have to plump for Neil and Stiliyan."

"He was perfectly happy with that, for the simple reason that because of his affection for Celtic during his upbringing in Ireland – an affection shared by countless other people there – he had genuinely set his heart on playing for the club."

I suspect that over and above those reasons, the challenge of being told he would not be an automatic first pick for Celtic would have been all the additional incentive required for a proud Roy Keane to offset any concerns he may have had about the move to Glasgow.

In any event, I thought he spoke excellently at his first media conference as a Celtic player.

"I gave other clubs a chance and was impressed with them all, but it's a great move for me. I feel that this is where I belong and I'm here to work hard and win games. I've been in the Premiership for a long time and feel I have proved myself there and needed a different environment. Different teams. Different grounds. Every boy in Ireland has an interest in Celtic, although my English team at the time was Spurs for some reason. I've been up to Celtic to watch a few games and always enjoyed my time here. This is not a financial move for me and I'm not coming here for an ego trip or to unwind. I had an important role in front of the back four at United, but I might be given more licence to play here. I push myself hard in training and try to push others hard, and people seemed happy with that until a few weeks ago."

A great day for me was made even better that evening when my teenage son and I headed over to the south side of Glasgow to watch the Pogues play the O2 Academy. I had been a huge fan of the band for many years without ever managing to see them play live. The atmosphere was incredible, party central as they ran through their playlist, congas in the aisles, a la Inverness a few years later. The works. About an hour into the set, Pogues frontman Shane McGowan grabs the microphone;

"So, you signed a Cork Bhoy today then?"

Cue bedlam. I thought the roof was coming off the place. One of the best days and nights of my life.

The football resumed three days later, Sunday, 18 December 2005, Celtic travelling up the A9 to face Inverness Caledonian Thistle, a first Hoops match for referee Stuart Dougal since sending off both Neil Lennon and Alan Thompson at Ibrox in September. Hearts had slumped to a second League defeat of the season 24 hours earlier, losing 1-0 to Rangers at Ibrox, meaning they had failed to cut into Celtic's three-point advantage at the top of the table. The changing face of football was once again illustrated by the sight of two Martin O'Neill lynchpins on the bench, Thompson joined by Chris Sutton for what would prove to be a significant afternoon for the big striker. Ross Wallace continued at left-back in the absence of the injured Mo Camara, as Gordon Strachan went with the following starting line-up:

Artur Boruc: Paul Telfer, Bobo Balde, Stephen McManus & Ross Wallace: Shunsuke Nakamura, Neil Lennon, Stan Petrov & Aiden McGeady: John Hartson & Shaun Maloney.

Only Stephen McManus had touched the ball for Celtic before the hosts took the lead, 30 seconds into the match, the big centre-half conceding a throw-in directly from kick-off, from which 39-year-old Caley player-manager Craig Brewster made a mockery of those who write off players of a certain age by head-flicking the ball on for Craig Dargo to slot home.

The hosts were enjoying a good run, unbeaten in six games, and threatened to add to that lead before Celtic settled, McManus perhaps lucky to escape with a yellow card after hauling Dargo down at the edge of the box. Gradually, the Hoops took command, Shaun Maloney volleying home on 20 minutes only to see Dougal rule the goal out for a perceived infringement by Bobo Balde, a harsh call at best. Within 60 seconds, Celtic were level, great work by Wallace down the left flank followed by a cross which picked out John Hartson on the penalty spot, the Welshman showing superb technique to chest the ball past his markers before blasting it beyond Mark Brown in the Caley goal. There was further drama and controversy 10 minutes later, McManus again catching Dargo, and Dougal pointing to the spot, the big Celt somehow remaining on the field despite his earlier booking. To add insult to Inverness injury, Artur Boruc then guessed correctly to save the Caley striker's attempt from 12 yards.

There would be no further goals in the game, although a significant event did take place in the second half. With 18 minutes remaining, Chris Sutton replaced Aiden McGeady, as Gordon Strachan looked for a winner. I suspect few, if any, of the watching Celtic support would have realised then that this would prove to be the Englishman's last appearance in the Hoops he had graced with so much power and style for more than five years, just one game shy of 200 for the Bhoys and 85 goals in his personal collection. He had scored his last goal for the club at the same venue as his first, Tannadice, in that crazy game where he managed to find the net at both ends in October. Sutton had been a tremendous signing, rated by Henrik Larsson as the best striker he ever played beside. Celtic praise doesn't come any higher. Back in Inverness, Strachan was fairly philosophical afterwards, albeit slightly frustrated.

"I was happy to get a point considering the performance. We made a lot of chances, but I can't remember us giving away so many. We were too anxious to win the game and, with our full-backs bombing on, our centre-halves were exposed too often, but they did well. The players maybe need to relax a bit and pick out the best pass."

The madness that is Scottish football sometimes also manifested itself on the sidelines that afternoon, as Gordon Strachan revealed in his post-match interviews, the Celtic manager seemingly avoiding what would have perhaps been the strangest sending-off in history.

"There's nothing I can do about referees' decisions but [the fourth official] threatened to send me to the stand if I put my hands to my head again. I asked if that was a rule, and then he said he never said that, [however] I had a whole bench and supporters behind me who heard him. I know it's silly and juvenile but when he threatens to send me to the stand for putting my hands on my head that's not great either. And to retract, that was why I had a problem."

There was one final game to be negotiated in the calendar year 2005, the Boxing Day visit of Livingston to Celtic Park. Over 57,000 festive followers made their way to the east to see the new King unveiled, Roy Keane given a hero's welcome from the Parkhead faithful before a kick-off delayed for fully 45 minutes due to a power issue. The Irishman would see a strong attacking performance from his new teammates go unrewarded until five minutes from the interval, Shaun Maloney teasing Livingston's Greg Strong into a tackle he had no hope of winning, then ignoring the protests to clip the ball expertly into the top corner to give visiting keeper

Roddy McKenzie no chance.

Celtic were comfortable until a calamitous mistake by Bobo Balde on the hour, the big Guinean trying to play his way out of trouble at the edge of his own box whilst under pressure from Hoops-mad Calton boy Robert Snodgrass. As the defender stretched then lost possession, the ball broke kindly to Paul Dalglish, who showed the composure of his father to stroke it past Artur Boruc at his near post. With 15 minutes remaining, Gordon Strachan introduced 18-year-old New Zealand-born striker Michael McGlinchey for his Hoops baptism, Aiden McGeady making way. The incessant home pressure finally paid off with just three minutes left on the clock. Paul Telfer cut out a dangerous Livingston through ball, the full-back immediately finding Shunsuke Nakamura with a lovely pass, allowing the Japanese genius to cut inside and unleash a perfect low shot past McKenzie to win the match.

McGlinchey's brief cameo would be his only first-team action at Celtic. Having played in the Under-20 World Cup for Scotland in 2007, he would be a member of the New Zealand squad which reached the senior version in South Africa three years later, McGlinchey an unused substitute as the Kiwis drew all three group matches against Slovakia, Paraguay and defending champions Italy. At the time of writing, Michael is currently playing with New South Wales outfit Weston Bears, having previously played alongside Tom Rogic at Central Coast Mariners in the Australian A-League, in Japan with Vegalta Sendai and with four different Scottish clubs, Dunfermline Athletic, Motherwell, Queen's Park and Clyde. Incidentally, the New Zealand striker's role for the three World Cup games in South Africa was handed to Chris Killen, then with Middlesbrough, whose club manager by that time was...Gordon Strachan! More on Chris later.

Livingston's player-manager, Paul Lambert, had missed the opportunity of an emotional return to the Parkhead pitch through injury. He was happy enough with what he had witnessed.

"We gave as good as we got, but that's what it's like playing here. They keep going for 90 minutes. That's why you pay the big transfer fees. There is no rocket science in football. That's what happens. If you have good players on the field,

the game becomes easier. But my team gave me everything they had, and I was proud of them."

His opposite number, Gordon Strachan, was thankful for the intervention of his Japanese superstar.

"We made a lot of first-half chances but didn't take them and we could have had another penalty. We eventually got through, but we didn't do enough at the start of the second half to put them under pressure. We allowed them back in it with a mistake and anxiety took over for 20 minutes but we're lucky to have Naka, who can stay above the nervousness."

There was a blow for Celtic as we moved into 2006. The opening of the January transfer window should have allowed Roy Keane's registration to go through in time for him to play in the vital New Year's Day fixture at Tynecastle, however, with thoughts of the ghost of Farry past echoing in the heads of Celtic supporters, we were advised that the offices would not be opened as it was a public holiday. Only in Scotland. Thus, the Irishman had to watch the most pivotal match of the season - a game which would have been tailor-made for him - from the Tynecastle stand.

At least he was there. I was visiting my in-laws in North Wales and so had to settle for a visit to a pub in St Asaph with my two Manchester United-supporting brothers-in-law and their Scouse friends. With both clubs winning their Boxing Day clashes – Hearts scoring five goals without reply against Falkirk at Tynecastle – the home side began the day four points behind Gordon Strachan's men, meaning it was a game they could not afford to lose.

It had been the strangest of opening halves to a season on the Gorgie Road, under their new Lithuanian owner Vladimir Romanov, or 'Mad Vlad' as the Scottish media liked to call him. He had sacked Hearts legend John Robertson as manager back in May, bringing in former Ipswich Town and Scotland star George Burley, in his place. Burley's nephew Craig had been a key player under Wim Jansen, as the 10 was prevented by Celtic eight years earlier. The new manager had started the season on fire, with the opening 10 games producing eight wins and two draws, one of those at Celtic Park in October, albeit they had suffered a shock League Cup exit at Livingston in September. Then the rumours commenced regarding some problems behind the scenes, with Romanov front and centre, culminating in Burley leaving the club one week after Hearts had maintained their unbeaten start in the east end of Glasgow.

At the beginning of November, Romanov appointed former Arsenal midfielder and Chelsea assistant manager Graham Rix as Burley's successor. Rix struggled to maintain that early-season momentum, with just three wins in his opening seven games, allowing Celtic to seize the initiative. Gordon Strachan made just one change from the Boxing Day win over Livingston, Alan Thompson coming in on the left side of midfield in place of Aiden McGeady, as he looked for the victory which would stretch the Hoops lead to seven points and strike a huge psychological blow to the Edinburgh side's hopes of a first Scottish title since 1960. Celtic lined up as follows at Tynecastle.

Artur Boruc: Paul Telfer, Bobo Balde, Stephen McManus & Ross Wallace: Shunsuke Nakamura, Neil Lennon, Stan Petrov & Alan Thompson: John Hartson & Shaun Maloney.

Hearts started as if their lives depended on the result, scoring twice in the opening eight minutes. First, Paul Hartley outpaced Paul Telfer down the left to knock the ball into the box with the outside of his foot, Lithuanian striker Edgaras Jankauskas getting the vital touch which beat Artur Boruc with the help of a huge deflection from the chest of the chasing Ross Wallace. Within two minutes, Celtic were in desperate trouble, Rudi Skacel's inswinging corner from the right clearing every Hoops defender and allowing Steven Pressley to head home, as the old Tynecastle ground shook to its foundations. With no further damage by half-time, other than to my liver in St Asaph as I looked on in horror, things then took another turn for the worse five minutes into the second half, star midfielder Stan Petrov limping off clutching his hamstring, Stephen Pearson coming on as a straight swap.

Within five minutes, the substitute had dragged Celtic back into the match, Pearson powering through from the edge of the box to meet Shaun

Maloney's delicious cross first-time and slip the ball past Craig Gordon. In St Asaph, a combination of alcohol and bravado has taken over as, totally out of character, I declare, "*We'll go on and win this now,*" ignoring the derision of the in-laws. But my faith is justified, as Celtic launch wave after wave of attacks in this proverbial 'game of two halves.' With 15 minutes remaining, the afternoon takes another twist, Hearts Greek full-back Takis Fyssas left with no option but to haul down Maloney as he raced clear, the inevitable red card following from referee Ian Brines.

The clock was showing 87 minutes as Shunsuke Nakamura weighed up his options from a free-kick on the main stand touchline. As always, the delivery was then perfect from the Japanese dead-ball expert, the cross coming in at speed to be met by the forehead of Stephen McManus and the ball is exploding past Gordon, and I'm racing up to hug a pub TV screen, for some reason, much to the amusement of the locals. There's smiles and relief all around, however, this is Celtic, and this is me with a few beers in my system.

"We're going to win this now, I'm telling you!"

We're in the 90th minute now and it is Groundhog Day, Nakamura bundled over needlessly by Hartley, who protests his innocence, on that same touchline. His whipped cross this time is headed on by Bobo Balde, before being blocked by McManus. Nine times out of 10 that ball is then cleared, however, fate has taken a hand and this time it has fallen for Stephen to get an unlikely yard of space at the angle of the six-yard box. The big central defender cuts across the ball and watches in delight as Gordon has not set his feet quickly enough to deal with the unexpected shot, the ball spinning across the big goalkeeper to nestle in the far corner of the net and win the match for Celtic, against all the odds.

In St Asaph, I have repeated my comedy routine and the place is in uproar. But I don't care. My faith has been vindicated and my team has won this crucial match in the race to regain our title. To strike the first blow since Black Sunday and the loss of Martin. And the others. It is a huge result for Celtic and it is a critical win for Gordon Strachan, who celebrates with his staff as if we have won the League. It was a much calmer Celtic manager, however, who addressed the media shortly afterwards.

"It was a classic. The game had everything. And to come from two goals behind to win is a good feeling. Give credit to Hearts. They bombarded us at the start and showed great power and lots of skill. We had a problem and to come back from that was excellent. We realised by half-time that we could not overpower them as they are big, strong lads, so we thought we could be quicker than them and put on some fresh legs."

And did the Celtic manager have a new selection dilemma, with Roy Keane now free to play and given the match-changing performance of Stephen Pearson?

"Stiliyan's injured, so there's a gap in midfield, but we certainly have options. With the way Pearo's playing, I don't know what I'll do."

Strachan shot down suggestions that the title race was over, his side now seven points clear of Hearts.

"It just makes us feel a bit better about ourselves."

We celebrate by staying on for a few beers. When we eventually arrive home, there is hell to pay, and I am genuinely sorry. But I cannot shake that sense of elation I feel on one of those magical Celtic days.

That feelgood factor took a dent a few days later, as the widely anticipated departure of Chris Sutton from Celtic became a fact, the English striker leaving Parkhead with the dreaded 'by mutual consent' tag accompanying news of his move to Birmingham City. Having failed to prise Sutton's old sparring partner, Henrik Larsson, away from Barcelona, Blues manager Steve Bruce had secured the services of the former England cap on Thursday, 5 January 2006, on a free transfer until the end of that season.

There had long been rumours of a less-than-healthy relationship between player and manager, and Chris Sutton's appearances for Celtic in the months since Gordon Strachan's arrival had been rare, albeit injury had accounted for many of those absences. He would also have been one of the top earners at the club whilst playing that bit-part role, at a time when Parkhead budgets were allegedly being revised. Nevertheless, I felt that

Sutton's carefully worded exit speech said it all - both what he did and didn't say - if that makes sense.

"It has been very disappointing for me to leave Celtic but under the circumstances, I felt that I had been left with no choice. I had five great years at Celtic under Martin O'Neill. I would like to thank the players and staff for making me and my family so welcome. I am now looking forward to getting started for Birmingham City."

No reference whatsoever to the current manager and not much sign of 'mutual consent' for me there. For his part, Gordon Strachan seemed genuine in his appreciation of what he was losing.

"It's obviously a huge disappointment to lose a player of Chris' quality. The club has granted Chris his wish to move on and I would like to wish him all the best for the future."

Despite the loss of another Martin O'Neill favourite, I was still on a high from the victory at Tynecastle and the prospect of watching Roy Keane in the Hoops as I drove back up the motorway three days later. I had taken the precaution of pre-recording that afternoon's Scottish Cup tie with Clyde at Broadwood, in the event we were late to leave Wales, radio silence maintained just in case someone inadvertently gave away the score before I watched it later, one of my pet hates. I have many of those.

The omens were all good.

Celts had won 5-0 at the same venue the previous March in the quarter-final of the Scottish Cup, Stan Varga hitting a rare double, an Alan Thompson penalty and goals from Stan Petrov and Craig Bellamy sending the Hoops into a last-four clash with Hearts and eventual success against Dundee United, in Martin O'Neill's final game as Hoops boss. None of those individuals would feature eight months later.

It had been almost 50 years since Clyde had knocked Celtic out of the Scottish Cup. You had to go back to March 1958, and a 2-0 victory for the Bully Wee in a third-round tie played at Celtic Park, due to safety fears around Clyde's Shawfield home following the death of a 9-year-old boy when a boundary wall collapsed at the previous meeting of the clubs three months earlier. Over 65,000 spectators had attended that day, Clyde going on to win the trophy the next month for the second time in four years.

There were only 8,000 in Clyde's current Broadwood home in Cumbernauld to watch Celts attempt to win the famous old trophy for a third successive season, something the most successful club in the competition's history had never previously achieved. Gordon Strachan's midfield dilemma appeared to be solved by the absence of Alan Thompson from the squad, presumably due to injury, the Geordie having been substituted in the second half at Tynecastle. His place wide on the left was taken by Stephen Pearson, whilst Roy Keane provided a direct replacement for hamstring victim Stan Petrov. The major surprise though, was a debut for Chinese defender Du Wei, starting instead of Bobo Balde, the big Guinean defender heading to Egypt to captain his country in the 2006 African Nations Cup.

Now hindsight is wonderful, absolutely, however, I do recall a certain seed of doubt on hearing that. To this day, I confess I still do not understand the logic of taking such a chance with team selection as Gordon Strachan appeared to do that day. A natural centre-half, Adam Virgo, was on the bench, and having featured six times since his summer transfer, he would presumably have offered less of a risk than Du Wei, a man who had never kicked a ball in Scotland. In a similar vein, I believed that for Roy Keane's return to first-team football, after a four-month injury lay-off, it may have made more sense to have saved that for the next game at Parkhead, away from the satellite TV circus which then ensued. Both Aiden McGeady and Maciej Zurawski were available, thus allowing Petrov's absence to be adequately covered without the Irishman's involvement. For me, it was just so out of character for Gordon to take those unnecessary risks, however, I accept, I am not in possession of all the facts here.

Celtic thus lined up at Broadwood Stadium as follows, on Sunday, 8 January 2006.

Artur Boruc: Paul Telfer, Du Wei, Stephen McManus & Ross Wallace: Shunsuke Nakamura, Neil Lennon, Roy Keane & Stephen Pearson: John Hartson & Shaun Maloney.

Clyde were managed by an unusual pairing of Graham Roberts – the man who famously conducted the Copland Road choir whilst playing in goals against Celtic – and Joe Miller, the scorer of the winning goal for the Hoops against Rangers in the 1989 Scottish Cup final. Miller had registered as a player and was on the home bench. They had taken Rangers to extra-time at Ibrox in the League Cup, back in September, and Roberts, in particular, had been making quietly-confident noises about the outcome.

"I played against Roy [Keane] when he was at Nottingham Forest and we knew he was a superstar back then. He is a wonderful player and it will be fantastic for Clyde and the people of Cumbernauld to see an actual superstar at their stadium, but he will know he has been in a game by the end of it. I can assure you of that. You like to pit your wits against the best players, and you like to pit your wits against the best managers. Gordon Strachan is probably the best manager in Scotland at the moment. [Both] myself and Joe Miller want to test ourselves and this is the biggest test we have had so far. When we played Rangers, people knocked us and said we were just going there to make the numbers up. When we went 2-1 up, it frightened the life out of them. In the end, we know we have 11 players against 11 players and our 11 players will run through brick walls."

The hosts came flying out of the traps to unsettle Celtic, something they did with great success. It is very rarely I watch a domestic game where you feel Celtic are just not at the races, however, sadly that was the case at Broadwood that sunny afternoon.

The writing was on the wall early on, as Tom Brighton outmuscled Du Wei to slide the ball past Artur Boruc, only to be pulled back for a foul on the Celt, a decision which appeared harsh on the Clyde man. The action continued to flow towards Boruc, with the green-clad Bhoys strangely – or perhaps not, given the changes – out of sorts, a second home goal ruled out for offside shortly afterwards, correctly on this occasion. Just after the half-hour, it was third time lucky for the Bully Wee, Boruc missing a cross from the left completely, allowing Craig Bryson a free header at the far post, which he duly dispatched for 1-0. It went from bad to worse for Du Wei minutes later. Beaten for pace by Brighton, he pulled the striker's jersey to concede a penalty, remarkably then allowed to remain on the field by referee Kenny Clark. As at Inverness recently, Celtic escaped natural justice when Boruc threw himself to his right to save superbly from Stephen O'Donnell, the nephew of former Celt Phil, who had scored from the spot in that League Cup-tie at Ibrox to put Clyde 2-1 up late on. That relief was temporary for the visitors, however, O'Donnell's corner met by Clyde full-back Eddie Malone to produce his career highlight, his shot rasping high past Boruc for 2-0 with eight minutes of the first half remaining.

With Celtic's cup hopes hanging by a thread, Gordon Strachan replaced Du Wei with Adam Virgo at the interval, the Chinese defender thus completing his only piece of first-team action at Celtic. Clyde then went close to making it 3-0, O'Donnell's header beating Boruc but crashing back into play off the post. Strachan made an early change, ending Ross Wallace's torrid afternoon by replacing him with Aiden McGeady, then with 20 minutes remaining he made his final throw of the dice, John Hartson making way for Maciej Zurawski. Finally, with just eight minutes to play, it was the Polish striker who made the breakthrough, Stephen McManus, now operating as an additional striker, heading the ball down for Zurawski to thrash past Clyde keeper Peter Cherrie from the edge of the box. For the first time, Celts looked like they might yet salvage the day, however, it would prove too little too late. Just as with his European debut in Bratislava, Gordon Strachan's first Scottish Cup tie would end in disaster.

It was hard to say anything other than the hosts had thoroughly deserved to win, an ecstatic Graham Roberts addressing the media afterwards;

"I think both myself and Joe Miller have tears in our eyes. It is the greatest day of my managerial career. I cannot quite believe it and at the moment I'm very emotional. I think we deserved it. We played from the first to the last and created all the chances. Every player gave it their best and we knew we were going to win. We could have won by four or five. Everyone was saying the

match was about Roy Keane making his Celtic debut, but Gordon Strachan came to watch us last week and knew what to expect. The players want to prove they are in a good team. They work hard and are always willing to learn. Our players worked to the plan and worked hard through the game. It would have been an injustice had we not won."

I had tears in my eyes too, Graham, I can assure you. For very different reasons, right enough. His opposite number, Gordon Strachan, was magnanimous in defeat.

"Clyde were the best team. They used the conditions well, played with common sense football and we did not. We laid the tactics down before the game, but they weren't adhered to. The players let themselves down and have to live with that. It is very hard to take everything in just now. The manner in which we got beat was disappointing. We think we have the answers, but we have to look into it even more. The start of the game was disappointing. Whatever tactics you use, if you have no crosses, no shots or don't even pressurise the goalkeeper to take some backpasses, then you will struggle. On the other hand, Clyde used the conditions well. They got crosses in, fired shots in and our keeper had to deal with backpasses. I wish Clyde all the best. They played with great spirit and deserved their victory."

The Celtic manager also refused to dwell on the performance of his new high-profile signing.

"He did fine, but it is hard to talk about Roy Keane because we have to look at a bigger picture than that. There were bad decisions on the pitch and problems before the game."

That last comment only served to increase the intrigue, with the conspiracy theorists convinced that the inclusion of Du Wei and perhaps even Roy Keane had more to do with commercial value than pure footballing logic. In his autobiography My Life in Football, published the following year, Gordon shines more light on the context behind his team selection at Broadwood. It makes very interesting reading.

"It is important for managers to look at themselves before anybody else when things go wrong and, in this instance, I have to hold my hands up and concede

that I did not choose the right team. Having watched Clyde at home in their previous match, and checked the weather forecast for the area for the two or three days before our tie, I fully expected the pitch to be heavy and lumpy. In anticipation of a gruelling, physical slog, I picked the biggest and strongest side I could get."

"When we arrived at the Broadwood Stadium, though, I was taken aback to find that the pitch, having been covered overnight to keep the rain and snow off, was like concrete, so hard and slippery in places that had it been a League match, I feel sure [that] the match would have been postponed."

"In my team talk, I said, "Right, let's keep getting the ball in behind their back men and turn them." However, it never really happened. Instead, John Hartson repeatedly came short for the ball to be played to his feet, which allowed Clyde to push up on us and deny us the space to properly feed off him. John, and the players on whom he tended to rely on the most to find him with the ball - the full-backs - were still locked into the style of play that had helped us recover from 2-0 down to win 3-2 at Hearts the previous week. It was a massive victory for us. It increased our championship lead over the Edinburgh club to seven points, and John's ability to take the ball in deep positions and link our play up front was a big factor in it. He caused Hearts central defenders Steven Pressley and Andy Webster a lot of trouble. But you could pass the ball more on the Tynecastle pitch than on the Clyde surface."

"As is often the case when a centre-forward is not stretching the play, John – one of our strongest runners in training – argued that the full-backs were not giving him the service necessary for him to do this, whereas they countered that he was not taking up the right positions. The bottom line is that Clyde were spot on with their personnel and tactics - they belted the ball forward and played on the knockdowns - and we weren't. The crucial difference between the two teams was Clyde's sheer hunger to run. For us, it was all a bit of a mess."

"If any Celtic player deserved sympathy, it was Du Wei, the centre-half and captain of China's national team. He made his full debut, along with Roy Keane, but like Mo Camara, when he was adjudged to have been partly responsible for two of the goals we conceded on his debut in Bratislava, the experience was a nightmare for him. Wei had been looking tremendous in training and, as he

certainly had the height [which] we felt we needed at the heart of our defence, all the coaching staff agreed that he should play. It was not entirely his fault that he did not do well. Usually, if one member of a back four is having a bad afternoon, he can rely on others to help him. Unfortunately for Wei, they were all struggling in this match. They could not even help themselves."

"Another problem for Wei was the language barrier. He could understand a bit of English but the noise from the crowd at Clyde made it difficult for him to hear or understand instructions from his teammates than had been the case in training and reserve team matches. That's why I had to substitute him at half-time. We were 2-0 down and I knew that the tactical changes I had to make to get us back into the game can only have made his communication headaches worse. That was his one and only game for Celtic. I would have liked to have kept him, but his club, whose asking price for him to join us on a permanent transfer was £700,000, were unwilling to give us more time to assess him."

Such was the crazy first week of 2006 as a Celtic supporter.

We had won a game we had no right to win, thanks to a forced but inspired substitution and an incredible desire from the players, then lost a game we had no right to lose, thanks to the strangest of team selections and a complete lack of that same fighting spirit against a side who had it in spades.

We had waved goodbye to a potential debut-season Treble for Gordon Strachan and to a much-loved player from a much-loved era.

There is definitely never a dull moment, following this team we love so much.

CHAPTER 8

Gordon gets busy in the January sales before reaching a first cup final with Celtic

Six days after the humiliation at Broadwood, Saturday, 14 January 2006, an incredible 60,000 fans rolled up to Celtic Park to witness the home debut of Roy Keane, as the Hoops continued the quest to regain the Scottish title by taking on Kilmarnock. The Irishman would line-up in an unfamiliar central defensive role, replacing the unfortunate Du Wei in Bobo Balde's continued absence on international duty in Egypt, whilst Stan Petrov came back into midfield, having recovered from his hamstring injury. Gordon Strachan's other change following the Scottish Cup exit saw Maciej Zurawski start up front with John Hartson, Shaun Maloney dropping back into the wide left position and Stephen Pearson moving to the bench. There was a wonderful Irish welcome awaiting the Cork man, with the entire Jock Stein Stand forming a fantastic tifo tricolour. This should always have been Roy Keane's debut.

Celtic lined up as follows.

Artur Boruc: Paul Telfer, Roy Keane, Stephen McManus & Ross Wallace: Shunsuke Nakamura, Neil Lennon, Stan Petrov & Shaun Maloney: John Hartson & Maciej Zurawski.

As well as Keane and the full-house Parkhead crowd, Kilmarnock were up against history, having failed to win at Celtic Park in more than half a century. Not since a Killie side led by Malcolm MacDonald and featuring ex-Celts Alex Rollo and Willie Toner had beaten Jimmy McGrory's Hoops 2-0 in December 1955 had the Ayrshire club returned from

Glasgow's east end with the spoils. That challenge became even greater within three minutes, Shunsuke Nakamura curling in a quite superb free-kick opener, after Petrov had been barged to the ground. The Bulgarian was again involved in Celtic's second goal, on 15 minutes, Petrov chopped to the floor by Killie full-back James Fowler, Maloney making an expert job of the penalty kick to give Alan Combe no chance. With Celts all set up for a convincing victory, the Rugby Park side decided to rewrite the script, albeit with the help of some slack home defending. Stephen McManus' reckless challenge on Colin Nish allowed Steven Naismith to reduce the deficit from the spot midway through the first half, and the scores were level within six minutes of the restart, Australian Danny Invincible living up to his name with a stunning headed finish at the back post.

The critical goal came along two minutes later, Keane's low shot fumbled by Combe with the keeper's error punished by McManus, who forced it home from close-range. And as the clock struck 67, Celts grabbed a fourth, this time Zurawski meeting a cross from Ross Wallace, after good work from the young winger-cum-full-back down the left. Combe did well to block the Polish striker's effort and knock the ball back out of the goal via the crossbar, however, the 'Jungle' linesman raised his flag, indicating it had crossed the line, the Bhoys then closing out the game for a very welcome 4-2 victory.

Whilst there were many positives to be taken from a much-needed win, there was concern expressed by Gordon Strachan afterwards, his side losing two goals for the second successive weekend.

"The crowd were anxious after last week's defeat by Clyde in the cup and we were anxious. We shouldn't have to score three goals to win a game of football and we have to sort it out. Individual errors are killing us at the moment. But while there can be question marks about the defending, there can be none about our commitment and general play."

The Celtic manager wasted no time acting on that concern, meeting the £500,000 release clause to sign Dundee United's 21-year-old right-back Mark Wilson, just two days later, on Monday, 16 January 2006, albeit Gordon Strachan was at pains to stress that the deal had been in the offing for some time.

"The decision to sign Mark was taken a long time ago. It's not a knee-jerk reaction, it's about the future of the club. When I first came to the club, [Celtic scout] Tom O'Neill said to me, "That's your man." I said, "Great but let me see for myself." This has been in progress for six months without actually speaking to Dundee United or Mark. The progress was me turning up and watching Dundee United quite a lot, seeing Mark play against us and then the decision was taken. We thought that we could afford it, we could do it and we should get on with it."

Would he go straight into the team?

"He must have a chance, but I can't guarantee anyone a first-team place when they come to the club. He can play football. He can get forward and he can tackle. He has the intelligence to take in information. He has hunger and an honesty about him. If you take into account all the factors, he is in with a half-decent chance."

The player himself was delighted.

"It's definitely a proud day. It's a club the family have supported all their life. I don't expect to break in right away, but I'll get my head down and try to impress the manager. I don't think it's really sunk in yet that I've signed for a club of this size. It's a privilege to get the honour and opportunity to come here and play for them. Over the next few days it will sink in a bit more when I get to meet the players and get into training. I'm looking forward to it."

Gordon Strachan then turned his attention to the other end of the field, three days later, confirming the pre-contract agreement which would bring Scotland striker Kenny Miller to Celtic in the summer. The Wolverhampton Wanderers player would thus become only the third man to play for both halves of the Glasgow 'divide' in my lifetime, following Jock Stein's audacious swoop for Tottenham Hotspur's Alfie Conn in 1977, then the infamous 'u-turn' performed by Nantes' Maurice Johnston 12 years later. Such transfers would cease to become a novelty item during Strachan's tenure at Celtic Park.

Having rejected several offers to remain at Molyneux, the 26-year-old Miller was happy to finally have his immediate future settled.

"I was fortunate enough to have options. But when Celtic made their interest known, this was where I wanted to play. It's a tremendous honour. Having spoken to Gordon and the club, I am delighted to have committed my future to Celtic. I am looking forward immensely to joining my new teammates in the summer."

His new manager echoed those sentiments.

"Kenny is a quality player and I am delighted to have secured his signing for next season. He is still a young player with his best years ahead of him and I am sure he will be a great addition to our squad from next season onwards."

Miller had spent four years at Hibernian before his move to Ibrox in 2000, and it was confirmed that another man with Easter Road connections would follow him to Celtic at the end of the season, current Hibs captain Gary Caldwell signing a pre-contract agreement 24 hours later, Friday, 20 January 2006. Caldwell had been the subject of abuse from his own supporters, after Celtic's interest had become known, booed and blamed for one of the goals as Aberdeen won at Easter Road the weekend before, something Gordon Strachan felt was unfair.

"People will have to get used to this happening in this country. These players have been honest and are not kidding anyone else on. They have been open in saying they are going to Celtic, but they still want to do a job with their clubs. Players are not doing anything wrong in this new 'free contract' system, and people will have to get used to it."

As Gary Caldwell and Kenny Miller looked forward to their summer moves, and Mark Wilson settled into his place in the home dressing-room at Celtic Park, another defender was moving out of Parkhead.

Despite the expectation of a permanent transfer expressed by all parties involved back in September, the 'on/off' saga of Du Wei took another, final twist, the Chinese defender now preparing to make the long journey home. The player's agent, Canada-based Edmund Chu, explained the rationale for the change of plans.

"Du Wei will go back to China because Celtic want an extension of his temporary deal and that does not suit Shanghai. It is very disappointing that it has ended this way, but Du Wei is a professional and after leaving Scotland in the next few days, he will concentrate on starting his career again in China. He is an important player for his club, and, under Celtic's new terms, it makes no sense for them to allow him to stay in Glasgow. It would take a miracle for anything to be resurrected at this stage, and I don't really believe in miracles. So, we are going through the process of arranging for Du Wei to return to Shanghai. There are one or two loose ends to be tied up, but I'd expect him to go back to Shanghai this week."

Whilst I wasn't inside Broadwood for his one and only Celtic appearance, I did meet Du Wei on one, memorable occasion, memorable perhaps for all the wrong reasons. I was with my daughter outside the main entrance at Celtic Park, presumably just before or after a game, when the big defender was signing some autographs for supporters. Now I'm guessing that Du Wei won't be far short of 6'3" plus there is the added complication that he is Chinese, however, that didn't stop the happy Hoops fan in the crowd from shouting over to him as he walked past, and I only ever-so-slightly paraphrase him:

"Haw. Nakamura. All right, big man?"

To which, in all fairness, given that he must have been cringing inside just like the rest of us present, Du Wei replied nonchalantly:

"Not Nakamura. I'm Du Wei!"

Only in Glasgow.

Events on the field then took a turn that weekend for the better, Kilmarnock's Danny Invincible on the scoresheet again after his equaliser at Celtic Park, his goal enough to defeat Hearts at Rugby Park and open up the possibility of a 10-point lead for Strachan's men, should they win at Fir Park the next day. It was a much-changed defence which lined up for Celtic on Sunday, 22 January 2006 at a ground which had proved so problematic for them recently. Roy Keane's injury coupled with a suspension for Steven McManus saw a new pairing in central defence, Stan Varga and Adam Virgo, a first outing for the Slovakian defender since the opening League game of the season at the same venue back in July.

Mo Camara had also been restored at left-back, Ross Wallace dropping to the bench beside new signing Mark Wilson, and Celts had the former Burnley defender to thank early on, his goal-line clearance preventing Irishman Richie Foran from opening the scoring for Motherwell. The Hoops would strike first, Maciej Zurawski running onto Stan Petrov's through ball to beat Graeme Smith low to the keeper's right. It was a lead Celtic retained until a few minutes before the interval, Artur Boruc helpless as Jim Hamilton's incredible first-time volley from the edge of the box screamed past him into the top corner. Goal of the Season material from the Motherwell striker, without a shadow of a doubt.

With an hour played, Gordon Strachan made his first change, Aiden McGeady for Shunsuke Nakamura, and the introduction of the teenager paid immediate dividends, as he danced away from his marker at the angle of the box to hit a shot which struck a defender before deceiving Smith in the home goal. That hard-earned lead was almost given up immediately, Motherwell's arch-villain Scott McDonald only inches out with his header, with Boruc hopelessly beaten. McGeady then turned provider, with five minutes remaining, his mazy run taking him past three defenders and along the byline to find John Hartson, the Welshman ending his recent goal drought by slicing the ball past Smith into the far corner, sealing the game at 3-1 and extending the Hoops lead over Hearts into double figures. It was a happy Celtic manager who addressed the media afterwards.

"Wherever we go, we have to put in a performance and that was another great game. Our discipline was fantastic because it got a bit tasty out there. Adam [Virgo] and Stanislav [Varga] were absolutely fantastic at the back. Aiden McGeady said his goal was a bit lucky, but it wasn't. Luck is when preparation meets opportunity."

The feelgood factor continued for Gordon Strachan on the following Friday, when midfielder Stan Petrov signed a contract extension which appeared to tie him to the club for at least the next three seasons. The 26-year-old Bulgarian captain had recently been the centre of much media speculation regarding a move to England, so this was a huge and welcome boost to the Hoops support. The player, now in his seventh season at the club, later spoke of his relief that the protracted negotiations had finally concluded.

"There has been a lot of speculation and I have had a lot of questions from my teammates and fans about when I would sign, when it would be over. Now I'm glad that's finished and the whole thing has been sorted out. It was not very difficult. It was important for me to make this deal. I knew it would take time, the chief executive and the manager knew it would take a long time and I'm happy to agree this deal and keep playing for Celtic. I've been speaking to the manager all the time and he has been very supportive to me. When you feel that someone trusts you and believes in you, you feel more welcome."

His manager was delighted at retaining the services of a player he considered a role model for others.

"He looks after himself and he is a professional. The younger players need to learn the way a professional behaves and that's what he gives us. That saves me speaking to the players about how you behave, not just on the pitch but also off it."

Another 60,000 packed into Celtic Park 24 hours later, Saturday, 28 January 2006, as the Hoops looked to maintain their advantage at the summit. Dundee United were the visitors, Mark Wilson handed his debut against the club he had left just a fortnight earlier. He replaced Paul Telfer, whilst Ross Wallace came back in at the expense of Mo Camara, the revised full-back pairing either side of the new Varga/Virgo partnership. Roy Keane and Stephen McManus returned to join Camara on the bench.

John Hartson started where he had left off at Motherwell, the Welshman opening the scoring within 10 minutes with a free header from Shunsuke Nakamura's delicious free-kick, after future Bhoy Barry Robson had fouled Maciej Zurawski. An ex-Celt would come back to haunt the Hoops on the day though, David Fernandez spinning quickly to equalise just before the break, the teams going in at 1-1. There was then a touch of deja-vu at the beginning of the second half, Zurawski finding himself in glorious isolation to place a header past the exposed Derek Stillie in the United goal for a carbon copy of Celtic's opener, and when Stan Petrov's wicked deflection made it 3-1 in the magical 67th minute it looked all over. However, as we all know to our cost, nothing is ever a given in football. Substitute Lee Miller pulled one back for United from a suspiciously-offside position with just eight minutes remaining, then with the home support growing increasingly anxious, it was that man Fernandez again with the killer blow, the Spanish striker the coolest man in Parkhead as he waltzed past Artur Boruc to slide home another equaliser for the Tannadice men. With Hearts exacting revenge for their earlier defeat at Easter Road by hammering bitter rivals Hibernian 4-1 at Tynecastle that same afternoon, those two late lapses saw Celtic's lead at the top now reduced to eight points.

Predictably, some Celtic supporters were questioning why the manager had not 'shut up shop' at 3-1. Gordon Strachan produced a bizarre and somewhat comical explanation. Deadpan humour, perhaps.

"At the first point, when we were going to put Roy [Keane] on, he disappeared to the toilet. We had one plan at 3-1 and another plan at 3-2. But by the time we had spoken to Roy about that one, another goal had gone in and I had to keep on all my attackers. It was going to be a 'shutting up' job at 3-1, but we didn't have the time to get him on. It's happened before. It's not Roy's fault. It was still 3-1 when he came back, and just as we were trying to get him on, the [second] goal went in. I felt a bit sorry for him, but he has taken it well."

To add to the surreal ending, it transpired that David Fernandez's goals were the first he had scored at Parkhead, despite spending three seasons at Celtic! The Spaniard was taking no pleasure at that.

"It was a weird feeling. I'd rather score against other teams. It's not the best feeling but that's my job. I was here for three years and I know I didn't play that much but I have friends here and the supporters have been kind to me, so I have to respect them. It's a great club and I have great memories."

As the end of the January sales drew closer, Gordon Strachan had one more item to drop into his shopping basket, the Celtic manager heading to Leicester to sign his old Coventry City striker, Dion Dublin, from the Foxes on a short-term contract. The now 36-year-old former England international had actually played for Leicester City against Celtic in the pre-season friendly the previous July, his early penalty kick saved by Hoops debutant goalkeeper Artur Boruc that evening.

The likeable Dublin was delighted to be off to Glasgow in the green, in the green, to meet old friends.

"Although I am 36, I feel fit and I am ready to go. I'm just happy to get the chance. What are you going to say? When you get to play for Celtic, it is an incredible experience. I know Alan Thompson from Villa, Paul Telfer from Coventry and Roy Keane from my Manchester United days. Hopefully, they will welcome me and make it easier for me because I am quite nervous. I may be 36 but I am still quite nervous to come to a place of this size. I know the fans are one of the biggest groups in the world. You don't get too much history of Celtic down south but having seen some games and played in friendlies against Celtic, I am just gobsmacked at the size of the place. I am just looking forward to being part of a good squad of players and, hopefully, I can add to that and help the team to success this season."

Dublin would provide cover for the now departed Chris Sutton and the overworked John Hartson as a target man, whilst he was versatile enough to fill in at the back should the need arise. Gordon Strachan had not had his January worries to seek, in terms of a regular central defensive partnership, with Du Wei's return to China, Stephen McManus' suspension and Roy Keane's injury all combining to stretch his resources in that area to the max, whilst Bobo Balde was out in Africa.

The big Guinean had been captaining his country through the group games of the 2006 Africa Cup of Nations finals in Egypt throughout the latter half of January, as the West African nation sought to make an impact on the competition for the first time in 30 years, a runner's-up spot to Morocco in the Ethiopian finals of 1976 by far their greatest achievement. Balde was joined in the squad by a familiar face, former Celtic teammate Mo Sylla. Guinea had been drawn in a tough section, the first match against South Africa in Alexandria taking place on Sunday, 22 January 2006, as Adam

Virgo and Stan Varga played in central defence together for the first time for Celtic at Fir Park. Balde was up against Porto striker Benni McCarthy once again, the pair having clashed as Celtic eliminated Celta Vigo on the Road to Seville just over three years earlier, and he would emerge triumphant again as Guinea won 2-0 with two late goals from Stoke City striker Sambegou Bangoura and Charleroi's Ousmane Bangoura. Tragically, Ousmane would be blinded in one eye after suffering a horrific injury in a Chinese Super League match six months later, following his move to Shenyang Ginde. Zambia were Guinea's next opponents, on Thursday, 26 January 2006 at the same venue, a double from St Etienne midfielder Pascal Feindouno - including a stoppage-time winner - seeing Balde's men come from behind to win 2-1. Ousmane Bangora and Feindouno would be on target again, as the side known as the National Elephants topped Group C with a 100% record, following a 3-0 win over defending champions Tunisia in Alexandria on Monday, 30 January 2006. Former Arsenal, Blackburn Rovers and West Ham United striker Kaba Diawara scored the final Guinea goal in injury time to seal that third win.

The reward for Balde's Guinea side was a quarter-final tie against Senegal, on Friday, 3 February 2006, once again at their happy hunting ground, the Harras El-Haddoud Stadium in Alexandria, on Egypt's Mediterranean coast. The big defender was happy with the progress his unfancied team was making.

"It is good that people keep thinking we are the underdogs. We have done something good to get to the quarter-final, but it's nothing. If the competition ends here [for us], then we have done nothing. It's not very important that we're here. We will see later. There are big teams still in the tournament. We don't feel any pressure. We are playing with a free mind. We have good players and we've had a good start. Our football history is brief. Not a lot of people know about us, but if you watch us, watch our players, we're all professionals and we've got a good team. We're not so bad. I hope we will go very far in the tournament. I hope this will help develop football in our country."

The Senegalese squad featured a number of players who would be familiar to football fans in these islands, including a couple with Celtic connections. Wearing the number seven jersey he never quite managed to secure at Parkhead was Henri Camara, then at Wigan Athletic, whilst his near-namesake Diomansy Kamara of West Bromwich Albion, wore 15. Kamara's Hawthorns manager Tony Mowbray at that time would later bring him to Celtic on loan, where he would make his debut with Robbie Keane in a 1-0 defeat at Kilmarnock in February 2010. El Hadji Diouf had infamously appeared at Celtic Park in the colours of Liverpool - spitting on a supporter in the front stand from memory - and would later do so again in the blue of Rangers, becoming the inspiration for the 'Broony.' Diouf was one of two Bolton Wanderers players in the Senegal team, Abdoulaye Faye being the other. Newcastle United's Amdy Faye – no relation to Abdoulaye, although bizarrely they would both sign for Stoke City on the same day in 2008 - would also play briefly at Ibrox, whilst Papa Bouba Diop built a reputation at Fulham, having scored the winner as Senegal beat defending champions France in the opening match of the 2002 World Cup finals, the West African country's first-ever appearance at that level. He would also be part of the Portsmouth side which won the FA Cup under Harry Redknapp in 2008.

Kaba Diawara gave Guinea the lead midway through the first half, a lead they held until the hour mark, when Bouba Diop converted Diomansy Kamara's cross for 1-1. Henri Camara then beat Bobo Balde to set Mamadou Niang up for Senegal's second before sealing the match in stoppage time himself. Pascal Feindouno's fourth goal of the tournament finished the scoring at 3-2, as the Guineans tumbled out.

Later that evening in front of 74,000 spectators in Cairo, Hossam Hassan scored the second of Egypt's four goals as they crushed the Democratic Republic of Congo to join Senegal in the last eight. Hassan had managed four against Celtic back in October 1991, as Swiss outfit Neuchatel Xamax inflicted a blow from which Liam Brady's Parkhead tenure would never recover, Celtic's worst European defeat prior to the events in Bratislava in July. The Egyptian striker was now in his 40th year and plying his trade back in his homeland in the green-and-white of Al Masry. Incredibly, given his four-goal haul against Celtic, he would only manage to score a total of three goals in his other 10 games for the club.

The other two quarter-final ties went to penalty shoot-outs, former Arsenal 'Invincible' Kanu scoring the decisive kick for Nigeria as they eliminated Tunisia in Port Said. His goal had also decided that 2008 FA Cup final. The other match featured perhaps the most remarkable spot-kick decider of all time, with all 22 players scoring as Cameroon faced the Ivory Coast in Cairo. The sudden death challenge then reverted back to the initial two takers, Chelsea's Didier Drogba and Barcelona's Samuel Eto'o, the tournament's star strikers. Eto'o blazed his second effort over the crossbar before Drogba sent the Ivorians into the semi-final. Earlier, Kolo Toure, another of the Arsenal Invincibles, who would later earn that title again under Brendan Rodgers at Celtic, converted the second penalty for Ivory Coast, another feat he would repeat in the final, played the following Friday in Cairo's International Stadium.

Drogba would score the only goal of the semi-final against Nigeria to take the Ivorians into a final against hosts Egypt, who beat Senegal 2-1. The goalless final would then also go to a penalty shootout, this particular Duel on the Nile won by the Egyptians, after the big Chelsea striker had missed the best chance of the 90 minutes, then seen his shoot-out effort saved by home keeper Essam El Hadary, the oldest player ever to play in the World Cup finals, following his appearance in Russia in 2018, aged 45.

Back home in sub-tropical Glasgow, a Celtic side minus Bobo Balde had followed up their 3-3 draw against Dundee United with a second clash in 10 days against Motherwell, this time in the semi-final of the League Cup at Hampden on Wednesday 1 February 2006. With Mark Wilson cup-tied from his time at Dundee United, Gordon Strachan shuffled his back four yet again, Adam Virgo and Mo Camara lining up either side of central defenders Stephen McManus and Stan Varga. Celtic's other new signing, Dion Dublin, joined his former Old Trafford teammate Roy Keane on the bench.

First blood on the night went to the Steelmen, after Artur Boruc appeared to stumble on his way to deal with Kevin McBride's high cross into the box, Richie Foran's looping header dropping agonisingly into the Celtic net within 10 minutes of the kick-off. With the Hoops looking out of sorts, it took a bit of magic from Shaun Maloney to conjure up an equaliser on the half-hour, his sublime pass inside the Motherwell defence releasing Maciej Zurawski, who finished clinically for his fifth goal in as many games. With extra-time looming, the Malaysian-born midfielder then won the game for Celtic. Under pressure from Zurawski, Motherwell defender Martyn Corrigan inexplicably played a back-pass to his goalkeeper with three minutes remaining, Graeme Smith having no option but to catch the ball to prevent an own goal. As the entire Motherwell team packed along the goal-line, John Hartson tapped the ball back for Maloney to sidefoot it with power through the onrushing defenders and into the top corner, taking Celts into the final, much to the relief and delight of the majority of the 33,000 crowd.

Motherwell manager Terry Butcher, an extremely happy man on Black Sunday eight months earlier, could not contain his feelings at the outcome of this latest clash with Celtic.

"We are bitterly disappointed. The lads have given so much and I'm proud of them all. I couldn't have asked for more. We created a lot of good chances and really should have taken more than one. And some of the Celtic players were saying to the lads that they deserved better from the game. Martyn has apologised to the lads, but, at the end of the day, we defend together and attack together. It is so hard to take for the lads because they have given me so much."

His opposite number, Gordon Strachan, was not much happier than Butcher, despite reaching his first cup final as Celtic manager.

"I'm not happy with the place in the final yet because I'm still angry and disappointed with the performance. It was a first semi-final for some of my players and there was a nervousness that spread like wildfire. But thank goodness for Maloney, Maciej and Hartson, who just kept running for us and were brave. We should have a few players right for the Falkirk game next week. We could have Telfer and Wilson back and Balde coming back soon, so we could have a reasonable back four again, similar to the start of the season, which can only be good."

The League Cup final opponents for Celtic at the same venue on Sunday, 19 March 2006 would be Dunfermline Athletic, the Pars having beaten Livingston 1-0 at Easter Road seven days earlier, preventing a Hampden reunion for Paul Lambert in his first season in management. Whilst he wouldn't know it at that point, John Hartson would not be part of that occasion either. He had picked up a third League Cup booking following an innocuous challenge on Motherwell goalkeeper Graeme Smith, ruling him out of the Hampden showpiece the following month. It was cruel luck on the big Welshman, who had suffered badly in the corresponding final of 2003. His legitimate equaliser against Rangers had been unbelievably disallowed for a quite ridiculous offside call, Hartson's pain then compounded as he struck a late penalty kick past the post, as Celtic lost out by 2-1.

Gordon Strachan had already picked up on that fact when he addressed the media afterwards.

"I don't think big John knows yet, but maybe the signing of Dion Dublin is not as mad as some have suggested."

Once his fate was known, in fairness, John Hartson was relatively philosophical about the situation.

"It is very disappointing, but I have always maintained that the most important thing in football is that the team win trophies and that the team win titles. These things happen in football. If it's any consolation, Roy Keane missed the Champions League final and at the end of the day, I am going to miss a League Cup final. I'll be there, I'll cheer on the boys and hopefully they can bring the manager his first trophy back to Celtic Park."

CHAPTER 9

Roy scores...even Lenny scores ...as the Irish Heartbeat drives Celts towards the title

The first Saturday in February 2006 was an unwelcome free day for Celtic, as those clubs still involved in the Scottish Cup played their fourth-round ties. Big winners on the day were the Edinburgh duo of Hibernian and Hearts, Aberdeen losing 3-0 at Tynecastle whilst Rangers' domestic season ended when they were beaten by the same score at Ibrox by Tony Mowbray's Hibs. Celtic's conqueror's Clyde survived to a replay, after a goalless draw with Gretna at Broadwood, their dreams of a fairytale run to Hampden over after a 4-0 hammering at Raydale Park 10 days later. Gretna would live that dream.

League business resumed in midweek, John Hughes' Falkirk the visitors to Celtic Park for the third time that season, on Wednesday, 8 February 2006. There were 56,672 inside the stadium that evening, however, sadly, I was not amongst them, having tried and failed to reschedule a 'leaving meal' for one of my team at work. Thus, I was dependent on messages from my kids as to progress, as I tried to look cheerful in a restaurant in Cumbernauld Village. As it transpired, I am so glad I 'took one for the team' that night. The lady we were honouring was lovely, hard-working and someone I had a lot of time for. A beautiful heart and a smile but, I always thought, the saddest of eyes, which I later found out masked some of the hurt, both physical and emotional, resulting from an unfortunate marriage. A few years later, I was really saddened to hear that she had passed away, after a short illness. She was one year younger than me, another beautiful soul taken far too soon. God bless and keep you safe, D.

Gordon Strachan had responded to the abject Hampden performance against Motherwell seven days earlier by ringing the changes. Back from his African Cup of Nations adventure was Bobo Balde to partner Stephen McManus in central defence, whilst Mark Wilson moved to left-back to allow Paul Telfer to return on his preferred right side. Roy Keane replaced Neil Lennon in midfield and new signing Dion Dublin made his debut up front, John Hartson dropping to the bench as this Celtic team lined up.

Artur Boruc: Paul Telfer, Bobo Balde, Stephen McManus & Mark Wilson: Shunsuke Nakamura, Stan Petrov, Roy Keane & Shaun Maloney: Dion Dublin & Maciej Zurawski.

The match is best remembered for the first – and as it transpired only – Celtic goal for Roy Keane, the Irishman picking up a headed clearance at the edge of the Falkirk box to rifle the ball home with the aid of a deflection 10 minutes before the interval, giving the Hoops a 1-0 lead. That advantage was doubled with seconds of the first half remaining, Balde getting his head to a Shaun Maloney cross to tee up McManus for a striker's finish at the far post. The score remained unchanged until the 83rd minute, Kenny Milne pulling one back from the Bairns with a glorious curling effort which beat Artur Boruc in his top corner, after great work on the right by substitute Pedro Moutinho. There was then a sharp intake of breath from the home support as an effort from Daniel McBreen rolled inches past the far post in the final minute with Boruc stranded, however, the 2-1 victory was enough to restore the 10-point lead at the top of the table for Celtic, Hearts having required a late Paul Hartley penalty to salvage a 1-1 draw at Tannadice, 24 hours earlier.

The Celtic manager was a bit happier with the improvement he had witnessed from last midweek.

"We're back in terms of freshness and imagination. We looked dangerous every time we went forward. The game should have been over and done with well before Falkirk scored and we were a little nervy at the end, but I'm pleased with the display and it's given me a few things to think about before the weekend."

Three days later, Saturday, 11 February 2006, the Gorgie men would slip up once more, losing an early lead to go down 2-1 to Aberdeen at Tynecastle, with Steven Pressley yet again scoring an own goal, offering Gordon Strachan's men the opportunity to stretch that lead to 13 points the following day. There was only the small matter of a trip to Ibrox to be negotiated before that could become a reality.

The build-up to that weekend's game with Rangers had taken a twist when under-pressure chairman David Murray had taken the unusual and some might say cowardly step of relieving that pressure by announcing on Thursday, 9 February 2006 that manager Alex McLeish would be vacating his position at the end of the current season. The previous evening, Aberdeen had inflicted another defeat on the struggling Ibrox outfit, by 2-0 at Pittodrie, leaving them a massive 18 points behind champions-elect Celtic with four months of the campaign still to play. That would prove a bridge too far for The People.

The smart money – no doubt other people's – was on former Olympique Lyonnais head coach Paul Le Guen taking over from McLeish, a rumour boosted by the appearance of his assistant Yves Colleu in the Ibrox main stand for the visit of Celtic on Sunday, 12 February 2006. How much a visit to the Govan stadium has changed over the years can be illustrated by the fact that I had tickets for myself, my two sons and my Old Trafford season ticket-holding brother-in-law, Mikey, whose latest visit to Scotland just so happened to coincide with his idol Roy Keane's first match for Celtic against Rangers, a fixture the Irishman himself had watched several times from the same Free Broomloan Road Stand we were currently occupying. Current Manchester United star Wayne Rooney, a guest of Keane's on the day and himself a huge Hoops fan, was seated just in front of us. Mikey asked my youngest Bhoy who he should back for first goalscorer and was immediately told, *"Maciej Zurawski."* Betting slip completed!

Maciej Zurawski was indeed in the team, partnering John Hartson in attack as Dion Dublin dropped to the bench after his midweek debut. The only other change to the Celtic line-up was the surprising omission of Shunsuke Nakamura to accommodate the returning captain Neil

Lennon, as Gordon Strachan included all three of his main central midfielders for the first time in this selection.

Artur Boruc: Paul Telfer, Bobo Balde, Stephen McManus & Mark Wilson: Stan Petrov, Roy Keane, Neil Lennon & Shaun Maloney: John Hartson & Maciej Zurawski.

Celtic made a strong start and were rewarded with a goal after 12 minutes. Contesting a high ball, Hartson found himself the meat in a Marvin Andrews/Sotirios Kyrgiakos sandwich, referee Mike McCurry waving play on as the ball broke to Stan Petrov, who in turn was fouled by Bob Malcolm. As the preacher-cum-football official continued to flap his hands skywards, Zurawski pounced on the loose ball at the edge of the box to stroke it away from Ronald Waterreus into the far corner for 1-0, his 11th goal of the season.

There was a Greek comedy moment shortly afterwards, as Kyrgiakos went in recklessly on Hartson before diving to the ground clutching his face as the big Welshman turned to confront him. McCurry – a minister famous for playing *Simply the Best* at his congregational gatherings – incredibly chose to take no action whatsoever. The referee then denied Bobo Balde another goal against Rangers when he spotted an infringement as the big Guinean backheeled the ball past Waterreus for what looked a legitimate second for Gordon Strachan's men. Keane then ticked another item off his Celtic bucket list, presumably, by clinically upending Croatian Dado Prso on the halfway line, taking a yellow card in his first experience of a Glasgow derby, perhaps the only time the Irishman broke sweat all afternoon.

The home side had one great chance, Thomas Buffel unsure whether to shoot or pass when one-on-one with Artur Boruc, however, my abiding memory of this game is watching the Irish Heartbeat of Roy Keane and Neil Lennon - both men now nearer 35 than 34 - stroll through the 90 minutes at Ibrox as if it were a training session. They could have been wearing slippers rather than boots to be honest.

A final blast on McCurry's whistle put the Ibrox men out of their current misery and saw Strachan's Celts move an unassailable 21 points ahead of Rangers, taking another giant step towards regaining their title, a traditionally difficult away fixture completed successfully and, indeed, with some ease.

The Celtic manager and captain were both keen - if you pardon the pun - to praise the contribution of the former Manchester United skipper, Gordon Strachan first up to the microphone.

"I picked a team for the heavy going. I thought it would be a physical game and so I picked physical players. Our discipline was excellent. It doesn't surprise me [that Lennon and Keane can play together]. We looked relaxed but that comes from having good players, and their touch makes them look that way but I'm not going to rule Rangers out of things. Roy's given us a presence and know-how. As I left the training ground on Friday, Dion Dublin and Roy Keane were sitting there speaking to a couple of the youth team lads and they were hanging on Roy's every word. It's that knowledge that's invaluable."

Neil Lennon, on the receiving end of a Keane rebuke at one point, as the Celtic midfield threatened to drop too deep for his liking, was also fulsome in his praise of his countryman, whilst recognising the significance of the weekend's results.

"There was a big swing for us this weekend. It's up to us to shore up that advantage now. You wouldn't want to change the way [Roy Keane] is. His shouting gets a reaction. It's up to you whether it's positive or not. The boys respect him for what he has done and what he is. He's a great player. If he wants to give you a rollicking, you respect that."

In his autobiography The Second Half, Cork Bhoy Roy Keane recalls that match and how he might not have stayed long enough at Celtic to make such an appearance.

"My hip had been causing concern and after my first training session, I drove back to my hotel in Edinburgh and lay on the bed. And my hip, I've never known pain like it. Just from the warm-up and the training. I lay there thinking, "I don't want to go back. But I need to. I have to. You should have retired. You should have just packed it in." But I couldn't leave after my first

*day. Imagine how that would have looked. I was man of the match [at Ibrox]. I got a yellow card for a foul on Dado Prso and they were baying for a red card. The atmosphere was brilliant, f****** electric. The hatred. I enjoyed all that."*

With the three points in the bag and the title now looking like the 1-33 certainty the bookmakers were quoting, there was only the question of what my Red Devil guest would pay the source of his windfall from the same brotherhood for his choice of first goalscorer. Sadly, I have to report, that despite 17 years of abuse dished out at every family gathering since that day, my son is still waiting for his reward!

The good times continued seven days later at East End Park, Dunfermline, in a dress rehearsal for the League Cup final the following month. The Celtic dress involved the all-green away kit worn with such devastating consequences at Bratislava and Broadwood, however, on a sunny afternoon in the ancient kingdom, any devastation would be inflicted on the home side. Gordon Strachan named an unchanged team from Ibrox and his side were ahead within three minutes, Stan Petrov drifting in from his new position wide on the right to tap home following excellent work down the left flank from Mark Wilson.

Artur Boruc had contributed the only negative headline in the positive few days following the win in Govan, allegedly criticising some of his teammates and goalkeeping coach Jim Blyth whilst back in Poland. If that had been the case, then the keeper would have been looking closely at himself after his misjudged attempt at collecting a hopeful cross ball allowed Andy Tod to equalise for the Fifers on 15 minutes.

Dunfermline Athletic had inflicted what would prove to be Celtic's only home defeat of the season back in November, however, there would no repeat of that as Strachan's men proceeded to run riot. Maciej Zurawski commenced his contribution to the cause by forcing Pars keeper Bryn Halliwell into a save at his near post midway through the first half, John Hartson first to react to slam the loose ball home. Eight minutes later, the Pole maker became taker, his delicious left-foot shot from the angle of the box rising past the Welsh goalkeeper to nestle high in his net, and five minutes from the interval, Zurawski sprang the home offside trap to finish clinically inside the post to send the Hoops in at 4-1.

The procession would continue in the second period. Ten minutes had elapsed when Hartson returned the favour to his striking colleague, the Welshman seemingly boxed in before swivelling to lay the ball off perfectly for Zurawski to complete his first Celtic hat-trick from close-range. With Hartson and Roy Keane making way for Dion Dublin and Alan Thompson, the goal of the game arrived with 15 minutes remaining. There seemed little danger when Zurawski looked up on the main stand touchline, then floated a pass fully 60 yards towards Shaun Maloney at the far side of the Pars penalty area, however, the little Scot adjusted his position to meet the ball with a sensational hitch-kick which flew past the Dunfermline keeper into the top corner, to the delight of the Celtic fans packed behind that goal. A few weeks earlier, the general consensus was that Jim Hamilton's strike for Motherwell against Celtic – a similar effort – would not be surpassed as the Goal of the Season in Scotland. Well we now had another contender. Simply sublime stuff from the skilful Maloney, and there was more to come.

With eight minutes left, the ball was worked towards Neil Lennon in an identical position. With the crowd crying *"shoot"* in unison, more in humour than expectation, the Irish midfielder did just that, his low drive finding the corner of the net as the roof threatened to come off the stand. If two goals at East End Park is prolific and one goal in every 100 appearances for Celtic is consistent, then Neil ticks both boxes. It would be a first goal for Lennon since a perfect chipped finish against Hibernian at Celtic Park back in December 2001, more than four years earlier. It would also be the third and final goal of his Parkhead career, his opening strike coming just three months after he signed in a 3-0 win at that same Dunfermline venue. Like the incredible Danny McGrain, Neil Lennon's goals will live long in the memory of Celtic supporters as the proverbial 'JFK moments.'

Despite my usual hunger for more Celtic goals, irrespective of opposition or occasion, I am usually happy to draw the line when we achieve that magical 7-1 scoreline, however, Maciej Zurawski would have other ideas with personal and club records there for the taking. In the 88th minute, he decided to go one better, showing electric pace to go past Andy Tod and slot home for his fourth of the day. Celtic would thus become the first side in the SPL era to score eight goals in one game. I have spent worse afternoons following this club of ours. Not surprisingly, the Celtic manager was cock-a-Hoops.

"I think Dunfermline were unfortunate because they got us on a day when our great players were great. Everything we hit went into the back of the net. The players had a reputation to uphold and I asked them to go out and do that against Dunfermline. I thought Mark Wilson and Stephen McManus were phenomenal in terms of their build-up play and Shaun Maloney's goal was tremendous. It was similar to Jim Hamilton's goal against us. He hit it very well."

Scoring sensation Neil Lennon was also a happy bunny...

"I'm delighted with the goal. It was a great day for us. I remember the last time I scored Martin O'Neill said he was pencilling in another for 2006 and I thought "cheeky get," but I don't know when the next one will come. Shaun's goal was great, and it sums up his season, and Zurawski was magnificent."

...whilst the normally bubbly Pars manager, Jim Leishman, was understandably shell-shocked.

"I've never experienced anything like this in my career. It hurts but we can't change anything now."

Celts enjoyed the rare luxury of a two-week mid-season break after the Dunfermline victory, albeit Gordon Strachan would have preferred to have been playing in the Scottish Cup quarter-final ties which completed the February schedule in Scotland. Runaway Second Division leaders Gretna continued to make the headlines, beating their First Division equivalents St Mirren 1-0 at Raydale Park to make the last four for the first time in their short history. Dundee, Hearts and Hibernian made up the final four but hopes of an all-capital final were dashed when the city rivals were drawn together.

Despite their scoring exploits in Fife, neither Maciej Zurawski nor

Shaun Maloney featured in the programme of international friendlies that midweek. Scotland faced Switzerland at Hampden on the first day of March with a starting line-up again devoid of Celts, albeit pre-contract signings Gary Caldwell and Kenny Miller both played the 90 minutes, the Wolverhampton-based striker scoring the goal in a 3-1 defeat. Bulgaria captain Stan Petrov led his team to a 1-0 win over Macedonia in Skopje the same night whilst 24 hours earlier, Shunsuke Nakamura set up both goals including a last-minute equaliser as Japan drew 2-2 with Bosnia & Herzogovina in Dortmund. The Bosnians featured Austria Wien defender Sasa Papac, who would win the League and Cup double that season in Vienna before moving to Glasgow to join Rangers. Another Celt in action in Germany was Artur Boruc, who replaced Jerzy Dudek at half-time and was beaten by Clint Dempsey three minutes later for the only goal of the night as Poland lost out to the USA in Kaiserslautern.

March opened for Celtic with the visit of Aberdeen on the first Saturday, more than 60,000 fans making their way to see if the Hoops could extend the lead at the top of the table to 16 points, with Hearts due to travel to Livingston 24 hours later. Gordon Strachan named an unchanged line-up and the Celts started where they had left off in Fife, with an exhilarating display of attacking football in the first half, only Dons keeper Jamie Langfield standing between his team and a hefty interval deficit. There was also some comedy refereeing from our old friend Mike McCurry, apparently the only man in the stadium who did not deem Zander Diamond's deliberate handball to block Shaun Maloney's left-wing cross a stonewall penalty kick. Aberdeen did suffer when they lost Barry Nicholson to injury following what can best be described as a robust challenge by Roy Keane. The Irishman was thriving in a more attacking role than usual, twice foiled by Langfield to stop him adding to his recent goal against Falkirk.

On the hour, Strachan made his first change, Shunsuke Nakamura replacing John Hartson, the move paying immediate dividends as Maciej Zurawski picked up a lovely forward pass from Keane to pull the ball back for Stan Petrov, the Bulgarian midfielder, having moved inside to accommodate the Japanese star, perfectly placed to smash a shot high past Langfield to finally open the scoring for Celtic. With 15 minutes remaining, Maloney made it 2-0 with a fortunate goal, Keane's right-wing cross being cut out by the Aberdeen defence but falling kindly for the Celt to knock it home. The icing was applied to the cake in the final minute, Keane and Petrov combining delightfully to send the Bulgarian through on the keeper, his unselfish pass allowing Zurawski the easiest of tap-ins for 3-0 and a 16-point lead.

Not surprisingly, the Celtic manager was beaming afterwards.

"We played excellent football in the first 45 minutes and their goalkeeper made some great saves. It was the most comfortable we've been in the first half for some time. Aberdeen had worked incredibly hard, but they were visibly disappointed by the second goal and gave us more room."

The gap at the top was duly reduced back to 13 points within 24 hours, as a late Roman Bednar strike saw Hearts edge a five-goal thriller with Livingston at Almondvale.

The following Saturday, en route to a family wedding in Aberdeen, I broke the habit of a lifetime and took jerseys to Celtic Park in an attempt to have a player autograph them, usually a definite 'no-no' for me. With me was my wife, which will help explain the fact that neither jersey was the sacred Hoops. My late father-in-law was from Hyde and the family are all huge Manchester United fans, something I might just mention when we get around to discussing Nakamura Night further down the line. Anyway, on that day we had an Irish top and a Manchester United jersey, with a view to producing some very special family gifts. On approaching the car park after training and enquiring as to which car was Roy Keane's, the security man suggested that he might not really be in the mood for doing this. However, I had previous, that photo opportunity at Hampden with my two sons back in 2002 surely enough to get me the nod from Roy the Bhoy.

Wrong! Catching him sneaking out of the security gate and jumping into a small black car, I managed to position myself 'papparazzi-style' in front of his by now moving vehicle, giving Roy the options of knocking me down or stopping. In hindsight, I'm guessing that may have been a 50/50 call, as he was not best-pleased. His mood then grew even worse when he saw the red jersey being handed through his open window. I may paraphrase slightly, however, the conversation went along the following lines.

"Why are you handing me that? I don't play for Man United any more. Why don't you give me a Notts Forest top, or a Cobh Ramblers one?"

My wife has gone quiet and I am totally taken aback. They say you should never meet your heroes and I don't do confrontation very well. In a voice several octaves higher than normal, I offer this gem.

"You're still a hero to a lot of United fans, Roy."

Really? That's it?

I'm chastising myself, however, in all fairness, something must strike a chord. Roy Keane's mood and tone instantly change as he signs both jerseys before handing them back with a smile.

"Ah how could I let that face down?"

Hers, not mine by the way, although both would probably have been appropriate.

The legendary Irishman then drives off and we both look at one another.

"Well that went well."

Gordon Strachan had been a Hibernian supporter as a boy and Easter Road would be the venue for Celtic's next match, 24 hours later, Sunday, 12 March 2006. Hearts had slipped up the previous day, following up their 3-2 win at Livingston with a goalless draw against Inverness Caledonian Thistle in the Highlands, thus offering the Hoops a chance to pull 15 points clear with a victory at the home of the Gorgie club's fiercest rivals. Shunsuke Nakamura retained his place in the team at the expense of the injured John Hartson, as Celts came under pressure from Tony Mowbray's young side from the off, Derek Riordan firing them ahead midway through the first half with a tremendous free-kick, which Artur Boruc touched but could not keep out. Ten minutes later, the black-clad Celts were level, totally against the run of play, when Shaun Maloney was hauled down from behind by Steven Whittaker as he prepared to fire home, a definite penalty and red card. Referee Alan Freeland awards the spot kick but settles for yellow, before Maloney whips a perfect shot into the top corner of the net for 1-1.

The game turned on the hour, with two crucial incidents. First, Nakamura's corner on the left is flicked on by Maciej Zurawski for Stephen McManus to sidefoot past Hibernian keeper Simon Brown to give Celtic the lead, a seventh goal of the season a nice reward for the central defender who had just been given an improved contract by the club. And within seconds of the restart, the Easter Road club were in big trouble, as Brown blocked a lob from Zurawski with his hands outside the box, the keeper on his way to the tunnel before Freeland produced the red card. His replacement, Zbigniew Malkowski, had the proverbial baptism of fire, his first job being to stop a free-kick from Nakamura and his second to face another Maloney penalty, after the little striker had once again been blatantly brought down by Whittaker. Incredibly, despite already being on a yellow card, the Hibernian defender was allowed to remain on the field. He would look on as his Polish goalkeeper produced his second outstanding save within two minutes, to parry Maloney's effort to safety. There would be no further scoring, as Celts extended their lead at the top to 15 points and that title win began to look more and more likely.

Shaun Maloney was certainly counting no championship chickens just yet.

"It's a big win for us so I think everyone will be happy after that, but we need to keep winning and, hopefully, things will take care of themselves. I was gutted [about missing the second penalty] but these things happen, and I'll just have to make sure the next one goes in."

Manager Gordon Strachan took time afterwards to acknowledge the performance of another of his stars, his on-form Polish striker, Maciej Zurawski, who probably should not have started the match.

"Maciej hadn't seen his teammates for the last few days because he had a virus, but he arrived this morning and said he'd give it a go. He's got huge heart. To turn up and play like that says a lot about him."

Strachan then received confirmation of the identity of one of his main adversaries for the following season, as word emerged from Ibrox later that afternoon that Frenchman Paul Le Guen had agreed to replace Alex McLeish as the next manager of third-placed Rangers.

Le Guen was well-known to Celtic supporters, both as a midfielder in the first great Paris St Germain side of the mid-90's then as the manager of Olympique Lyonnais, several years later. Tommy Burns Bhoys came up against the French Cup-holders for the first time in the European Cup Winners' Cup in October 1995. My dad had just received some dreadful medical news as he approached his 70th birthday, my siblings and I attempting to cheer him up by arranging for him to travel to Paris for the first leg, accompanied by Yours Truly, of course. We were part of a 10,000-strong Hoops army in the French capital for Celtic's first competitive match there, most of us caught up in horrendous crushing outside the stadium before kick-off. It was also an emotional trip for one of the Celtic players, Albanian Rudi Vata, who had faked injury in that same Parc des Princes arena four years earlier to trigger his substitution in an international match with France, the big defender then grabbing a bag and heading to the nearest police station as he defected from his native country.

The PSG support inside the stadium created an electric atmosphere that evening, which lives with me to this day. Behind one goal were the so-called 'left wing ultras', whilst their bitter rivals, the 'right-wing ultras' presumably, in a script which would have sat well in Monty Python's *The Life of Brian*, competed song by song and fan display by fan display to secure the bragging rights for that night. It was a show of co-ordinated supporter performance art which I have never seen bettered in any stadium in Europe in all of my travels since then. The Celtic support, mostly packed into one corner of the stadium, would show their appreciation at full-time, bursting into a spontaneous rendition of *La Marseillaise*, which went down a storm with the Ultras to our left, if not so much with the Popular People's Front at the far end.

On the field, Celtic did well to contain an excellent PSG team, which featured Paul Le Guen in midfield besides the wonderful Youri Djorkaeff, whilst future Celt Stephane Mahe was at left-back. Those two would combine for the only goal of the game, with 15 minutes remaining, Mahe's cutback dispatched past Gordon Marshall by Djorkaeff to give the French a narrow first-leg advantage. Early in the game, Pierre van Hooijdonk had passed up a glorious chance of a vital away goal by heading past the post when it looked easier to score, whilst the French had struck woodwork twice.

That was my first sighting of Youri Djorkaeff, who would go to enjoy a marvellous career, winning the UEFA Cup with Inter Milan in 1998 just before lifting the World Cup in the Stade de France following the hosts' 3-0 victory over Brazil. He would claim a European Championship with France two years later in Rotterdam, after their 2-1 extra-time defeat of Italy.

Before that, there was the small matter of the 1995/96 European Cup Winners' Cup. Despite the quality of the opposition, I still fancied Celts to turn the tie around in Glasgow two weeks later, in what was the first big occasion at the newly redeveloped Parkhead arena. Just under 35,000 packed into the two completed stands creating a cauldron of noise, and they watched their team compete well until a dreadful blunder by goalkeeper Gordon Marshall 10 minutes from the interval, his fumble from Lauren Fournier's weak effort at goal allowing PSG 'Bad Boy' Patrice Loko to fire his team ahead. And within seven minutes, Loko struck again with a neat near-post finish after Djorkaeff had provided the cross. Perched high up in the north-east corner of the stadium, I had a bird's-eye view of the third PSG goal, midway through the second half, as Djorkaeff showed sublime skill to take a pass on the run with the outside of his boot then leave John Hughes for dead, before setting up a tap-in for substitute Pascal Nouma. This would be Celtic's worst home defeat in Europe to date, however, rather than a storm of booing, the Parkhead crowd rose as one to acclaim the attacking quality of PSG at the finish.

Le Guen, Djorkaeff et al would go all the way to the final the following May at the Heysel, where they would meet our old Cup Winners' Cup adversaries Rapid Vienna, the Austrians twisting the knife a bit further by wearing green-and-white Hoops in Brussels for their second such final in 11 seasons. PSG defender Bruno N'Gotty would score the only goal of the game on the half-hour, as the French won their only major European trophy to this day. Le Guen stepped back into a defensive role 12 months later, as PSG lost the 1997 final to Bobby Robson's Barcelona in Rotterdam, the Catalan side including Pep Guardiola, Luis Figo and Ronaldo winning courtesy of a penalty converted by their Brazilian star.

Paul Le Guen would play over 300 League games for PSG between 1991-1998, having earlier enjoyed lengthy spells at both Brest and Nantes. In May 1995, he scored the winning goal in the French Cup final for a PSG side which included George Weah – better known as Timo's dad – and David Ginola, just weeks before the brilliant winger ditched signing talks at Celtic Park to join Newcastle United. Their opposition in the Parc des Princes was Racing Club de Strasbourg, who featured the two Francks, Leboef and Sauzee, who would later make their names with Chelsea and Hibernian respectively.

On his retiral in 1998, Paul Le Guen picked up his first coaching post at Stade Rennais, where one of his players was a young El Hadji Diouf, before taking over as manager of French champions Olympique Lyonnais in May 2002. Having retained Ligue Un in 2003, he would make a return to Celtic Park with his new club the following September, matchday two in the Group Stage of the Champions League. The Hoops won 2-0 in one of the finest European performances by Celtic I had witnessed in decades, thanks to second-half headers from Chris Sutton and the late Liam Miller, both from pinpoint crosses from the King of Kings, Henrik Larsson.

The critical matchday in the group was the final one, played on Wednesday, 10 December 2003. Celtic were in Lyon requiring just a draw to qualify, whilst the hosts needed a win, locked on the same points as Martin O'Neill's men but having lost in Glasgow. Goals from John Hartson and Chris Sutton levelled the match twice for Celtic, who were four minutes from a first-ever qualification to the Last 16 before the harshest of penalty calls was given against Hoops defender Bobo Balde. Lyon's Brazilian genius Juninho was the coolest man in the Stade Gerland as he stroked the ball home to eliminate Celtic.

Le Guen's men would show their quality in the next round by winning both legs against Real Sociedad to reach the quarter-final of the Champions League. There they would come up against Jose Mourinho and Porto, conquerors of Celtic in Seville and Manchester United in the previous round of the Champions League – the famous Mourinho touchline sprint celebration. Goals from Deco and Ricardo Carvalho in Oporto would prove too much of an ask for the second leg in Lyon, the clubs sharing four goals a fortnight later. Porto would go on to beat AS Monaco in the Gelsenkirchen final, a second successive European triumph for Mourinho in his last game before he left to manage Chelsea.

Olympique Lyonaiss and Le Guen would take some domestic comfort for the retention of their French title in 2004, repeating the feat the following season, a fourth consecutive championship for the club and a third personally for the manager. He then left Lyon on 9 May 2005 to take a year away from football management, his role taken up by the former Liverpool boss, Gerard Houllier.

With that track record, Paul Le Guen would provide a serious challenge to Gordon Strachan at Celtic.

But that would have to wait until next season. There was still a bit of work to be done before that would be an immediate consideration or concern for those in charge of matters at Celtic Park.

CHAPTER 10

Passing time: The end of the line for Celtic's greatest-ever player

The week leading up the Scottish League Cup final got off to the worst possible start for those with Celtic in their hearts, when the news came through on Monday, 13 March 2006 that Lisbon Lion Jimmy Johnstone had lost his five-year battle with that dreadful Motor Neurone Disease at 6am that morning. He was only 61 years old.

Tributes immediately poured in from all areas of society, however, for me by far the most touching and personal were from those men who had lined up alongside 'Jinky' for so many of those magical days or nights in the sacred green-and-white Hoops.

Celtic legend Billy McNeill paused briefly to say a few words as he headed across to visit Agnes, Jimmy's wife of 40 years, and her family.

"This is a very sad day for myself and all his family, for the game and Scotland. We all had so much admiration for this wee man. He faced up to this illness the way he faced up to everything in his life, head on. He campaigned for stem cell research knowing [that] any cure would come too late for him just so other people could get some relief. The world has lost a fantastic man. Jimmy was a brave, powerful little man, a magnificent player with unrivalled courage. He was an absolutely fabulous player. Over his career, this wee man produced some of the most magnificent performances ever seen in the game. We won't see a man like him again."

Well said, Cesar.

Still very much our leader.

It's so very poignant writing these words now, after the sad events of spring 2019, when we lost Billy himself. Then Stevie. Then Harry. We had also said farewell to another of the winger's great friends just two years earlier, during the Invincible Treble season of 2016/17. That was Tommy Gemmell, Jimmy's former teammate, and indeed manager, during his brief spell at Dundee. Back in March 2006, whilst not enjoying the best of health himself, Tommy spoke from the heart about the loss of his old partner in crime.

"He fought motor neurone disease with great courage. He stood up to it well. He was deteriorating physically but he's at peace now. He had the heart of a lion and the ability of a maestro."

Whilst I never had the pleasure of meeting him, as my parents had many times socially, particularly back in the 1960's at one of many supporters' functions, I had been fortunate enough to see some of Jimmy's greatest performances, for Celtic against Dundee United in a midweek match as a kid and for Scotland, well it had to be that match against England back in 1974. Hell, I even had his single, Passing Time, back in the day. He was even a great singer. The full package. I felt real sadness at his passing.

In over 50 years of following Celtic, for me there are three stars who shine just that bit brighter than any of the rest - Henrik, Kenny and Jinky. They don't require surnames. These guys just epitomise everything that is great about Celtic. This thing we love so much. Which you either get or you don't.

Born a 'war baby' in Viewpark, Uddingston on 30 September 1944, appropriately enough a Saturday, James Connelly Johnstone had spent countless hours as a youngster honing the dribbling skills so wonderfully demonstrated by his hero, legendary England winger Stanley Matthews. A schoolboy footballing sensation and Celtic youth player by his early teens, Jinky managed to get a job as a ballboy at Parkhead in 1957, in the aftermath of Hampden in the Sun, through one of the scoring heroes of that day, Sammy Wilson. Life was good.

On Saturday, 7 October 1961, Jimmy turned out as a trialist for Celtic reserves, scoring one goal and making the other three as the Hoops beat St Johnstone 4-2 in front of manager Jimmy McGrory, who signed two players immediately afterwards, Jimmy Johnstone and Tommy Gemmell. The gifted but tiny winger was then farmed out to a junior club, as was the custom back then, in his case to Blantyre Celtic, to toughen up and develop physically, ahead of a career in the professional game.

He was capped by Junior Scotland against Ireland in a 4-1 win at Newtownards on St Patrick's Day 1962 but it did not start well at senior level for the 18-year-old Jimmy Johnstone, drafted into a makeshift Celtic side for a difficult midweek trip to Rugby Park 12 months later, on Wednesday, 27 March 1963 Jinky was one of three debutants on a night where the only positive thing was the full-time whistle, meaning that Kilmarnock could not add to their current 6-0 lead. Jimmy McGrory - or perhaps Bob Kelly if you believe those stories - chose the following 11 in Ayrshire:

Dick Madden; Ian Young & Jim Kennedy; Dunky MacKay, John Cushley & Billy Price; Jimmy Johnstone, Bobby Craig, Stevie Chalmers, Charlie Gallagher & Frank Brogan.

The three new Bhoys – Dick Madden, John Cushley and Jimmy Johnstone - would go on to have very different football careers, although they had all followed the same route to that Rugby Park debut and there would later be a tragic correlation for two of the three in death.

Hamilton-born centre-half John Cushley had preceded Jimmy at Blantyre Celtic, before signing up at Parkhead in 1960. John had one of the tougher gigs in football, as understudy to Billy McNeill. This would restrict him to just 42 first-team appearances for Celtic before he left for West Ham United in the aftermath of Lisbon. However, his 12 League appearances in 1965/66 included the 5-1 victory over Rangers where Steve Chalmers scored a hat-trick and earned John a Championship medal in the first of THE Nine-in-a Row seasons. And a similar run in the team in the autumn of 1964 saw Cushley appear in his beloved Hoops in the League Cup final at Hampden – Jimmy Johnstone scoring Celtic's goal in a 2-1 defeat to Rangers – and against Barcelona in the Camp Nou on Ronnie Simpson's debut, a few weeks later. A fluent Spanish speaker, John famously accompanied manager Jimmy McGrory in the bold but ultimately unsuccessful bid to tempt Alfredo Di Stefano to sign for Celtic that same year.

John Cushley's final appearance for Celtic was against the same club where it all began, Kilmarnock, this time in the closing match of the 1966/67 League Championship on Monday, 15 May 1967, the last game played by the club before Lisbon. John lined up beside Billy McNeill, who was wearing number eight shorts for some reason, as goals from Bobby Lennox and Willie Wallace made it a winning finale.

Following the glory of Lisbon, John signed for West Ham United in June 1967, swapping one legendary skipper in Billy McNeill for another, England's World Cup-winning captain Bobby Moore. He would spend three seasons in London's east end before returning to Scotland to join Dunfermline Athletic. John's final club would be Dumbarton, moving to Boghead in 1972. He would enjoy his most consistent run of appearances there before retiring in 1976.

Beyond his playing career, John moved into teaching full-time, a role which allowed him to do some coaching with the youngsters at Celtic. He would enjoy seeing one of his recruits finally join the club in January 2006, right-back Mark Wilson. In 2003, John became Celtic's Education & Welfare Officer.

Having commenced his senior career beside Jimmy Johnstone, John would suffer from the same illness which claimed the life of his friend and colleague. On 24 March 2008, two years after we lost Jinky, brave John Cushley lost his own battle with Motor Neurone Disease. He had just turned 65 years old.

In goals for Celts at Kilmarnock was another 18-year-old, Dick Madden, replacing the injured Frank Haffey. He famously made two appearances for Celtic that night, his first and his last, as he watched six goals fly past him without reply. Blantyre-born Richard Michael Madden was the latest on the conveyor belt between the local junior Celtic and the more famous

Joy unconfined on and off the pitch after Stephen McManus scores a last-minute winner at Tynecastle. Hearts had taken an early two-goal lead in the vital League clash played on New Year's Day 2006.
(Photos by Jeff J Mitchell/Getty Images)

Top: Clyde knock holders Celtic out of the Scottish Cup on Roy Keane's debut on 8 January 2006.
Bottom: Du Wei looks on as Artur Boruc is beaten for Clyde's second goal. The disastrous first half at Broadwood would be the only first-team appearance at Celtic for the Chinese national captain.
(Photos by Ian Stewart/AFP via Getty Images)

Top: Roy Keane makes his home debut in the League clash with Kilmarnock on 14 January 2006.
Centre: Stan Petrov congratulates Shunsuke Nakamura after his superb free-kick gave Celts the lead.
Bottom: Maciej Zurawski turns away after scoring Celtic's fourth goal that day in a 4-2 win.
(Photos by Jeff J Mitchell/Getty Images)

The Irish Heartbeat of Roy Keane and Neil Lennon dominated proceedings at Ibrox on 12 February 2006 as Celts took another huge step towards the title with a 1-0 win.
(Photos by Jeff J Mitchell/Getty Images)

Majic moments at Ibrox!
Maciej Zurwaski scores the winner on 12 February 2006 before being engulfed by his teammates.
(Photos by Aubrey Washington/SNS Group via Getty Images and Jeff J Mitchell/Getty Images)

An emotional farewell to a football genius.
The man voted Celtic's greatest-ever player makes his final journey to Paradise on 17 March 2006.
(Photos by Jeff J Mitchell/Getty Images)

Top: The Celtic players acknowledge one of their own ahead of the Jinky League Cup final at Hampden on 19 March 2006.
Bottom: A fitting moment as Celtic's current number seven Maciej Zurawski opens the scoring.
(Photos by Glenn Campbell/AFP via Getty Images)

Happiness is a cup final goal at Hampden for Celtic.
Maciej Zurawski and Shaun Maloney savour that special feeling with their teammates.
(Photos by Jeff J Mitchell/Getty Images)

Top: Dion Dublin beats Dunfermline goalkeeper Allan McGregor to score Celtic's third goal in the League Cup final victory at Hampden, then turns away to take the acclaim of the supporters.
Bottom: The first trophy of a new era.
(Photos by Glenn Campbell/AFP via Getty Images and Jeff J Mitchell/Getty Images)

Bobo Balde emerges triumphant against Hearts on 5 April 2006 as Celtic clinch the League title.
(Photos by Jeff J Mitchell/Getty Images)

Celtic captain Neil Lennon and Birthday Bhoy goalscorer John Hartson lead the celebrations after a 1-0 home win over closest challengers Hearts secured the League flag with six games still remaining.
(Photos by Jeff J Mitchell/Getty Images)

Action from the League clash with Hibernian at Celtic Park on 16 April 2006.
Top: Roy Keane weighs up his options as Paul Telfer makes his trademark run down the right flank.
Bottom: John Hartson beats future Celt Gary Caldwell in the air to threaten the Hibernian goal.
(Photos by Stringer/AFP via Getty Images)

Top: Stan Petrov and Hibernian's Kevin Thomson slug it out in midfield at Celtic Park on 16 April 2006.
Bottom: Roy Keane congratulates Maciej Zurawski after the Polish striker's equaliser against Hibernian.
(Photos by Jeff J Mitchell/Getty Images)

The new Scottish Champions return to the field to take the acclaim of their support on 16 April 2006.
(Photos by Jeff J Mitchell/Getty Images)

There's nothing quite like that champion feeling!
The Celtic players, backroom team and support celebrate their title win together on 16 April 2006.
(Photos by Glenn Campbell/AFP via Getty Images)

An incredible Celtic support descends on Old Trafford for Roy Keane's testimonial game on 9 May 2006.
(Photos by Laurence Griffiths/Getty Images)

Glasgow version, signing on at Parkhead in August 1962. Having made that solitary appearance in March 1963, he was freed at the end of the following season, someone – often attributed to Jimmy Johnstone himself - later joking that *"Dick Madden was the only thing Frank Haffey managed to keep out during his time at Celtic!"*

On leaving Celtic, Madden joined Albion Rovers, where he played for three seasons. Whilst details of his career there are sketchy, he did feature in one of the most bizarre and memorable games in the Coatbridge club's history. The League Cup draw of 1965/66 paired Albion Rovers with local rivals Airdrieonians in a four-team section, together with southern Scottish clubs Queen of the South and Stranraer. Having lost 6-1 at Broomfield two weeks earlier, I'm guessing that the Rovers players were not holding out huge hopes of turning that position around when they met again at Cliftonhill on Wednesday, 1 September 1965. However, a team featuring Dick Madden in goal and future Blackpool and Scotland inside-right Tony Green defied the odds to win 8-2 on the night, Madden saving a penalty from Paul Jonquin at 2-0. Can't be too many 9-8 aggregated scores which played out on that basis.

After three seasons in Coatbridge, Dick made his debut for Clydebank in a 2-0 victory over Brechin City at New Kilbowie Park on Saturday, 12 August 1967. He would make 93 appearances for the Bankies over three seasons, enjoying 17 'clean sheets' before playing his final match against Forfar Athletic at home on Saturday, 7 March 1970, Clydebank suffering a 1-0 defeat.

Some mystery remains as to his movements after that, however, what is known is that Dick Madden had a significant win in the football pools at some time after leaving Celtic, so perhaps despite the fact that he was still only 26 years old, it is just possible that he chose to give up the game at that point.

Despite the heavy defeat at Kilmarnock, Jimmy Johnstone fought his way back into the Celtic side for a Monday night trip to Tynecastle at the end of April, his first goal for the club on the hour mark sealing a comeback from two goals down to put the Hoops 3-2 ahead. A late rally from a Hearts team featuring three future teammates at Parkhead – Gordon Marshall, Chris Shevlane and Willie Wallace - saw the hosts edge home by 4-3, however, Jimmy's performance earned him a surprise place in the starting line-up for the Scottish Cup Final against Rangers the following Saturday.

The first clash of the old Glasgow rivals in that showpiece match since 1928 would be played out in front of 130,000 supporters at Hampden. Celtic lined up as follows, on Saturday, 4 May 1963, for the biggest game in the teenage Johnstone's life.

Frank Haffey; Dunky MacKay & Jim Kennedy; John McNamee, Billy McNeill & Billy Price; Jimmy Johnstone, Bobby Murdoch, John Hughes, John Divers & Frank Brogan.

Jimmy showed up well in a fighting Celtic performance, as did oft-maligned goalkeeper Frank Haffey. A Bobby Murdoch equaliser on the stroke of half-time secured a 1-1 draw against the Ibrox favourites, Ralph Brand having opened the scoring minutes earlier. Somewhat inexplicably, Jinky was then dropped for the midweek replay, 10 days later, as was left-winger Frank Brogan, their places going to Bobby Craig, an inside-forward who had never played on the wing previously, and Stevie Chalmers. Rangers would run out easy 3-0 winners on the night, with Brand netting a double and Davie Wilson also on target. Tens of thousands of Celtic supporters streamed towards the Hampden exits long before the final whistle, unable to bear the sight of their team going down to a fourth successive Scottish Cup Final defeat in just nine years. Drastic change would be required at Parkhead, and soon.

Jimmy would enjoy his breakthrough season in 1963/64, as despite Rangers domestic dominance, the Bhoys enjoyed a run all the way to the semi-final of the European Cup Winners' Cup, Celtic, ironically, only participating in the tournament on the back of that Hampden failure. The diminutive winger commenced his remarkable scoring run in continental competitions by netting the opener against FC Basel in a 5-0 victory at Celtic Park on Wednesday, 9 October 1963, in front of what remains our lowest home attendance in European football, just 8,000 hardy or mad souls braving a horrific night in the east end of Glasgow. There would be 51,000 in the old ground for the first leg of the semi-final on Wednesday, 15 April 1964, Jinky repeating the feat by opening the scoring against MTK Budapest just before the interval, a Stevie Chalmers second-half double giving the Hoops one foot in the Brussels final. However, rather naively, as the song goes 'Celts went all out to attack' in the second leg and paid the ultimate price, a 4-0 defeat in the Hungarian capital meaning that the long wait for silverware since dragged back to Hampden in the Sun in October 1957 would stretch into an eighth season. On a personal level, with 10 goals from 42 starts, it had been a successful campaign for Jimmy Johnstone.

The 1964/65 season would see the dawn of a new era for Celtic, albeit not immediately. Jimmy celebrated the end of his teens by gaining his first cap for Scotland, lining up with club colleagues Jim Kennedy and Stevie Chalmers at Ninian Park, Cardiff on Saturday, 3 October 1964 for the Home International match with Wales. Despite a Chalmers strike helping the Scots to a 2-1 half-time lead, a Welsh side featuring legends Ivor Allchurch and John Charles fought back to win 3-2. A first World Cup match for Johnstone would follow shortly afterwards, 55,000 spectators rolling up to Hampden for the qualifier with Finland on Wednesday, 21 October 1964. Chalmers was again on target as Scotland won 3-1, keeping them in the hunt for the English finals of 1966 in a section which also included Italy and Poland. Three days later, Jimmy was back at the national stadium for his first League Cup final, Rangers again the opposition, in front of 91,000 spectators. Celts had won their only two previous finals in this competition, an inaugural replay victory over Partick Thistle in October 1956 followed by the famous 7-1 game 12 months later. Sadly, that run would end here, a double from Garngad man Jim Forrest enough to win the trophy, despite a 70th minute strike from Jimmy giving the Hoops some hope, after Ibrox keeper Billy Ritchie had blocked a shot from another son of Royston, Stevie Chalmers.

The new year would bring a new experience for Jimmy Johnstone, as he suffered the first ordering off of his career in the Ne'erday derby at Ibrox. Having had enough of the treatment being dished out to him, he sought his own retribution on Rangers Icelandic inside-forward Tottie Beck, referee Tom 'Tiny' Wharton sending him down the tunnel with 10 minutes of the first half still remaining and the home side 1-0 up through another Forrest goal, scored a few minutes earlier. Ten-man Celts then produced one of those stirring performances against the odds for which they are renowned, Bobby Murdoch passing up a glorious chance to save a point when he blazed his spot kick high over the crossbar with just six minutes remaining, after Ronnie McKinnon had chopped John Hughes down in the box. Presumably under the instructions of Bob Kelly, who abhorred any kind of foul play by his team, Jimmy would sit out the home draw with Clyde the following day before returning to the team for the next three matches, as the winless start to 1965 stretched to five games. He was then dropped to make way for the returning Steve Chalmers for the Parkhead clash with Aberdeen on Saturday, 30 January, the famous match where the aforementioned 'Big Yogi' scored five goals whilst wearing white trainers, as Celts crushed the Dons on the icy pitch by 8-0.

The appointment of Jock Stein as Celtic's new manager in March 1965 would be the catalyst for Jimmy Johnstone's world-class career, however, that change did not bear fruit immediately. As the Hoops continued to win, racking up seven consecutive victories, the little winger could only watch from the sidelines. He would be restored to the team following the first defeat under Stein, a 1-0 home loss to St Johnstone, Jinky setting up a goal for Bobby Lennox at Dens Park before making it 3-1 with a solo effort, before a late rally saw Dundee salvage a 3-3 draw. Jimmy also picked up a thigh injury, which would rule him out of the visit of Jock's old team Hibernian, two days later, a game where Neil Martin became one of the few visiting players to score a hat-trick at Celtic Park, as the Leith men won 4-2.

Johnstone was back on the right-wing for Jock's first game at Hampden as Celtic manager, the Scottish Cup semi-final against Motherwell on Saturday, 27 March 1965. Well striker Joe McBride twice put his side ahead, with first Bobby Lennox then a Bertie Auld penalty levelling the tie. Jimmy was then given offside in the dying seconds as he set Auld up for the winner, a decision which was marginal. McBride would impress enough to become Jock Stein's first major signing as Celtic manager in the close-season.

Jimmy Johnstone's thigh injury prevented him playing in the replay four days later, Stevie Chalmers again wearing the number seven shorts and opening the scoring before second-half strikes from John Hughes and Bobby Lennox sealed a 3-0 victory for Celtic which set up a rematch of the 1961 Scottish Cup Final against Dunfermline Athletic, a night when Jock Stein was in the Pars dug-out at Hampden. Jimmy would also miss Third Lanark's last-ever visit to Celtic Park, when former Parkhead captain Dunky MacKay scored the late own goal past future Hoops goalkeeper Evan Williams which consigned the relegation-haunted Thirds to a 1-0 defeat. Another former Celt, Billy McNeill's best friend Mike Jackson, also lined up for the 'Hi Hi' on that historic afternoon. The famous old club from Glasgow's south side, Celtic's opponents in their first-ever Scottish Cup final back in February 1889 at what would become their Cathkin home in 1903, would then go on a downward spiral which would sadly result in their liquidation in June 1967. The Football Gods had treated the two clubs very differently in the intervening eight decades, before twisting the knife by overseeing the demise of Third Lanark just weeks after the most glorious day in the history of the club they had defeated in that 1889 showpiece.

As the 1965 Scottish Cup final loomed closer, Jimmy featured in two successive defeats, a 6-2 mauling at Brockville followed by a 2-1 loss to Partick Thistle at Celtic Park. He would then miss out at Hampden as Jock Stein brought Charlie Gallagher back into a reshuffled attack, with Stevie Chalmers again moving to the right flank. Gallagher's contribution would be massive, setting up two Celtic goals. His incredible 30-yard drive rebounded from the crossbar for Bertie Auld to make it 1-1 in the first half, then with just nine minutes remaining, Charlie's corner kick from the left wing was met by the flashing head of Billy McNeill to begin a golden era which would never be surpassed in Scotland. To add insult to injury, Jimmy was restored to the team for a visit to East End Park just four days later, the Pars taking a measure of revenge as they dished out a 5-1 thrashing to their cup conquerors, the fifth goal falling to a certain Alex Ferguson - whose younger brother Martin had played alongside Jimmy in that Junior International in Ireland - as Celts conceded 11 goals in the final two away games in the League.

Season 1965/66 would see Jimmy establish himself as a first-pick under Stein, the winger scoring twice on the eve of his 21st birthday, as the manager's debut European match at Celtic ended in a 6-0 victory in the Netherlands over the Go Ahead Eagles of Deventer in the first round of the Cup Winners' Cup, Jinky having done the same four days earlier in a 7-1 League hammering of Aberdeen at Parkhead. And the following month, Johnstone won his first major honour in senior football, as Jock's Celts added the League Cup to the growing collection after an eight-year gap, two John Hughes penalties beating Billy Ritchie and Rangers at Hampden. The sight of jubilant Celtic players celebrating with the trophy would prove too much for some of the spectators packed into the Mount Florida terracing, as on to the pitch they came to intimidate and confront the Parkhead men, creating dreadful scenes which would see the traditional laps of honour banned for many years at the national stadium.

There would be mixed fortunes as the season reached its conclusion, Jimmy recalled to the Scotland team and scoring yet another double - his first two goals for his country - in a 4-3 defeat by England at Hampden. And the national stadium would provide a sad backdrop just three weeks later, as a late Kai Johansen goal won the Scottish Cup final replay for Rangers, after Celtic had dominated the first match, thus preventing a first Parkhead Treble. Jock Stein's Celts had also been denied a European Cup Winners' Cup final appearance at the same venue, when a late Bobby Lennox goal was incorrectly ruled out for offside at Anfield the previous midweek, thus allowing Bill Shankly to bring his Liverpool side to Hampden, where they would lose 3-1 to Borussia Dortmund. Jimmy would then score crucial goals against Morton and Dunfermline Athletic as the flag race went all the way to the wire, Bobby Lennox's last-gasp winner at Fir Park on

Saturday, 7 May 1966 finally sealing the first of the nine titles.

Under Jock, Jimmy Johnstone would win every honour in the game, culminating in the European Cup Final in Lisbon in May 1967. He had been a key figure on the Road to Lisbon, memorably terrorising the French champions Nantes both home and away to earn the 'Flying Flea' accolade, before scoring the vital first goal in the semi-final against the Czech Army side, Dukla Prague. Three weeks before the final, Jimmy had scored both goals as Celtic got the single point required at Ibrox to clinch a second successive League title and first-ever domestic Treble in front of the watching Inter Milan manager, Helenio Herrera. His second goal is a thing of beauty, Jinky cutting in from the right to hit a screamer into the top corner with his left foot, the ball then sticking in the goalmouth mud in one of those iconic Celtic moments. That season, the little genius was voted third in the Ballon d'Or, behind Ferencvaros star Florian Albert and Manchester United's Bobby Charlton, Jimmy finishing ahead of European footballing legends such as Franz Beckenbauer, Eusebio, Gerd Muller and George Best, plus his friend and team-mate Tommy Gemmell, who came in a very creditable sixth, as Celts won all five trophies for which they had entered for an unprecedented and still unrivalled Grand Slam.

The last game of that magical season also provided one of his career highlights, on and off the park! The new European champions Celtic were invited to play in the testimonial match for the one and only Alfredo Di Stefano, his final appearance for Real Madrid attracting 120,000 fans to the Estadio Santiago Bernabeu. It was the night when the six-time continental masters and 1966 champions would show the new Bhoys their place, however, a little redhead from Viewpark, Uddingston had not read that particular script. Jimmy had the game of his life that balmy evening, tormenting the Madrid defenders throughout, as the vast crowd roared their approval, before sending his great pal Bobby Lennox through late on to score the only goal of the game. There is a fantastic moment at full-time, captured on film forever, as Jinky holds the ball above his head with one hand to take the acclaim of the home support, who rise as one in his honour. His next move is also legendary, albeit for other reasons. Having booked a taxi from the Madrid stadium to take his bride of 12 months Agnes on a well-earned holiday, Jimmy stepped into the cab and uttered the immortal words, *"Benidorm, mate"*, an eight-hour car journey across Spain being a better option than a one-hour flight for the aeroplane-fearing winger.

That fear of flying had been triggered on a flight back to Scotland from San Francisco the previous summer, Jimmy returning early from the club's post-season tour to marry his childhood sweetheart, the passengers terrified as the jet experienced severe turbulence. The most famous story associated with his subsequent phobia is perhaps the Red Star Belgrade episode of November 1968. The previous month had included a week which said it all about the Jimmy Johnstone package. In midweek, he had been outstanding in putting the latest French champions St Etienne to the sword, Celts recovering from a 2-0 deficit to score four without reply, in one of only four games I can recall the team wearing that all-white kit with green trim on the collar and cuffs. Three days later, he was replaced late on by George Connelly against Dundee United, Jimmy responding by throwing his jersey towards Jock Stein in the dugout, an act he regretted instantly as the Big Man came charging down the tunnel after him!

Although that incident resulted in a club suspension, Jimmy was back in Stein's side for the next round of the European Cup, against the dangerous Yugoslavs, the home first leg level at 1-1 at the interval. In one of those psychological mind games in which Jock excelled, he promised Jinky that if Celts had a four-goal lead he would not have to fly to Belgrade for the second leg. Cue a Johnstone masterclass, setting up two goals and scoring a double himself as the Bhoys won 5-1. *"I'll no need tae go!"*

If these stories had been passed down, then I was fortunate enough to witness the next Jimmy classic personally. I recall clearly standing at the back of the old Celtic End on a cold Wednesday, December night 11 months later, to watch him 'terrorise the Terrors,' as Dundee United, playing in their new all-tangerine kit, were blown away 7-2. Former Rangers winger Davie Wilson waited on the pitch at the end of the match to congratulate him, whilst Tannadice manager Jerry Kerr described Jimmy's display as the finest he had ever seen, although I believe he possibly surpassed even that performance the following April, in both legs of the European Cup semi-final against Don Revie's great Leeds United side. England left-back Terry Cooper endured a torrid time, Jimmy running riot as Jock's Lions roared to their second 'Big Cup' final in four years, in front of a European competition record attendance of 136,505, before tamely losing out in Milan to a hungry Feyenoord team which included Wim Jansen.

Four years later, I watched Jimmy tear another England full-back 'a new one' on the same Hampden pitch. This time, the late Emlyn Hughes was his victim, as Johnstone inspired Scotland to a 2-0 victory, in front of a paltry 95,000 drenched supporters. His performance was all the more remarkable, as just four days earlier, we had the infamous 'Rowingboatgate' incident, as Jinky headed out across the Irish Sea from Largs on an impromptu early-morning solo crossing, minus those helpful oar 'thingymybobs.' That episode is now mostly a source of anecdotes and fun, however, the press of the day did not miss him, and were duly rewarded with a personal victory sign from the mercurial winger, following his man-of-the-match performance on the Saturday. Sadly, the blazers would have the last laugh, the SFA selection committee ensuring he took no part in that summer's World Cup finals tournament in West Germany, his last such opportunity on that stage before, essentially, retiring the following season. By that time, the English FA had appointed Don Revie as their new national team manager, the Hampden torture inflicted by Jinky on caretaker boss Joe Mercer leading to a public campaign to install the Leeds legend in the hotseat. That would not end so well, following England's failure to reach Argentina four years later, with Revie becoming public enemy number one south of the border following allegations that he was already planning his exit to take up the manager's post in the United Arab Emirates. Revie later retired to Scotland, where he was diagnosed with Motor Neurone Disease in May 1987. He would pass away in Edinburgh exactly two years later. Like the man who had done more than most to ruin his dreams of European glory over that two-legged tie in 1970, he would succumb to that illness whilst just 61 years of age. Sometimes the parallels of life are stranger than any fiction one can write.

As Jimmy Johnstone's career and reputation had developed, the punishment he endured on the field often led to the little winger seeking his own retribution, leading to a further four ordering-offs to add to his initial dismissal in the 1965 Ne'erday fixture at Ibrox. On Saturday, 23 September 1967, Jimmy reacted angrily to a nasty challenge from former Celtic colleague Kenny Aird in a League match with St Johnstone, referee Bert Padden sending the winger down the Parkhead tunnel for an alleged punch. He was subsequently summoned to a disciplinary hearing at the SFA's Park Gardens HQ at Kelvingrove Park and given a 21-day suspension, which ruled him out of the forthcoming League Cup Final with Dundee, an opportunity lost to collect his third successive winner's medal in the competition. Sadly, the ban did not extend to the brutal World Club Championship games with Racing Club de Avellaneda of Argentina, Jimmy a constant source of disgraceful treatment before, incredibly, being one of four Celtic players dismissed by an incompetent Paraguayan referee in the farcical Play-off in Montevideo.

Jimmy was on target in the following season's Scottish Cup semi-final against Morton at Hampden on Saturday, 22 March 1969, my eighth birthday, Celtic kindly wearing their 'St Etienne' all-white kit to mark my first visit to the national stadium as they won 4-1. Both he and I would miss the April final against Rangers, me due to the size of the crowd and the fact that *"you don't go to that game, son,"* whilst Jinky had picked up yet another costly suspension, a two-week ban for accumulating bookings. Thus, he would miss out on the final leg of a second domestic Treble secured within just three weeks in April, young George Connelly wearing the number seven shorts as he waltzed around Ibrox keeper Norrie Martin to coolly score the third goal in Celtic's wonderful 4-0 victory.

Following the infamous Davidson final of 1970 against Aberdeen, Jimmy would be back at Hampden to pick up winner's medals in the Scottish Cup finals of 1971 and 1972. His performance in the replay against Rangers in May 1971 was sublime, a virtuoso display best summed up by the sight of Ronnie McKinnon rugby-tackling him for the penalty which Harry Hood converted for 2-0, the Ibrox centre-half then sportingly but sheepishly shaking the winger's hand as if to say, *"What else could I do?"* And 12 months later he lined up against Hibernian for the greatest game of my childhood, the 1972 Scottish Cup final, as Dixie Deans bagged his first Hampden hat-trick against the Edinburgh men in what I often think of as the last great performance of a truly wonderful Jock Stein Celtic era, a 6-1 win.

Johnstone's final two dismissals in the Hoops came along in a five-month spell in 1973. I remember the first one particularly well, on St Patrick's Day, in a Scottish Cup quarter-final tie against Aberdeen at Celtic Park. The referee who had done more than most to ensure the Dons would win the 1970 final against Stein's men, Robert Holley Davidson of Airdrie, was again at the centre of the game's two most controversial incidents. Within the first minute, he had disallowed a Jinky goal after consulting with the stand-side linesman, then on the hour, with the game still goalless, he infuriated the majority of the 40,000 crowd by sending the little winger to the dressing-room, after a chat with his assistant on the Jungle touchline, allegedly for violent play. The Celtic winger departed the scene as a Hail Hail of missiles flew onto the pitch. The decision would later be overturned on appeal, with no action taken!

The last ordering-off of Jinky's career was against the same opposition as his first, Rangers, in a League Cup-tie at Celtic Park on Saturday, 25 August 1973. Once again, retaliation was the alleged offence, Alex MacDonald the Ibrox player involved, as he would be on the same field six years later, when one of Jimmy's successors, the late Johnny Doyle, took the same walk in that memorable 4-2 title victory.

The winner's medals would continue to stack up in the Johnstone trophy cabinet, Jimmy completing a ninth successive League Championship success in April 1974 beside the other survivors of that first title-clincher at Fir Park back in 1966, Billy McNeill and the winger's best pal, Bobby Lennox. Johnstone would miss the game at Brockville which sealed the historic achievement, having been the recipient of a death threat in Madrid three days earlier, as the disgraceful behaviour of Atletico's players in the first leg of the European Cup semi-final in Glasgow went unpunished. He would be back in his normal berth the following Saturday to help Celts win a fifth League and Cup double under Jock Stein with a comfortable 3-0 win over a Dundee United team appearing in its first-ever national cup final.

There would be one last Indian Summer for Jinky at Celtic, as season 1974/75 commenced with a first Drybrough Cup triumph for the Bhoys at the fourth attempt, Johnstone scoring the winning penalty in the 4-2 shootout victory over Rangers at Hampden. The winger's glittering European career in Hoops would end in the heat of Piraeus in early October at the hands of Greek champions Olympiakos, his 16 goals from 67 continental appearances a Celtic club record only surpassed by Henrik Larsson, Jimmy's tally equalled by Chris Sutton on the night the Swede came back to torment his old club with Barcelona in September 2004. However, by the end of that month of October 1974, Johnstone had won another League Cup-winner's medal, Jimmy opening the scoring himself then inadvertently laying on the hat-trick goal for his good friend Dixie Deans against Hibernian in the final. From my angle at Hampden, Jinky's shot was heading for the North Enclosure before the striker threw himself to meet the ball with his head, the little redhead looking to the heavens in mock protest as the net bulged. The pair would then feature in a double-header for Scotland at the same venue within the next month, the games with East Germany then Spain proving to be the only caps awarded to Deans and the last to Johnstone. Jimmy scored four goals in a paltry 23 international appearances spread across 10 years for Scotland.

My final memory of Jimmy Johnstone the player is a wonderful one, as you would expect. On Saturday, 14 December 1974, the Hoops travelled the road and the miles to Dundee for a game we would never forget. Jimmy scored a first-half brace whilst Kenny Dalglish went one better with a hat-trick, as Celts beat the Dark Blues 6-0 in front of the watching Rod Stewart, great pals of the pair from his affiliation to the Scottish national team. I sat enthralled in the main stand at Dens Park as the Celtic supporters around me belted out the old Pilot hit, 'Magic,' the words suitably adapted to tell the world and anyone who would listen that

10-in-a-row was imminent. But from being almost home and hosed, the Hoops inexplicably collapsed after the turn of the year, so handing the title to Jock Wallace's Rangers.

Despite those wonderful performances in the closing three months of 1974, Jimmy would make just five further starts in his beloved Hoops following the calamitous 3-0 defeat at Ibrox on Saturday, 4 January 1975, the last of those in the final League game of the season against St Johnstone at Muirton Park on Saturday, 26 April 1975. Jock Stein went with the following line-up that afternoon:

Peter Latchford; Danny McGrain & Andy Lynch; Steve Murray, Billy McNeill & Roddie MacDonald; Jimmy Johnstone, Ronnie Glavin, Dixie Deans, Tommy Callaghan & Kenny Dalglish.

An injury to Jimmy saw him replaced by Harry Hood on the hour mark, Saints scoring the third and final goal of the day just five minutes later. That would subsequently rule him out of the following week's Scottish Cup final against Airdrieonians, where his captain Billy McNeill brought his own glorious 18-year Celtic career to an end by lifting the famous old trophy aloft at Hampden. Although he had made 31 appearances in that final season, Jimmy had not managed a single minute on the pitch during that Scottish Cup campaign, the winger restricted to a couple of substitute slots. And he would start on the bench at the same venue seven days later, eventually seeing some action as Celtic and Rangers shared four goals in the Glasgow Cup final, his last appearance for Celtic. On Tuesday, 10 June 1975, a distraught Jimmy was handed a free transfer by Celtic chairman Desmond White, an outcome the player would later describe as akin to a death sentence. In many ways, sadly, it was.

For all the honours won and glory nights enjoyed together, there was perhaps an inevitability for Jock Stein that the player he regarded in many ways as an errant son would have to be on his way. It had been coming for some time, but the manager later paid him the most incredible, loving tribute.

"People might say I will be best remembered for being in charge of the first British club to win the European Cup or leading Celtic to nine League

Championships in a row, but I would like to be remembered for keeping the wee man, Jimmy Johnstone, in the game five years longer than he might have been. That is my greatest achievement."

Post-Parkhead, Jimmy endured some difficult times as he tried to fill that huge Celtic gap in his life. He had a brief spell in the NASL with San Jose Earthquakes in 1975, famously coming up against Pele, the Brazilian legend at that time carving out another career with the New York Cosmos. Before the end of that calendar year, Johnstone had been signed by new Sheffield United manager Jimmy Sirrell, the former Celt. Whilst at Bramall Lane, he would team up with another Scottish winger, John McGeady. Many years later, his son Aiden would wear the number seven jersey for Celtic with some distinction.

In May 1976, Celtic supporters would have a final opportunity to watch the legendary winger play in the Hoops, as Tommy Docherty brought his Manchester United team to Glasgow for a joint testimonial match for those old pals, Jimmy Johnstone and Bobby Lennox. Almost 50,000 fans turned out for a highly emotional night, as we had the sight of Jock Stein returning after his near-fatal car crash the previous July, just weeks after Jimmy had left Parkhead. And there was the sight of David Hay in Hoops once again, a player many of us felt had never truly been replaced since his move to Chelsea two years earlier. I was in the Jungle that night to watch the current captain, Kenny Dalglish, steal the show with a hat-trick, after Bobby Lennox had got his own party started with the opening goal in a 4-0 victory. Magical stuff, even if I didn't manage to catch either of the boots he threw in towards us at full-time.

His next stop, in the latter half of 1977, was that same Dens Park, Dundee where he had enjoyed his last moments of brilliance in the Hoops of Celtic, three years earlier, teaming up with new manager Tommy Gemmell, his old partner-in-crime from Parkhead, and his teenage captain Gordon Strachan. That spell would end, as Sheffield had, in disappointment, just 14 League games managed across both.

With his drinking becoming more and more of an issue, perhaps Dublin was not the ideal place to try and resurrect his career, Jimmy signing for

Shelbourne in November 1977, together with another old Celtic friend Dixie Deans. Johnstone would remain with the Shels until the following March, training in Scotland then flying in for the weekend. One can only imagine the shenanigans involved as Jinky and Dixie enjoyed the craic in the Irish capital. On the pitch, there were glimmers of the genius, with the highlight a winning goal for Johnstone in a League Cup-tie against a Shamrock Rovers side featuring former Leeds United playmaker Johnny Giles. Allegedly, there was no love lost between the pair. There would be one final throw of the dice in terms of Jimmy's playing career, a spell in the Highland League with Elgin City in season 1978/79, a final 18 appearances before it was all over at the age of 34.

Jimmy's life after football was largely spent battling against alcohol addiction and working in a variety of labouring or driving roles before being diagnosed with the dreadful Motor Neurone Disease in 2001. Showing the same courage that he had done over many years of taking punishment on the field, the legend bravely battled the illness, a film of his struggles inspiring Sarah Faberge, great-granddaughter of the famous Carl, to create 19 precious jewelled eggs to raise funds to help the stricken winger, one for each of the major honours he won as a Celt . An excellent singer, as mentioned earlier, Jimmy also recorded 'Dirty Old Town' with Jim Kerr, Celtic-daft lead singer with the Simple Minds, in an attempt to promote the work being done to seek a cure for MND.

Sadly, Jimmy Johnstone passed away in the early hours of Monday, 13 March 2006, at home with his beloved Agnes and surrounded by his family. Four days later, on St Patrick's Day no less, thousands stood outside Celtic Park as his cortege passed his spiritual home, and the League Cup Final on the Sunday would become 'the Jinky Final,' the Celtic players all wearing the number seven on their shorts in his honour and the crowd continually chanting his song, *"Oh Jimmy Johnstone on the wing."*

On Saturday, 13 December 2008, a bronze statue of Jimmy in classic pose was unveiled in front of the main stand at Celtic Park, beside those of two other men who changed the course of Parkhead history forever, the immortal Jock Stein and the Irish Marist with the huge heart who gave us

Celtic, Brother Walfrid. It was a fitting tribute to the red-headed winger from Viewpark, Uddingston who was voted the club's greatest-ever player in 2002, the Big Man still managing to keep an eye on the Wee Man.

I'll leave the last quotation to Jinky himself.

"I was always an entertainer. The pitch was my stage. The whistle meant it was showtime."

It certainly did. There was only one Jimmy Johnstone.

A little man with a big heart and a huge talent, who will never be forgotten by the Celtic family.

God bless him

Jimmy Johnstone - Celtic Roll of Honour

Appearances 529 Goals 135

European Cup 1966/67

Scottish League	Scottish Cup	Scottish League Cup
1965/66	1966/67	1965/66
1966/67	1970/71	1966/67
1967/68	1971/72	1968/69
1968/69	1973/74	1969/70
1969/70		1970/71
1970/71		1971/72
1971/72		1973/74
1972/73		1974/75
1973/74		

The original 9-in-a-row.

CHAPTER 11

Seven is the magic number as Strachan's Celts win The Jinky Final

Jimmy Johnstone was still very much to the forefront of the thoughts of many of the 50,090 spectators who made their way to Hampden on the afternoon of Sunday, 19 March 2006 for the 59th Scottish League Cup Final, a first meeting at that stage between Celtic and Dunfermline Athletic.

The two clubs had met in the Scottish Cup Final three times previously, each one an historic occasion in its own right, albeit for very different reasons. The first national cup final of my lifetime had seen a young Jock Stein mastermind Dunfermline's inaugural major trophy success at the expense of his old club Celtic, following a 2-0 replay win at Hampden in April 1961, which saw the trophy drought extend yet further for the Parkhead faithful since that greatest of all League Cup Final days, the 7-1 thrashing of favourites Rangers, all the way back in October 1957.

Four years later, Stein would end that dismal run and embark on his own unprecedented silverware conquest as the manager of Celtic by winning the famous old cup against that same Pars outfit. The Hoops would twice come from behind to equalise through superb Bertie Auld goals before the flashing blond head of Billy McNeill thundered Charlie Gallagher's corner kick behind Jim Herriot with just nine minutes remaining to kick-off the first of so many celebrations across the worldwide Hoops diaspora.

Almost four decades would pass before the third cup final clash between the two clubs. This time, another Celtic legend was taking centre-stage, Henrik Larsson appearing in his final competitive match for the Hoops after seven magnificent seasons. The Swedish hitman turned the game on its head by netting a second-half double to turn a losing position into a winning one, Stan Petrov applying the icing as Martin O'Neill's men secured a second Double in four years by winning the 2004 Scottish Cup.

The man in the middle for that Scottish Cup Final, referee Stuart Dougal, would again be in charge of proceedings for the fourth Hampden showpiece between the Bhoys and the Pars. His whistle kicked off a thunderous minute's ovation for the late Jimmy Johnstone, the Celtic players having emerged in white tracksuit tops with 'Johnstone 7' printed on the back, and all wearing shorts with that magical green seven on the side. There wasn't a dry eye in the national stadium as our thoughts turned to the little genius in Hoops who had given us so much pleasure and a thousand anecdotes over the years.

For his first cup final as Celtic manager, Gordon Strachan again adapted his normal formation to account for the loss of striker John Hartson, the big Welshman's harsh booking in the semi-final against Motherwell having cruelly ruled him out of the Hampden showpiece. Stan Petrov would play in a more advanced midfield role than usual to support Maciej Zurawski, as the Celts lined up as follows:

Artur Boruc; Paul Telfer, Stephen McManus, Bobo Balde & Ross Wallace; Shunsuke Nakamura, Neil Lennon, Roy Keane & Shaun Maloney; Stilian Petrov; Maciej Zurawski.

The most obvious change to the Dunfermline side who had shipped eight goals to Celtic the previous month was, unsurprisingly, between the sticks, Ibrox loanee Allan McGregor replacing Bryn Halliwell. Former Celt Mark Burchill would lead the Pars line, whilst another Parkhead striking favourite, Simon Donnelly, whose goal at East End Park in May 1998 had come within minutes of clinching a first League title in a decade for the Hoops, was on the bench. In central defence for the Fifers was Englishman Aaron Labonte, a survivor of the 3-1 Scottish Cup Final defeat two years earlier. It was his slip which had let the great Larsson in for the sublime finish which had tied the match up at 1-1, the 20-year-old Middlesbrough-born stopper then beaten again as the magical Swede gave the Hoops the lead. He would perhaps feel some need to put things right today, albeit the consensus at the time had been mostly favourable in terms of his overall performance against such a world-class talent that afternoon.

The League Cup final has been a graveyard for the hopes and ambitions of many Celtic supporters over the years, however, this never felt like one of those days, as the Hoops took control from the outset. Shunsuke Nakamura was the first to provide a threat to McGregor's goal, the latest in a series of delicious corners from the dead-ball expert crashing back off the Dunfermline crossbar after Bobo Balde had connected with a combination of his shoulder and a defender's back. Then the Japanese maestro found the head of Roy Keane with another superb delivery, the Irishman doing everything right but looking to the heavens as the Pars keeper stretched a hand up to fingertip the ball to safety.

As often happens, a goalkeeper stopping everything he shouldn't then loses the softest of goals. With the half-time whistle imminent, there seemed little danger when Shaun Maloney's flick saw McGregor favourite to reach the ball ahead of Maciej Zurawski, however, the Football Gods can be cruel when they decide to intervene. As the Pars keeper scooped the ball into his arms, he collided with the aforementioned Labonte, and suddenly Zurawski was presented with an open goal from a matter of yards out. The Pole made no mistake to give Celtic a rather fortunate lead. There would be no real surprise that the current owner of the iconic seven jersey would open the scoring with the seventh cup final goal against Dunfermline on the day we honoured the greatest of all Celtic number sevens. The crowd immediately burst into a chant of *"Jimmy Johnstone on the wing."* Hollywood doesn't write scripts which even remotely compare with the magic moments produced as we follow the Celtic.

That one was for you, Jinky.

Having been denied his own Roy of the Rovers moment in the first half by McGregor's save, Keane then saw his first cup final with Celtic end just after the hour. The Irish legend had been immaculate before pulling up as he chased a Nakamura pass, clutching his troublesome hamstring. Cork would be off in the green for Dublin, fellow veteran Dion coming on in search of his own moment in the sun.

With 15 minutes to play, the League Cup was won, the move started with a piece of trickery Jinky would have appreciated as Nakamura spun brilliantly away from two Dunfermline defenders before feeding Maloney, the little winger weaving his own way through the defence before returning the pass and watching the Japanese playmaker upended at the edge of the box. As Maloney, Nakamura and Stan Petrov all stood poised around the free-kick, it would be Shaun who stepped up to curl the ball expertly over the wall and into McGregor's right-hand corner. It was a goal fit to win any game by a player who had done more than most to take Celtic to Hampden, his glorious strikes in the quarter-final against Rangers and the last-four clash with Motherwell absolutely crucial in the run to the final.

And once again the chant rang around the national stadium.

"Jimmy, Oh Jimmy Johnstone, Oh Jimmy Johnstone on the wing."

Simon Donnelly came on immediately to form an ex-Celt striking partnership for the Pars, but this match had already been decided, I would suggest, earlier in the week with the passing of Jimmy. There would be a final fairytale moment before the whistle though. Paul Telfer had made another of those trademark 40-yard runs down the right flank to support Nakamura. Released by the Little Emperor, Telfer's low, teasing right-wing cross was met perfectly by Dublin, whose flick across McGregor found the same bottom corner as the second goal, the big Englishman staking his claim to be the oldest cup final scorer in history, his first strike for Celtic coming just 34 days short of his 37th birthday.

And away we went again.

"Jimmy, Oh Jimmy Johnstone, Oh Jimmy Johnstone on the wing."

Within seconds, Stuart Dougal's final blast of the whistle signalled a first trophy for Gordon Strachan as a manager, the Celtic boss exchanging a few words with his Dunfermline counterpart Jim Leishman before warmly embracing his players as they left the pitch. To the strains of Daft Punk's *'One More Time,'* a Hampden post-match favourite for some years now, the victorious Celts then changed into special Hooped jerseys with *'Johnstone 7'* on the back for the trophy presentation, another lovely touch on this most emotional of afternoons.

Then to a huge roar from three-quarters of the ground, Neil Lennon waited until all the players were on the podium before lifting his own first silverware as club captain, the Pogues' '*Fiesta*' accompanying the individual roars as one-by-one the Celts showed the League Cup to the vast Hooped support.

And then our heartstrings are tugged massively once again, as the voices of Jimmy Johnstone and Jim Kerr belt out '*Dirty Old Town*' from the Hampden speakers, and images of the great man appear on the giant scoreboards at either end of the stadium he graced so often for club and country. One of the pieces of tickertape lands in a corner of my eye, presumably. This is classic Celtic theatre at its most poignant best.

"I saw Jimmy Johnstone, set the night on fire."

We did, indeed. Many times. And we will never forget how privileged we were to do that.

There were new heroes in green-and-white now, trying to make their own mark on this great club. Today would be the first deposit down on that lofty ambition. The Class of 2006 lined up to share their thoughts on what this afternoon had meant to them, firstly the winning manager, an old teammate and, briefly, a drinking buddy of Jimmy Johnstone at Dundee.

"You cannot really have a game of football which befits Jimmy, because he was above everyone else playing on that football field. It's hard to play like Jimmy Johnstone. You cannot do that, but what we tried to do was play with imagination."

"Our priority was to win the game, and if we could, entertain. I thought our movement at times was smashing. Some of the football was excellent, which the wee man would have liked. There were bits of the game Jimmy would have loved, and the bit at the end he would definitely have loved, winning the trophy. The Celtic boardroom is full of Jimmy Johnstone medals. Jimmy won first and through that he entertained and made us happy. We have to remember who we are talking about here, a genius who made you smile on

the field and somebody who made you chuckle when you thought about him. We had to get over the death, then smile about how he played the game. It got to the stage where everyone was telling Jimmy Johnstone stories around Celtic Park, so there was a lot of laughter. Jimmy has left that legacy, so we could smile and think about the football and be upbeat. It was not all doom and gloom, although we wish he was still here. There has not been a depression hanging over us, as people thought there maybe would be. It was not as claustrophobic as people thought."

"We had to play with patience and move the ball about the pitch. We knew if we did that, Dunfermline would eventually tire. They played 4-5-1 and we had to find a way to move them around and drag them out. We did that. The funny thing is we had more possession and more attempts at goal – and their keeper played smashing – than the 8-1 game. I'm pleased, because all the pressure was on our players. There was a big build-up to the game. We had to win, and we did it. Roy Keane and Neil Lennon did well, driving people on. I thought Nakamura was fantastic, playing in areas where they could not get hold of him. He's brave and is not afraid to take a kick. Our discipline was fantastic, because we took some heavy tackles, which is understandable. Our reaction to that was to get up and play. That's what Jimmy did, he got up and played. There were people in there who inspired in their own way. Lennon as captain and Zurawski kept on running and tired them. That allowed us to play near the end of the game. The philosophy at the clubs I have been with before, 90% of the time it was simply not to get beaten. Here, it's 100% you must win – and it's nice to win something. It's fantastic watching people enjoying themselves in the dressing-room and celebrating. And that's what I have enjoyed today. It is the first trophy I have won and the first as a new group so, hopefully, there will be more. When the second goal went in, I knew that was us on the way. The supporters are fantastic, and it was good to see people enjoying themselves."

Skipper Neil Lennon continued in that vein.

"It was everything I thought it would be. A magic moment. That's for Jimmy. I am delighted because it is my first major honour as captain of the club. It takes on an extra significance because of all that has happened over the week and the emotion that was involved in the game. There was extra pressure on

everyone, and I am delighted at the way we handled it. The lads were brilliant and dominated the game. There were some good individual displays out there, but I felt the team as a whole was excellent. We scored three good goals and we couldn't ask for any more from the players. I thought we were unlucky not to score earlier in the game. Right from kick-off, we took the game to Dunfermline and held them back for long periods. Their keeper made some outstanding saves. We just kept waiting and hoping that the goals would come, and we got that bit of luck just before the break. Shaun produced a trademark free-kick for the second and that sums up the kind of season he has been having. He is a really conscientious boy and if he hits one bad shot in three, he will worry most about the fluffed one. Shaun has a great attitude and worked really, really hard to get back into the team. Once we got the second, the game opened up. Dion just put the icing on the cake and the big man could have had a hat-trick. I'm delighted for the manager. He stuck by me through thick and thin and I'm glad the players rewarded him."

"I was nervous myself because of the extra responsibility, but I think Jimmy would have enjoyed it if he had been there himself. The fans were in great voice and, with the extra emotion out there, it was great. Jimmy was an absolute legend. I know that word gets bandied about a lot but you have to put into perspective just what he meant to so many people attached to the club. He was before my time, but he was a mythical figure and, growing up, I remember hearing so many stories about him back home. It was a privilege for me to meet him here and be at his funeral on Friday. He was a great Celtic man and was always really encouraging when he came into the dressing-room. A couple of words from Jimmy Johnstone were like 50 from anyone else."

"It was always in the back of my mind that there was so much focus on the tribute to Jimmy that we might be a little distracted, but I spoke to the boys before the game. As much as it was for Jimmy Johnstone, I said to them that it might be the first final for some of them and the last for others and that we had to make the most of it. It could be my last, too. You never know. You have to enjoy it and remember it is a cup final. I've lost a few finals and know the feeling afterwards. So, I wanted them to make the most of it. Above all else, we needed to win."

"I think this week has shown some of our newer players what being a Celtic player is all about, and what the fans think about us. If you can't enjoy this kind of occasion, with the support we have, there is something wrong. But the League is the big one for us. It was a good result for us at Tynecastle today. Inverness will give us a hard game in midweek, but we'll have ourselves ready for that. We will enjoy tonight and then regroup for the rest of the League. The League now is the priority. The one we want. We are getting closer to the title, but we still have to win the games."

The result Neil Lennon referred to - an earlier 1-1 draw at Tynecastle between Hearts and third-placed Rangers – saw the home side fail to take any real advantage of Celtic's day-off from League duty. His midfield partner over the past six seasons, Stan Petrov, a League Cup-winner under Kenny Dalglish all the way back in 2000, was also heavily focused on the next big prize up for grabs.

"This gives us a great lift for the rest of the campaign. The League has always been the main priority and we want to win it as quickly as possible."

And Man-of-the-Match Shaun Maloney pitched in with his take on the significance of the win.

"We all felt the pressure and knew we needed to win it and we played well to achieve that. It is great to win a first trophy for the manager as well."

Striker 'Majic' Zurawski had the honour of inheriting Johnstone's number seven in The Jinky Final, something not lost on the talented Pole, who was enjoying a productive debut season with Celtic.

"It's the first cup for me in Scotland and I am very happy. It was great to score and wearing that number seven jersey is very special to me because of the players that have worn it before, such as Jimmy Johnstone and Henrik Larsson. It is a special number and I love to play in it. I didn't know much about Jimmy before I came here, and it might take me a little longer to really know what he was about. I know what a big legend he was, though. The atmosphere around the stands was great and I am waiting for the championship to go with the cup."

And the remaining goalscorer, Dion Dublin, was still in a bit of a daze after his cameo appearance had secured a first-ever cup-winner's medal at the grand old age of 36.

"It was great to have a cup final at my age and I showed there are still goals in me, even if I missed some chances. It's massive for me to win the trophy. I've never seen anything like it before. The tributes to Jimmy. I knew Jinky was a legend before I came here but I don't think I knew how big. I have realised what a player he was since coming to Celtic and I am just pleased we gave the fans something to cheer about on what was a very special day. To come on and get the third goal was superb. It was a massive moment for me, because I'm 36 and I'm not going to get another cup final under my belt. The gaffer had faith in me and it's nice to score"

Shunsuke Nakamura spoke through an interpreter, the Japanese midfield star clearly taken aback by the outpouring of love and emotion following Jimmy Johnstone's death.

"This is the first time I have been at a club and really understood what a deep and rich history exists around it. It was really special for us all to have the number seven on our shorts as a tribute to Jimmy Johnstone. He was a player for this club so long ago and it just tells you what a special person and player he was that he is still held in such high regard by so many people. This kind of thing would never happen in Japan, where you wear another player's number as a mark of respect."

It was an emotional day for young defender Stephen McManus, one of the last visitors at the bedside of the stricken former Celtic winger.

"It was an important week for the fans and the club and lifting the cup gave it a nice ending. That was my first senior medal as well and it all went in so quickly. I hope it is just the first of many. No-one wanted to win more than the guys in the team, and I am sure all the fans will be every bit as delighted as we are."

Amidst the celebrations, there was one Celt feeling the frustration of an injury situation which refused to ease off, Roy Keane acknowledging that he would be forced to review his situation in the close-season.

"It was a little tug on my hamstring. Hopefully, it should only keep me out for a week or two. We will know more by Tuesday, when I get a scan done on it. I had not felt it earlier in the game. Will I be back at Hampden? I am enjoying it

but the older you get in any sport, the more you've got to listen to your body when you are picking up injuries all the time and we will have a look at things in the summer, as I have said from the very start. I don't feel too bad, but we need to have a look at my hip because there is no doubt it is leading to the hamstring injuries I am suffering. There is sometimes a side-effect. It is about what it is leading to. I made runs into the box today but maybe that was the problem. Perhaps that is why I had the hamstring injury later. With Neil Lennon sitting back, I have the opportunity to get forward. And I should have scored with the header. I enjoy that part of my game but maybe I've made one forward run too many. Everyone is getting side-tracked, but I am enjoying myself and the occasion today was good. It has been an emotional week for Celtic. I am very fortunate to be playing for Celtic. I just said I would look at things again in the summer. I've got to be fair to everyone with this. We will see how things go. When you are picking up injuries all the time, you must be fair to everybody. It is more a case of how my body is. I will see how my hip is at the end of the season. Hopefully, I will be able to continue."

Keane also took time out to comment on Jimmy Johnstone and the next generation of Celtic players, with some rare personal insight thrown in.

"It was a brilliant tribute to Jimmy. It was a really sad week, what with the funeral and the response from the fans. It was good to see and important to win. If you don't win a game like that, then you remember it a lot longer."

"It was nice for one or two of the younger lads at Celtic to get their first real winner's medal. Winning a trophy will definitely improve guys like Shaun Maloney and Stephen McManus. I pulled wee Shaun aside beforehand today and told him that these are the occasions where he must make his mark. He has certainly done that on his last two visits to Hampden. I get more satisfaction from seeing them happy at the final whistle and for the manager to get off to a good start with his first trophy. I hope it is the first of many for him at Celtic. We have two or three here who are still young, but they are coming on in leaps and bounds. You are judged by how you perform on the bigger occasions and winning trophies is a great habit to get into. It is always nice to pick up a trophy and when you get to the final of a competition like this, you want to win it. I maybe haven't appreciated every medal I have won earlier in my career the way I should have.

Today was nice. It is satisfying, particularly for the fans and the younger players. I wish I did enjoy these finals and medals more, but that's just the way I am."

His manager, Gordon Strachan, was slightly more upbeat about the midfielder's current problem.

"Roy has done his hamstring near the back of his knee. It's at the bottom of his hamstring, which is not so bad, as it is not right on the muscle."

His opposite number, Jim Leishman, was not for throwing any of his players under the bus, despite the disappointment of that opening goal.

"It was always going to be very difficult for us, even before the sad news of Jimmy Johnstone's death. Everybody at Celtic was galvanised, it made this game even more significant to them. It hurt when people were saying 7-0 would be a great tribute to him, because we are a professional club and we have pride. When we lost 8-1 to Celtic, we took some stick - deservedly."

"It was unfortunate how we lost the first goal. Allan McGregor had been magnificent, but to catch the ball and bump into Aaron Labonte and for the ball to break loose was just unfortunate. All of a sudden it broke loose and I'm not sure if the Celtic striker knew it was going to come to him. Aaron is a young lad and he's got to learn from that. Bobo Balde made a mistake in the UEFA Cup Final and that doesn't stop you shaking yourself down and getting on with it."

"I am very disappointed. We were not creating many chances, but we were containing them. We wanted to make sure it was not over by half-time in the final. It might have been a wee bit different if we had got into the second half and frustrated them again, but when we lost the goal it was game over. It wasn't a hill to climb it was Mount Everest."

Last word goes to Gordon Strachan, to sum up his first trophy success as the Celtic manager.

"We won it with a little bit of style and a little bit of patience. We had to beat four Premier teams to win this, including Rangers. Don't forget that."

CHAPTER 12

Birthday Elf Maloney delivers for Celts as the title party looms closer

It's always a bit special when Celtic have a game on your birthday.

I was born in Robroyston Hospital on the northern outskirts of Glasgow at 7.30am on Wednesday, 22 March 1961. That night, the two young stars of the current Celtic team, Pat Crerand and Billy McNeill, would play key roles in a 3-2 win for Scotland's Under 23 side against their English counterparts at Ibrox. These games were a big deal back in the day, I recall Kenny Dalglish and Martin Buchan starring in the same fixture, probably a decade later, in the quagmire which was the Baseball Ground in Derby.

Billy and Paddy were back in their normal places on the following Saturday, for the first Celtic game of my lifetime, a home League match against Dunfermline Athletic. Looking at that side, it would appear to be a mix of hardened pros and young talent, with future Lions McNeill, John Clark and Stevie Chalmers lining up alongside the great Willie Fernie. Captain Bertie Peacock's injury enabled young Clark's initial introduction to the first team to continue, a run which included an extra-time winner in the Scottish Cup quarter-final replay at Easter Road, where Ronnie Simpson was the beaten keeper. Charlie Gallagher and Alec Byrne were on the wings, providing the ammunition for a young John Hughes in the centre. That well-established early 60's defensive trio of Frank Haffey, Dunky MacKay and Jim Kennedy completed the line-up. Second-half goals from Fernie and Byrne saw Jimmy McGrory's Celts come from behind to win 2-1, in front of 20,000 fans. In the opposing dugout, a young manager watched carefully, his thoughts very much on a bigger day to follow, just one month later.

As discussed in the previous chapter, the Pars would have their early revenge, in the final of the Scottish Cup. On a rainy night at Hampden, underdogs Dunfermline Athletic ruined Celtic hopes of a first trophy since the 7-1 League Cup triumph four years earlier, the Fifers winning the replay 2-0 after a goalless first match. Goalkeeper Frank Haffey, badly at fault for the second goal, looked disconsolate at the end. Both he and Cesar had been part of Scottish football's biggest humiliation thus far, a 9-3 defeat by England at Wembley just 10 days earlier. They looked on as Jock Stein, resplendent in white overcoat, ran onto the Hampden pitch to hug the hero of the hour, Pars keeper Eddie Connachan. On a cruel, sad night for Celtic, a chain of events had been kicked off which would lead to glory in Lisbon.

The biggest of those events would take place just before the first match Celtic played on my birthday. Saturday, 6 March 1965 was Scottish Cup quarter-final day, with two ties in particular relevant to this story. At Easter Road, that same Jock Stein masterminded a third Hibernian victory of the season over defending champions and cup-holders Rangers, to send his current club through to the last-four. The Edinburgh side were also in a three-way fight with Hearts and Kilmarnock for the League title, so the prospect of a first-ever Double would see the good citizens of Leith licking their lips.

At Parkhead, Jimmy McGrory's inconsistent young Celtic team was knocking Kilmarnock out of the Scottish Cup, edging a five-goal thriller with goals from Bobby Lennox, Bertie Auld and John Hughes, whilst 'Rambo's Dad' – Jackie McInally – scored twice for the visitors. On that Saturday, they were not wearing the Hoops, of course. This would be the last outing for that fabulous Shamrock change kit, which many supporters, myself included, would love to see back at some point in the future. Ironically, that game against his old club Killie was also the last outing for the great McGrory as Celtic manager.

Two days later, it was announced that Jock Stein would be leaving fellow cup semi-finalists Hibernian to take over at Celtic with immediate effect, and our lives would change forever, although it may not have felt like it at the time. Stein's first match in charge was a 6-0 victory over Airdrieonians at Broomfield, with the player he had allegedly insisted be bought prior to his arrival, Bertie Auld, scoring five of those goals. The next two games saw the new manager lose his home debut to a single St Johnstone goal then blow a 3-1 lead against Dundee at Dens Park to drop another point.

The fourth game of the Stein era took place on my fourth birthday, Monday, 22 March 1965, and saw the Celtic manager quickly reunited with his old players, as Hibernian visited Glasgow's east end. The game was considered a potential dress rehearsal for the Scottish Cup Final, Jock's current and former clubs both favourites to progress at the expense of Motherwell and Dunfermline Athletic respectively in that weekend's semi-final ties. With the benefit of hindsight, I think it is interesting to see the players and formation adopted by Jock that night, only three Lions placed in the roles in which they would create history in Lisbon just two years later, as he sought the solutions and winning formula required to take the club forward. Jock Stein's Celts lined up against his old side as follows:

John Fallon; Ian Young & Jim Kennedy; Jim Brogan, Billy McNeill & John Clark; Stevie Chalmers, Bobby Murdoch, John Hughes, Hugh Maxwell & Bobby Lennox.

Stein would no doubt learn some valuable lessons over the 90 minutes which followed, but it would be at the expense of the two points, Hibernian winning 4-2 with Neil Martin becoming one of the few visiting players if not the only one to score a first-half hat-trick at Celtic Park. The completion of the League programme would see a third home defeat for the new manager, from Partick Thistle, then a 6-2 loss to Falkirk at Brockville and a 5-1 reverse as Jock returned to East End Park. Celts trailed home a miserable and distant eighth in the table, as Kilmarnock stole the title on goal average from Hearts and by a point from Dunfermline Athletic. Jock's old Hibernian players would finish fourth, their Double dreams long gone after losing their semi-final clash with the Pars at, of all places, Tynecastle.

Despite the desperately poor League form, history will record that before the curtain came down on the 1964/65 season, Jock Stein had won two trophies as the manager of Celtic. The Scottish Cup returned to Paradise for the first time since he had lifted it as captain 11 years earlier, following a 3-2 victory over the Dunfermline side he had managed to victory in April 1961. And within three weeks, the same 11 men retained the Glasgow Cup in that same national stadium, albeit with around 90,000 fewer spectators in attendance, as amateurs Queen's Park were dismissed by 5-0 on their home turf.

My eighth birthday, four years later in March 1969, brought a very special present, that rite of passage for every Bhoy, the first trip to Hampden. I clearly remember the excitement, walking up Prospecthill Road with my dad to take our seats high up in the North Stand for the Scottish Cup semi-final against Morton. I also remember the boos as the first team came running out of the Hampden tunnel, clad all in white, then the total confusion, as a second side emerged wearing blue jerseys and red socks. Where were Celtic? For only the second occasion I could recall, the other being that famous night against St Etienne, Celts had elected to wear an all-white strip, with thin green rings around the collar, cuffs and socks. It was a classic, if not a particularly well-thought-out change strip, given that the majority of opponents requiring a change from the Hoops would have white as a predominant colour.

The early surprises continued with a Morton goal in the opening minute and suddenly the spectre of a second major tournament exit in 10 days - Pierino Prati's strike at Celtic Park having taken AC Milan into the semi-final of the European Cup after a goalless draw in the San Siro - loomed large. However, the Lions roared once again that fine day, goals from Willie Wallace, Stevie Chalmers, Jimmy Johnstone and yet another Hampden counter from Billy McNeill, ensuring that Birthday Bhoy Matthew Corr from Springburn, his dad, and the vast majority of the near-50,000 crowd went home happy.

In the final they would meet old rivals Rangers, who had beaten Aberdeen 6-1 at Celtic Park in the other semi-final tie the same day. Jinky's suspension and an injury to Yogi prompted many within the media to tip the Ibrox side for the cup, however, just as he had done back in 1961 and so many times since, Jock Stein came up with a plan. In came young George Connelly for Johnstone, the young Fifer rewarding the manager's faith in him by casually taking the ball from John Greig and waltzing around Norrie Martin to put Celtic three goals up before half-time. Cesar had scored with a classic header in the opening minutes, a goal which would cost his supposed marker Alex Ferguson his Ibrox career. Bobby Lennox, in his favourite fixture, sped away from the Rangers defence to make it two and Stevie Chalmers cheekily popped one in at the rapidly emptying Mount Florida end in the second half, the cue for the obligatory pitch invasion by The People. It was one of the definitive games in Stein's illustrious career and allowed him to enjoy his second domestic treble in just three years, a feat unsurpassed until the arrival of Brendan Rodgers half a century later. Remarkably, this Treble was secured within just three weeks within the month of April 1969, a fire-delayed 6-2 League Cup final win over Hibernian at the start of the month and a great fightback from two goals down at Rugby Park to earn the required title-winning point completing the set. My own abiding memory of that cup final day is walking out of Dallas' store in Glasgow's Cowcaddens with my mum and sisters to watch as the Celtic buses sped past, the fans singing and waving in scenes of unsurpassed joy. More than 50 years later, that vivid picture remains in my memory's view.

Three years later, on Wednesday, 22 March 1972, another special gift was discovered in my 11th birthday card, an Upper Stand ticket for that night's European Cup quarter-final match against the Hungarian champions Ujpest Dosza. Those of you of a certain vintage will remember the old stand briefs, a yellow paper ticket, which unfolded like an Evening Citizen. There was no better sight to behold. Two weeks earlier, I had run home from school to watch the first leg which was shown live on television, a rare occurrence in those days. A late Lou Macari goal gave Celtic a precious lead to bring back to Glasgow, in a game perhaps best remembered for the after-match party with Richard Burton, Elizabeth Taylor and the travelling Celtic support! The significance of that tremendous result was emphasised in the return game, in front of 75,000 Celtic fans, as Ferenc Bene gave our defence a torrid time, setting up a tie-equalising goal in the opening five minutes. My young heart sank into the seat, as a purple tide threatened to sweep Celts out of the tournament. But then there was Jinky. Parkhead erupted as he came off the bench on the hour mark, as yet again Jock Stein flexed his tactical muscles. Within a few minutes, Lou had scored again, lobbing the goalkeeper gloriously at the packed Celtic End to kick off celebrations which would continue until full-time. Celtic marched through to their fifth European semi-final, four of them under Jock, to face old foes Inter Milan in a repeat of the 1967 final. Sadly, there would be no third European final, as the Football Gods turned their back on Dixie Deans.

My 14th birthday, in March 1975, was memorable for a slightly different reason, in that I had taken a season out from watching football to playing it. Following in the giant footsteps of Celtic's Jimmy McGrory, I turned out for St Roch's Boys Guild in the Garngad. Thus, a day which began with my first 'proper' haircut, a feather-cut from the Barber of Hutcheson Street, continued with a trip behind enemy lines to the remote outpost of Penilee, to take on a team from Our Lady and St George. Despite playing in the colours of Our Lady - or Aston Villa to the heathens amongst you - no respect was shown to the Blessed Lady's team, as we recorded a rare awayday triumph, winning 4-1, thanks to fantastic performances from our wingers, James Divers and Arthur Jamieson. Much like Celtic's European record, our results were pretty much predictable, unbeatable at Fortress Garngad - where the men would leave the Hibs Club to roar us on at the red blaze pitch across the road - contrasting with an abysmal away record. My joy at our result was short-lived, however, on hearing that Celtic had lost at Broomfield, courtesy of a first-half Willie McCulloch strike. This was part of a desperate League period for Celtic, with our nine-in-a-row run about to end and only Cup Final wins over Hibernian - with Dixie Deans adding a second Hampden hat-trick against them in a 6-3 victory - and then Airdrieonians, in what would be Cesar's Last Stand, providing a degree of compensation for the season's efforts. As an aside, the late Paul Wilson would become the only player ever to score in four Hampden Cup finals in the same season when he netted a double against Airdrie, just days after the sad death of his mother.

My final recollection, my birthday in 1986, involves another memorable occasion, as Celtic fought out an eight-goal thriller at Ibrox. Celts had taken an early two-goal lead before Willie McStay was sent packing for a second booking on the half-hour mark. This was quickly followed by a Cammy Fraser goal, to reduce the deficit at half-time. Despite an early second-half strike by the Blessed Tommy, where he rolled the ball deliciously in at the post, we then contrived to lose three goals in 10 minutes to face a costly defeat in the final throes of Jock Wallace's 'pre-Souness' Ibrox tenure. Then Murdo MacLeod gathered the ball outside the box to fire in a classic goal and the party in the Free Broomloan was in full swing again. As the ball nestled in the top corner in front of us, the prevailing emotion was one of relief. It would be six weeks later, on a rainy afternoon at Love Street, before the significance of that strike and the resulting point it earned would be fully appreciated, as eight straight League victories by David Hay's heroic Bhoys snatched the title from Hearts in the dying embers of the season.

Anyway, I digress.

Twenty years on from that 4-4 draw at Ibrox, my latest birthday clash saw the visit of a club who did not exist back in 1986, Inverness Caledonian Thistle. There was a lovely touch pre-match as Agnes Johnstone, Jimmy's wife of four decades and now his widow, brought the newly-won League Cup onto the turf her husband had graced so often in the green-and-white Hoops, supported by those remaining Lions from that unforgettable night in Lisbon, as an emotional wave of applause rang around the old stadium. Gordon Strachan made two changes from his victorious Hampden line-up, the cup-tied Mark Wilson and suspension-free John Hartson replacing Ross Wallace and the injured Roy Keane, the Celtic manager then forced into a substitution as Stan Petrov limped off on the half-hour. Stephen Pearson would still be warming up his muscles when the Hoops took the lead five minutes later, Stephen McManus rising high to connect with Shunsuke Nakamura's floated corner and direct his header perfectly over Caley keeper Mark Brown, the ball striking both crossbar and post on its way in. With 10 minutes remaining, Shaun Maloney replicated his Hampden masterpiece by curling a free-kick into the corner of Brown's net to seal the match at 2-0. The only blight on the evening was the stoppage-time strike from Richard Hart, which somehow squirmed through the grasp of Artur Boruc, thus preventing a clean sheet for Poland's Number One. Other than that unwanted late gift from the Holy Goalie, it hadn't been a bad way to 'celebrate' turning another year older.

The three points earned restored Celtic's 17-point lead at the top of the table with just eight League matches remaining, the calendar geeks amongst the support quickly working out that only two wins would now be required to clinch the flag, the second of those being against closest challengers Hearts at Celtic Park in a fortnight's time. Remarkably, that third League meeting of the country's top two clubs would see Celts face a third different Hearts manager that night, the strange goings-on at Tynecastle having continued earlier in the day. Having mutually consented one new manager out of the door in October - George Burley leaving four months into the job, whilst at the top of the table - Hearts' owner Vladimir Romanov had advised Graham Rix that his services were no longer required. The Lithuanian then installed his countryman Valdas Ivanauskas as the latest interim Head Coach.

That would be a matter for another day. Whilst the 2-1 victory over Inverness Caledonian Thistle had not been a vintage performance from the champions-elect, as comfortable positions go this was right up there, a fact not lost on the Celtic boss.

"You can't play fantastic [football] all the time, but that's us 17 points clear and the players should be congratulated for that. We started well and their goalkeeper has made three unbelievable saves. But they are a good side. They are fit and well-organised and have only been beaten once in 14 months away from home and that was by us. Bobo Balde has a bad stomach problem and he's making it difficult for himself. He seems to think he needs to keep playing all the time and [he] put Paul Telfer in difficult situations a couple of times. We'll talk about that on Friday. Yes, we got a scare at the end but apart from that, I felt we were really comfortable."

His Inverness counterpart, Charlie Christie, on the books at Celtic as a youngster under Billy McNeill but failing to get a first-team opportunity, was not too disheartened by the night's events. He was still finding his feet in the new role, having replaced Craig Brewster in the Caledonian hotseat two months earlier, after Dundee United had come calling for their former player. Christie had enjoyed happier evenings at Celtic Park, notably his man-of-the-match performance on Wednesday, 8 February 2000, as second-tier Caledonian Thistle knocked John Barnes' Celtic out of the Scottish Cup after a 3-1 win, an early 5th birthday present for his son Ryan. He had also featured in a five-minute cameo role three years later, a late replacement for Barry Robson as the Highland side repeated the feat to eliminate Martin O'Neill's Hoops from the same competition, in the aftermath of that great victory at Anfield.

"Celtic came out the blocks, but I thought we had weathered the storm before we lost a disappointing goal from a corner. We played second fiddle but took the game to them in the second half. We were without Craig Dargo and, while we had chances, the only thing missing was a cutting edge in the box. We played a team that I thought could trouble Celtic and I think we achieved that, but now we need to go to Easter Road on Saturday and get something out of that game."

Celtic's next match, four days later, saw them up against yet another newly-appointed manager. Paul Lambert had vacated the Livingston hotseat on 11 February, the former Hoops skipper having enjoyed just two League wins since commencing his first managerial post back in June, on the same day Gordon Strachan took over at Parkhead. Ironically, the man who had recently taken over from Lambert, John Robertson, had managed both Hearts and Inverness Caledonian Thistle previously, as the Scottish football cartel merry-go-round continued.

Strachan made one change from his midweek line-up for the trip to West Lothian, Dion Dublin starting a second game in the Hoops after four appearances from the bench. He replaced John Hartson, whilst Stan Petrov had recovered from the injury sustained against Inverness Caledonian Thistle to regain his spot at the expense of Stephen Pearson. Celts would fail to break the deadlock in a fairly even first half, Maciej Zurawski going closest with a header which struck the crossbar. The Pole would then strike within two minutes of the restart, Shunsuke Nakamura stretching to reach

Shaun Maloney's clipped cross, distracting the attention of two home defenders who could only look on helplessly as Zurawski followed up on the blindside to beat Roddy McKenzie for his 18th goal of the season. Within five minutes, the points were secured. At first glance, the penalty awarded by Kenny Clark for the challenge of Emmanuel Dorado on Dublin seemed harsh in the extreme. Later clips would show that the French defender with the golden name had clearly grabbed the big Englishman's jersey as they challenged for a high ball. Despite the protests, Maloney remained the coolest man on the park as he side-footed the ball firmly past McKenzie into the corner for 2-0. Celts would have chances to increase their lead as the game opened up, however, there would be no further scoring, the Hoops now just one win away from the title.

Livingston manager John Robertson felt his side had not received the benefit of the two contentious calls in the game, the penalty against Dorado and a challenge by Stephen McManus which saw the Celtic defender yellow-carded.

"We were terrific in the first half. We got about Celtic well and could and should have been ahead. Celtic were maybe fortunate to keep McManus on the park and it's wee things like that you need to go your way. At the start of the second half, Celtic finished us with a quick goal and a soft penalty - Dion Dublin went down very easily. We asked the referee before the game to watch Artur Boruc at crosses. We'd noticed that he has a habit of barging people in front of him out of the way, but it happened at the first corner and we got nothing."

Gordon Strachan was more upbeat as his first Championship win as a manager loomed ever closer.

"We've got a big chance to win it in 10 days. It's in our own hands. For 15 minutes we were really hot, so it's been a good week for us, with the League Cup win last week and the win over Inverness on Wednesday. I'm happy with the points. Livingston were excellent in the first half. They should be pleased with their display."

CHAPTER 13

It's emotional and bittersweet for the Celtic family as the flag is secured

The month of March ended with a dreaded feeling of *deja-vu* for the Celtic diaspora.

Just two weeks after we lost one of our own, the incomparable Jimmy Johnstone in the run up to the League Cup final, and as the countdown commenced to the hoped-for title party, news broke of a serious illness concern for another great Celtic redhead, Tommy Burns. On Wednesday, 29 March 2006, it was confirmed that Celtic's first-team coach was undergoing treatment following discovery of a malignant melanoma. It was a huge blow for the former player and manager, a much-loved character with the Hoops support, who had already undergone surgery following his original diagnosis in 2005. The sad news about Tommy was released in a brief official statement from the club, which added.

"It goes without saying that Tommy will receive every possible support from the club and his many friends. Anyone who knows Tommy will be aware of his determined and positive attitude. His doctors are optimistic."

Still nine months short of his 50th birthday, Burns was currently combining his duties at Celtic by acting as assistant manager to Walter Smith with the Scottish national team. Smith too was making positive noises in terms of his recovery.

"I am aware of the situation and feel it is a very private matter for Tommy and his family. We have spoken in the last day or two and he is very upbeat. He and his family have the best wishes of all of us and, knowing the sort of guy he is, I'm

confident he will be back with Celtic and Scotland as soon as humanly possible. Tommy is a great guy, first of all, and then a terrific coach and all the players and international staff are fully behind him."

And old friend and colleague Danny McGrain added his words of support.

"I visited him the other day and he looked great. He seemed his chirpy and happy self but he's always like that. Our thoughts are with him, but nobody knows at the moment how bad things are. But, whatever happens, he will continue to look to the future because that's the kind of man he is."

The first weekend in April saw champions-elect Celtic watching from the sidelines, as the Scottish Cup semi-finals took centre stage. Borders outfit Gretna had earlier dispatched of Celtic's conquerors Clyde and now became the first third-tier outfit ever to reach the final by disposing of First Division Dundee by 3-0 at Hampden. Whilst this was a remarkable feat, the attention of most football observers was focused on the second match, a Sunday meeting at the same venue between Edinburgh rivals Hibernian and Hearts, another bizarre choice of location by the game's administrators. The Tynecastle men had already scored four goals against their Easter Road counterparts on two previous occasions this season, and they would do so for a third time, thanks mainly to a hat-trick from former Hibernian midfield star Paul Hartley, as they cruised into a final showdown with Gretna after a 4-0 victory.

Three nights later, on Wednesday, 5 April 2006, Hearts would be back in Glasgow, this time trying to prevent a title party at Celtic Park. They would be missing captain Steven Pressley, withdrawn at Hampden after suffering a head injury and not risked tonight. The Hoops were an impressive 17 points clear of the Gorgie side with just seven games remaining, meaning a win would be enough to see the flag return to the east end of Glasgow after a one-year absence, another huge step in the long and painful recovery process from the events of that Black Sunday at Motherwell, just 11 months earlier.

Birthdays were again to the fore, John Hartson celebrating his 31st such occasion by returning to lead the attack in place of Dion Dublin, the only change made by Gordon Strachan following the 2-0 win at Livingston, 10 days earlier.

Artur Boruc; Paul Telfer, Stephen McManus, Bobo Balde & Mark Wilson; Shunsuke Nakamura, Neil Lennon, Stilian Petrov & Shaun Maloney; john Hartson & Maciej Zurawski.

There was a magical atmosphere in Paradise, 60,000 expectant supporters packed into the old ground under the lights, and the noise level was racked up several decibels within four minutes as the Hoops scored a most atypical Celtic goal. Goalkeeper Artur Boruc's lofted clearance was met by the head of his compatriot Maciej Zurawski, the Pole's clever flick dropping neatly for his advancing strike partner John Hartson. The big Welshman took the ball first time, catching Hearts keeper Craig Gordon completely unawares, the Celt's volley bouncing on the six-yard line before shooting up into the net past the despairing fingers of the Scotland stopper. It was a throwback to his 'Crazy Gang' days at Wimbledon, where 'Route 1 Football' had been utilised to devastating effect. Hartson then slid on his knees across the Parkhead turf to take the acclaim of the supporters in the Lisbon Lions Stand, producing one of those unforgettable iconic Celtic images. It was a dream start for the title-chasing Hoops, and for the Birthday Bhoy in particular.

If we expected an onslaught from a rampant Celtic, then that failed to materialise. Instead, it was the visitors Hearts who responded to their early setback, Boruc called into action immediately to deal with a low shot from Roman Bednar before Andy Webster's 'equaliser' was ruled out for offside just before the break. The second half produced several more anxious moments for the home support, as their favourites looked unusually edgy, so often the case when you are so tantalisingly close to the prize. Having missed a great opportunity to seal the points, Bobo Balde came close to gifting Hearts a way back in at the other end, his fresh-air swipe at the ball taking out Cech striker Rudi Skacel, sharp intakes of breath all round as referee Dougie McDonald failed to award the penalty kick, a decision which incensed Tynecastle coach Valdas Ivanauskas so much he was dismissed to the stands by the official. 'Dougie Dougie' would have his day in the sun a few years later at Tannadice, to square that circle off.

With 94 minutes having come and gone, it was with a huge collective sigh of relief that the final blast on the referee's whistle was received. After the last-gasp heartbreak of Fir Park, we have clinched the title before the League split, an implausible 20 points clear with six games still to go. There are huge celebrations on the pitch – with an impromptu Huddle in the centre circle led by Neil Lennon, winning his first Championship as Celtic captain. And on the touchline, a bittersweet moment as Gordon Strachan and his backroom team minus the stricken Tommy feel the release and reward for their work over the past nine months. And in the stands, as once again that emotional full-time ritual of thoughts of my dad flood in, and for a few minutes there are three generations of jubilant Corrs taking in the moment. It never fails to kick in at that point of triumph. Dad is always a huge part of these occasions, forever in our hearts and thoughts. He always will be. Suddenly, there is something in my eye again.

Half an hour later, it is a title-winning Celtic manager who shares his thoughts with the media.

"To win by 20 points is scary. Nobody could have dreamt that after the start we had. After we got beat by Dunfermline here, we've gone 16 games - 14 wins and two draws - that's not bad going. I don't care who you are, to keep up with that you need to be a good side. These players have been fantastic. We're not saying that we're a great side - far from it. What we're saying is that we are a side that is improving all the time. We wanted to try and get the Championship back after last season and we wanted to get respectability back from the start to the season - and they've done that. Over the season, we've been involved in some great games. It was exciting tonight but not a great game. Hearts did very well and will be great adversaries over the next couple of years."

In the absence of Valdas Ivanauskas, it was left to his assistant John McGlynn to plea the Hearts case. Not surprisingly, he opened up with a complaint regarding Balde's crude challenge on Roman Bedmar.

"Roman hasn't just fallen to the ground for no reason. If it was a dive he should have been booked, but he wasn't. There are a few newcomers to Scotland at our club and they don't realise yet that you don't get those decisions. It wasn't the best of starts – losing a goal so quickly, but once we settled, we played well and created three or four good chances. That's the most possession we've had at Celtic Park for a long, long time and with a wee break we might have got something from the game. If we keep playing like that and show the same determination and courage, I'm sure we will hold on to second place."

Reflecting on how the season had progressed, 24 hours later, Celtic chief executive Peter Lawwell was glowing in his praise of the job done by his manager, despite the difficult beginning to his tenure.

"It was a tense night against Hearts, and we were not at our best, but it was not about that one game, it was about the fantastic turnaround there's been this season. I don't think Gordon has received the credit he deserves from various quarters."

"The Celtic job is a massive job. People don't realise how big a job it is until they're working here. The fans demand victory every week and there's a great deal of media pressure too. Gordon also had to cope with following Martin O'Neill, who was a magnificent manager and a legend. He had 10 players up on the board when he arrived, as 13 had left. And he had to bring new players in whilst reducing the wage budget. In terms of blending those players and adding to them, Gordon has done a great job. He went to Bratislava and we had a disastrous start, but I think the game came too early. Apart from that and one or two other blips, Gordon has had a great season and come through an amazing set of circumstances."

"If you look back to the start we had, then you would have really queried whether or not we would have won the title so early, with that sort of margin. It shows brilliantly well on Gordon, in terms of how he's turned the whole thing around. I mean, if there is a Manager of the Year award, then there is absolutely no doubt that Gordon Strachan, with the general pressures and the job that he had to do here, should win that. There's no debate about it. With the greatest respect to all the other managers – you know you've got Tony Mowbray, Jim Jefferies – the Celtic job, frankly, it's at a different level and

the specific task that he had to do. It's been a transitional year for us. He's had to rebuild a squad and get the wage bill down. It's a massive job and Gordon has performed magnificently in his first season. I think anyone who is close to football, and who is judging football, could only have one decision there. If he doesn't get it, there will be reasons other than football."

And did the club's ambitions stretch to making an impact on the Champions League next season?

"This club needs to be in the Champions League. It's not only the financials, short-term financials, it's the exposure. You're a big club if you're playing in the Champions League. And for us, we want to get in there and make an impact. We'll try and do as much as we possibly can, certainly in the Group Stage and let's see where we go beyond that. What we will do, within our resources, we will be doing everything we can to strengthen the club, strengthen the squad, that will allow us to have a good account for ourselves in the Champions League. That's what we'll be doing over the close-season. We've already strengthened. We've got two signings and we'll be looking to strengthen the squad over that period."

What about the anticipated challenge from south of the river?

"We understand what's going on elsewhere. Clearly, Paul Le Guen coming in at Ibrox is really exciting. It's a major coup for Rangers. Fantastic excitement, I think, in the build-up to next year now, so we need to be ready for that challenge. Gordon wants to work with a pool of 22/23 players, so really, between now and the close-season, it will depend on who goes and who comes. But the objective is definitely to strengthen from what we have."

Could Celtic afford to lose a player such as Neil Lennon?

"What we decided with Neil was "Let's wait. Let's get the title out of the way and let's then sit down and talk." And that's what we plan to do in the next couple of weeks. Just to see where he is, let the dust settle and see where we are, and hopefully we can come to an agreement there."

And Tommy Burns? How is he?

"Well, I spoke to Tommy last night after the game. He was in great spirits. Thrilled

as everyone. I'm particularly delighted for him. Clearly, Tommy has his health issues at the moment but last night he was in great form. We want Tommy back here as soon as he possibly can and I'm sure he'll be here before long."

With the title secured, Gordon Strachan now had to field questions about the future of the man who scored the goal which finally delivered it, John Hartson. Rumours regarding the Welshman's imminent return south of the border after five years in Scotland refused to go away, with a well-publicised marital split adding fuel to the flames. Whilst the Celtic boss had shot those down, Hartson himself was slightly less emphatic, leaving Hoops supporters to draw their own conclusions, of which my own would subsequently be proved correct.

"I need to sit down with the manager and talk with my family, but it would be a massive wrench to leave. I don't know how long I'll be here, but I'll cherish the next few weeks. Even at 31 I am still feeling good and I can have a few more years at the top if I keep my sharpness. Then I will be happy, but I don't want to play for ever. I'll have another two or three years in the game but then I will be hanging up the boots."

Hartson would be in his normal place up front four days later, Sunday, 9 April 2006, as Celts returned to Rugby Park, the scene of their previous title triumph, two years earlier. Stan Petrov's goal had reclaimed the flag that day on the venue where the Hoops championship dreams had died in the aftermath of Seville, 12 months before that. Today would prove a much more comfortable afternoon in East Ayrshire, as the fixture Gods sent Celts to the other ground Tommy Burns graced as both player and manager.

There were three changes to the midweek line-up. With Artur Boruc injured, David Marshall returned between the sticks after a six-month exile, his first appearance since losing four goals at Motherwell on the opening day of the League season. Young Irish keeper Michael McGovern was promoted to the bench, whilst Bobo Balde and Maciej Zurawski made way for Stan Varga and Aiden McGeady.

McGeady was lively early on, combining well with Shunsuke Nakamura before the Japanese playmaker found himself the meat in the Kilmarnock sandwich. It would be a costly foul, as Nakamura drew back his deadly left wand to send the ball curling past the outstretched fingertips of Killie keeper Alan Combe, yet another masterpiece in a season packed with sensational Celtic goals. There was a major let-off for the visitors as the interval approached. Gary Wales quickly-taken free-kick releasing Steven Naismith to beat David Marshall with a low shot. The linesman's flag had shot up as he shaped to shoot, with television replays later showing that the Kilmarnock youngster was clearly onside. Naismith's bad day at the office would continue after the break, twice clean through on goal only to produce two identical finishes which trickled past the same post. Those misses would come back to haunt his team, when just after the hour mark, John Hartson was perfectly placed to tap home after Combe had parried a shot from Shaun Maloney. Marshall then produced a stunning save to prevent Gary Wales pulling a goal back for the hosts, the Celtic keeper diving low to save bravely at his far post. With eight minutes remaining, Nakamura added a goal of real quality to his earlier effort, showing wonderful presence of mind to slot home after great work between Maloney and substitute Dion Dublin. And there was still time for a fourth goal, Maloney and Dublin again combining beautifully to allow the big Englishman to send his drive into the far corner.

As both sets of supporters spontaneously erupted into a chorus of "*Tommy Burns,*" there was a final defiant act from Kilmarnock, Colin Nish finding himself in the clear to finish the scoring at 4-1. Whilst one of my pet hates is losing these goals at the death, it was hard to be anything but happy with such a powerful Celtic performance, Gordon Strachan's men sealing a 10th consecutive victory. The Celtic manager still found time to fire a shot across the boughs of his title-winning players.

"Kilmarnock have done fantastically well this year considering their resources, so, to come here and score four - and both sides could have had more - is great. But, at times, I thought we took liberties at the back and you cannot do that with Kilmarnock, as they have good, determined forwards."

Strachan then singled out his Japanese star for special praise.

"He has a touch of an angel and he was fantastic out there. He must have been

one of the lads who stayed in after the title win on Wednesday."

Skipper Neil Lennon admitted that Celtic had perhaps dodged a bullet at 1-0.

"It probably would have changed things. Goals do change the course of the game and, at the time, it looked touch and go whether he was offside or not. But we got the benefit of the doubt and we were happy going in at 1-0 up. But I felt we were in control of the game for the most part and maybe overcooked it in the final third, but we got our rewards in the second half for our good football. We went 4-3-3 and it worked well for us, although maybe the scoreline flatters us a bit. The shackles are off and I told the players before the game just to relax and enjoy themselves."

Kilmarnock manager Jim Jefferies was in less forgiving mode.

"Decisions like that can change the course of a game. He was clearly onside, and the linesman was right in line with it. You look at the incompetence of that decision, but they get away with it. There should be a form of punishment. Celtic scored with every chance they had. We had plenty of chances ourselves and had a perfectly good goal chopped off. But I had warned before the game that, if you don't take your chances against Celtic, they will punish you."

Next up for Gordon Strachan and Celtic was a trip to Coventry, two nights later, to face his old club in a testimonial match for Sky Blues' long-serving defender Richard Shaw. Paul Telfer, John Hartson and Dion Dublin would also be returning to honour their former colleague, a huge Hoops contingent within the crowd of 25,000 packed into the Ricoh arena. Shaw had enjoyed a long and varied career since debuting for Crystal Palace back in 1988. Two years later, he started both matches as the Eagles lost out in the FA Cup final replay to Manchester United, Alex Ferguson's first trophy win at Old Trafford. The Red Devils would also feature in Richard's other claim to fame from his spell at Palace. In January 1995, a frustrated Eric Cantona lashed out at Shaw before receiving his marching orders, promptly attempting a Kung Fu challenge on one of the home supporters. That summer, he would sign for Ron Atkinson at Coventry City, remaining there as Gordon Strachan moved up from his assistant manager role the following season. Shaw would make over 300 appearances in Sky Blue over the next decade.

The Celtic boss named an unchanged side from Kilmarnock, the Bhoys caught cold as former England midfielder Dennis Wise curled a free-kick past David Marshall within three minutes. Weekend hero Shunsuke Nakamura delivered his own masterclass five minutes later to level the match at 1-1, Celts enjoying the better of things before the half-time whistle, following which the usual batch of mass substitutions took place. Man-of-the-moment Shaw then departed the scene just after the hour to a rousing ovation, youngsters Kevin Thornton and Liam Davis then staking their claim for a regular place in Micky Adams' Championship squad with superb goals as the hosts ran out 3-1 winners on the night. An emotional Richard Shaw had parting words of praise for his former gaffer in the West Midlands.

"I played under Gordon and I count him as one of the best, if not THE best, manager I've played under."

As if to amplify those words, just two days later, Gordon Strachan was voted the Scottish Football Writers' Association Manager of the Year, apparently in the closest-ever finish despite the Celtic boss winning two of the three available domestic trophies in his debut season in the most trying of circumstances. Scotland, eh? Wha's like us?

Typically, the Celtic boss played the individual honour down, preferring instead to claim it on behalf of the wider group.

"Receiving the Manager of the Year award reflects the major achievements of the team this season. The effort and commitment by the players, backroom staff and everyone at the club has been tremendous."

There was another celebratory occasion the following Sunday, as it was announced that the SPL trophy would be presented to Celtic after their home game with Hibernian, despite the fact that their last such Parkhead fixture, the traditional slot for such a ceremony, would take place seven days later against Rangers. Yet again, more than 60,000 supporters rolled up to Celtic Park for the party, even the weather getting into the spirit as we were given a glorious sunny afternoon as the backdrop.

Strachan made three changes for the match against his boyhood club. Artur Boruc returned, and with compatriot Zbigniev Malkowski doing likewise for Hibernian, we thus had a headline-writers' dream of two Poles between the posts. I'll get my coat. Roy Keane saw action for the first time since leaving Hampden injured during the League Cup Final, Aiden McGeady making way, whilst Maciej Zurawski partnered John Hartson up front with Shaun Maloney, perhaps surprisingly, dropped to the bench.

As often with these occasions, the game itself was a bit of an anti-climax, in many ways getting in the way of the party we had all come to enjoy. Celts had created and missed several chances before the visitors took the lead 10 minutes from the interval. As the Hoops attacked, a mix-up between Maciej Zurawski and Shunsuke Nakamura allowed Stephen Glass to launch the ball forward, finding teenage striker Steven Fletcher in space at the edge of the Celtic box. As both defender and goalkeeper hesitated, Fletcher took advantage to calmly stroke the ball between the legs of Boruc for 1-0. This was not in the script. I could not help but cast my mind back 12 months, to when an unexpected home defeat by many of these same players ultimately set us up for Black Sunday.

The half-time break saw Shaun Maloney introduced for Stan Petrov, as the Celtic manager looked for a reaction, and he almost got his reward immediately, the substitute's first attempt beating Malkowski but shaving the upright. Suddenly, it was one-way traffic as the new champions sought to ensure that the afternoon's proceedings would not end in disappointment, new Celtic signing Gary Caldwell and his Hibernian defensive colleagues pulling out all the stops to preserve that slender lead. There was a touching moment with 20 minutes remaining, as young Irish midfielder Dean Shiels replaced Kevin Thomson for the visitors, just three months after having an eye removed, the Celtic supporters warmly applauding his introduction. Within six minutes, the Bhoys were level, with the most straightforward of goals, Paul Telfer's beautifully-weighted cross from the right wing finding Zurawski unmarked 12 yards out, the Polish hitman's header duly directed into the bottom corner of Malkowski's net.

With the game ending 1-1, it was finally time for the party. The SPL trophy appeared first, carried by Howard Brown, the singing bank clerk from those Halifax TV adverts of the time, and Billy Connolly. Then came the players - all wearing the number 06 on the back of their jerseys – first up to receive their medals on the rostrum from the presentation party. And finally, the title-winning manager and captain, Gordon Strachan and Neil Lennon, striding out together to huge applause from the packed stands. Neil then turns conductor, building up a crescendo of noise before lifting the huge trophy high above his head to signify that Celtic are the champions of Scotland once again. The domestic trophy we desire most has come home. The obligatory ticker tape and burners add to the colour and spectacle as, one by one, the players take their turn of raising the trophy for their own personal moment of glory. For many it will be the first time. For others it will be the last. For some it will be both.

Then Gordon Strachan takes his moment to do something I guess would have felt like a stretch after his first match in charge, the nightmare of Bratislava back in July. One can only guess what is going through his mind as he holds the giant silver trophy aloft, and 60,000 Celtic supporters roar back their approval. Having gathered his thoughts, he shared some of those with the media on the pitch, as the party continued around him, the manager's focus already on the challenges which lay ahead.

"There was no life in the game in the first-half and I thought it was going to be a bit of a damp squib, but the second-half was as good as we've played against Hibs this season. We never dreamed of this. I thought we could win the Championship but not as early as we did. It has been a wonderful effort from everyone here. I already know that we need to improve in this League alone because Hearts and Rangers are getting stronger, using money, and when Hibs get their players back, they will also be stronger. We will need to get better and hopefully we can also do well in Europe. I know right away that we need more players for that. The wheels are in motion. We are doing a few bits and bobs behind the scenes."

Striker John Hartson had seen it all before, the big Welshman picking up his third Championship medal. Time would tell if this would be his last as a Celt, however, meantime he was savouring the moment.

"It's a fantastic achievement to have won the title as early as we did. It wasn't a vintage performance from us, but we showed what we can do in the second half. And that was against a resilient Hibs side, who are still playing for something."

As the Celtic team and backroom staff embark on the traditional walkaround to thank the support, *"It's a grand old team to play for"* rings around the vast stadium, followed by *"You'll never walk alone."*

There is no finer sight and sound in world football.

It is quite uniquely Celtic.

CHAPTER 14

A time for farewells

The old saying that *"a week is a long time in politics and a lifetime in football"* came to mind on the Friday after Trophy Day, as news of Stan Petrov's transfer request filtered through. The Bulgarian international captain had failed to reappear for the second half against Hibernian five days earlier, triggering suggestions of an exchange of words in the dressing-room, and had also seemed alone and somewhat detached at the title celebrations afterwards. Stan had agreed a new deal as recently as January, committing his future to the club until at least the summer of 2009 – Celtic having an option to extend that by a further year – so it was really disappointing to hear that he now wanted to leave.

Having had his request turned down by the club, the powerful midfielder explained his position, just 48 hours ahead of the visit of Rangers to Celtic Park.

"It's my wish to leave at the end of the season. I hope Celtic are going to respect my wishes. The manager told me he knew exactly how I was feeling. He said he is going to respect my wish, but he is going to fight to keep me at this club. I want to test myself on a different level and learn what I can't here. I can't do that here. I have always been loyal to Celtic and I hope they recognise what I have done. I have given Celtic the chance to get money so they can be active in the transfer market. If I hadn't signed a new contract, the club would not have got a lot of money. Now they are going to have enough money to go and buy a player. There are two winners here. I told them when I signed [that] I had thoughts about playing somewhere else. They knew this could happen. We could have let it go on, but it wasn't right. I have given my best here, but I am the

type of guy who wants to learn and better himself all the time."

Gordon Strachan had not had too much time to enjoy his Double triumph of the previous week before facing his next big challenge. He was taking a pragmatic stance, citing his own personal experience.

"It might be a worry that this could have an effect on the player and those around him, but, despite him wanting to move on, we are relaxed about it. You are talking to someone who asked Alex Ferguson for a move in 1982 and I was told to go forth and multiply. I was there the next two years, won a few more trophies and just got on with it. Ultimately, we have the power to decide how and when he leaves."

Strachan had more immediate and pressing matters on his mind as he prepared for the Sunday clash with Rangers, a final derby fixture for his old Pittodrie colleague Alex McLeish. Having rested Shaun Maloney against Hibernian, the Celtic manager brought him back for this one, the only change from the eleven who kicked off against Hibernian. Surprisingly for me, this time it was another flair player, Shunsuke Nakamura, who would make way, the Japanese genius taking a seat on the bench. Stan Petrov retained his starting slot, despite the current transfer speculation.

Maloney would be involved in the two highlights of a rather dull first half, his curling free-kick forcing an excellent save from visiting keeper Ronald Waterreus, then his superb through ball freeing Maciej Zurawski inside the box, the Belgian again coming to the rescue of the Ibrox side with a great block. The stalemate continued after the break, this time the visitors passing up the better chances, Chris Burke firing over from a great position then Artur Boruc producing the save of the match to deny Dado Prso. Nakamura was finally introduced on the hour mark, replacing Roy Keane, and Celtic immediately looked more threatening. Maloney again tested Wattereus with a long-range swerving drive which the keeper stopped low at his post, before the winger made way for Aiden McGeady, and Dion Dublin was introduced for John Hartson as a final throw of the dice to secure a winner. All to no avail as the game ended goalless, Celts thus failing to chalk up a fourth consecutive victory in the derby fixture. It was a somewhat frustrated Gordon Strachan who faced the media afterwards.

"Giving the boys a few days off after our title celebrations was maybe not a good idea. We did things that we've been working on this week that saved us, but it was obviously not our best day. We will be giving it a full working week before the Hearts game. We had a crazy period over on the right-hand side of the defence at the start of the second half, but we became a far better side when Shunsuke Nakamura came on for Roy Keane. I am not being derogatory to Roy, but I just think he held the ball better in that position. I had left him out because of the physical nature of the game, but I will have to think about that now. I decided a few weeks ago to rest Shaun Maloney for the Hibs game and Naka for the Rangers game, but the Championship is won."

It was a farewell interview from Alex McLeish, in terms of this particular Glasgow derby fixture.

"I think we should have won, but, at the end of the day, it is one point closer to Hearts. I asked for a performance and I'm proud that I got a performance. We have to rely on Hearts dropping points now, but I think teams are capable of taking points from us both. Rangers will be looking to strengthen next season, but a lot of the players will have done themselves no harm today."

And how would McLeish look back on his experiences in these games as Rangers manager?

"When you win, there is no better feeling in the world, but it is horrifying when you lose. It hurts like hell, but I relish the Old Firm games because the occasion at Ibrox or Celtic Park is something to look forward to. It's just something that's fantastic to be involved in and my career would have been all the poorer had I not experienced it. I told the players that they shouldn't let this pass them by and, although we can't guarantee winning, we caused them problems."

The last day of April 2006 saw Scotland's top two sides clash in the Sunday sun at Tynecastle. The previous meeting of the clubs there, on New Year's Day, had seen Stephen McManus emerge as the unlikely goalscoring hero with a late double which capped a superb second half fightback from Celtic, the Champions recovering from the loss of two early goals to win 3-2. In my view, this had been THE decisive result of the campaign, with Celts powering away from their Edinburgh rivals to clinch the flag.

McManus would again find himself in the centre of the action, albeit not for the same reasons. Within two minutes, a delightful flick from Dion Dublin – in for John Hartson – found the big defender with only Craig Gordon to beat, a feat he failed to achieve as the Scotland keeper brilliantly blocked his point-blank effort. Seven minutes later, he lost his bearings completely, rising majestically to meet Paul Hartley's wicked free-kick to power a header home...past the despairing Artur Boruc to give the hosts the lead. Before the 10-minute mark, Hearts had repeated their start from the January fixture, by taking a 2-0 lead. Stan Varga once again conceded a free-kick just outside the box, the Slovakian perhaps fortunate to avoid a card. The punishment would be both swift and brutal, Hartley reacting quickest to curl a beautiful effort into the far corner whilst Boruc and his defenders were still preparing for the set-piece. It was a 16th goal of the season for the Hearts man, enjoying the form of his life.

Tynecastle can be a cauldron when the home side are doing well in these games, a thrilling atmosphere to witness, albeit the other side of Scottish football was sadly to the fore on this afternoon. With Stan Petrov dropped to the bench to accommodate the returning Shunsuke Nakamura, the Irish Heartbeat of Neil Lennon and Roy Keane were patrolling the central midfield roles for Celtic, as they had done with such aplomb at Ibrox in February. Both players were roundly booed for every touch they took on the ball from the kick-off, presumably for the heinous crime of being Irishmen playing for Celtic, a shameful reflection on an attitude which sadly still prevails in many sections of our Scottish society.

It was sad that this behaviour detracted from an excellent Hearts performance, as they chased the three points which would take them within touching distance of the Champions League slot on offer for Scotland's runners-up. Before we had played 15 minutes, Rudi Skacel's shot had come crashing back off Boruc's near post with the keeper beaten. Keane then had an opportunity to deliver a perfect response to the baying mob, the Irishman finding himself alone in the six-yard box following yet another free-kick. As the ball dropped over his left shoulder, the Celt failed to connect properly, a grateful Gordon able to pick it up. At these moments, you just know it is not going to be your day.

If there was any lingering doubt of that, it would finally be confirmed just after the hour, Roman Bednar looking for all the world in an offside position as he picked up a through pass, stumbled at the edge of the box, then still had time to recover and clip the ball past Boruc for Hearts third goal. The unpleasant afternoon being endured by Neil Lennon had continued after the interval, the Lurgan Bhoy booked for pushing Skacel to the ground after the Czech striker had appeared to spit in his direction. Skacel would then seek his own retribution after Bednar's goal, lunging at the Celtic captain from behind to join him in referee Alan Freeland's notebook. Both players would be quickly withdrawn by their respective managers to prevent the inevitable red card as the poisonous atmosphere intensified, Stan Petrov joining the fray for Celtic. Gordon Strachan would make his remaining two changes in a final, desperate attempt to salvage something from the game, Stephen Pearson and Hartson replacing Maciej Zurawski and Dublin, however, this day would belong to the Gorgie men, their comprehensive 3-0 victory inflicting a first League defeat on the Scottish Champions in five long months.

Gordon Strachan appeared to be anticipating some veiled criticism from some quarters, judging by his final post-match comments, the three points for Hearts all but consigning Rangers to third place.

"I said beforehand the game would be decided on free-kicks, and I was right. We didn't defend them properly. I'm disappointed their power-play was so damaging to us. Hearts took their chances better than us and Craig Gordon made some great saves. Our attitude was good enough, we fought hard, showed character and we kept trying to play football, but anyone looking at that game could see we were trying."

The Celtic manager also commented on the distasteful incident involving his captain and Rudi Skacel.

"I took Neil off because I didn't want to take any chances with him after he got booked. It wasn't so much Neil, but there may have been people round about him who were trying to take advantage. He's an angry man, Lenny, at the moment.

But my advice to him is to put it away now. The pictures say it all. I think you need no words after that, but, whatever happens, I can't do anything about it."

For his part, Neil Lennon insisted that he had been the victim of an unprovoked and disgusting attack.

"I'm not in the business of making things up or trying to get people into trouble. I know what happened and I'm adamant about that. I would not have reacted unless something did happen. The referee told me he did not see anything, so I will leave it at that, but it's important I set the record straight. He is a total disgrace and it's not the first time he has done this since he moved to Scotland [Stuart Duff of Dundee United had made the same accusation against Skacel three months earlier]. I've been involved in plenty of Old Firm games, heated matches, but never had to deal with anything like this. The guy is the lowest of the low."

Skacel had suggested that Lennon's reaction was simply down to the fact that his team were 3-0 down, a statement immediately shot down by the Irishman.

"That's funny, because the score was still 2-0 at the time and that had nothing to do with what happened. I went in and won the ball. The pictures clearly show me moving up the park as Skacel is getting up from the ground and then I turn around and confront him after the spit has flown over my shoulder. That's the truth and if he says anything different then he is a liar. I don't mind going on record saying so, because I know what happened."

In the interests of balance, Hearts denied the allegations via an unnamed spokesperson.

"There doesn't appear to be any proof of these allegations on television pictures. As for Rudi himself, he is very angry and strenuously denies that he spat at Neil Lennon. Rudi finds the comments attributed to Neil Lennon extremely offensive."

On a more positive note, the transfer speculation surrounding Celtic took another twist, this time for the better, it would appear, with John Hartson vowing to play on for another season at Parkhead, despite constant links with a return south of the border for the big Welshman.

"I spoke with my family about staying with Celtic for another year and they gave me their full support. It is a huge weight off my mind to know exactly what I'm doing. There has been speculation for months that I might be going here, there or the next place, but this puts it all to bed - I'm staying where I am. There is no doubt the manager has been influential in my decision. He made it clear in a meeting with my agent he wanted me to stay and I was pleased to hear that. Now I can play the remaining games this season and enjoy the summer break without any speculation."

Interim Hearts Head Coach Valdas Ivanauskas was understandably upbeat following his side's first victory over the Champions in four attempts. There was no doubt who he viewed as the key player.

"That was the perfect performance, but it's just one step to the Champions League place. We know Aberdeen are strong and we need the same performance again. It will be a very difficult game on Wednesday. As for Paul Hartley, I haven't a word for him. He is a leader, he scores important goals, he is the best player in Scotland and one of the best in Europe."

Football being the theatre it often is, a few hours later the controversial Skacel would find himself once again competing with a Celtic midfielder. Well two in fact, as Stan Petrov and Shaun Maloney joined the Czech forward at the awards ceremony for the 2005/06 SPFA Player of the Year. Skacel's Hearts teammate, Craig Gordon had picked up the Writers' nomination, however, the night would be a personal triumh for Maloney, becoming the first man ever to win both the main and Young Player of the Year awards. In doing so, he also became the third Celt to win the major prize in consecutive years, following in the footsteps of fellow Parkhead hitmen Chris Sutton and John Hartson. It was a proud Maloney who addressed the assembled throng in Glasgow's Thistle Hotel, Shaun generous enough to compliment both his rivals for the accolade and his manager for showing such faith in him.

"It's not been done before, so it's a big honour and I feel quite proud. There is no better accolade than to be voted for by your peers and it does mean a lot to me. Individually, they've all had great seasons. When you play against them, you can see what great players they are. It just makes it even more of an honour when

you look at the players I was up against. I've got a lot of time and respect for these players and it makes it all the more special. At the start of the season, I didn't know what was happening and [Gordon Strachan] gave me the opportunity to play. If I played well, he would stick with me. If not, I'd be straight back out the team. But, as a manager, I've got a lot to thank him for this season. It's been a tremendous season for the team and I just feel privileged to be part of that team."

Having been the tormentor-in-chief of Maloney and his fellow Celts on the Sunday, Paul Hartley was at it again three nights later, his second-half penalty enough to defeat Aberdeen at Tynecastle, thus securing second spot in the SPL for Hearts. Their final day clash with Rangers at Ibrox would now be a dead rubber, allowing them to prepare for the Scottish Cup Final with Gretna the following weekend.

The same night, Wednesday, 3 May 2006, Celtic's final home League match of the season, against Kilmarnock, surprisingly drew one of the lowest crowds of the campaign to the east end, albeit it was still around the 49,000 mark. It was a special night for Roy Keane, wearing the captain's armband for Celtic for the first time, with regular skipper Neil Lennon on the bench, one of six changes made by Gordon Strachan following the weekend defeat in Edinburgh. In came David Marshall, Ross Wallace, Alan Thompson, Stephen Pearson, Stan Petrov and Aiden McGeady, with Artur Boruc, Paul Telfer, Shunsuke Nakamura, Shaun Maloney and Dion Dublin joining Lennon on the sidelines. The goal action on the night would be squeezed into an eight-minute period early in the second half. First, Polish hitman Maciej Zurawski would be in the right place at the far post as the ball broke off a defender, hammering it past Alan Combe for his 20th goal of an excellent debut season. Then just after the hour, we had the sight of Stan Varga rising high to nod Ross Wallace's left-wing cross into the net for his only goal of the campaign and, as it transpired, his final strike for the club. Maloney immediately replaced McGeady, and there would be late cameo roles for Adam Virgo and Dion Dublin as Strachan's Bhoys sent the supporters home happy with a 2-0 victory, a first win in four games, to bring the curtain down on a successful Celtic Park season with another three points.

The 38th and final League fixture would take place at Pittodrie four days later, Sunday, 7 May 2006. With no sign of Neil Lennon or Roy Keane in the squad, Alan Thompson became the third different Celtic captain in three games, leading the team out for what would turn out to be his final competitive appearance for the club he had served with such distinction for six seasons. Paul Telfer and Mo Camara came in for Mark Wilson and Ross Wallace at full-back, whilst there was a first senior start for Paul Lawson after three earlier appearances from the bench, the youngster replacing Keane in midfield. Shaun Maloney and John Hartson were chosen to play in the advanced roles at the expense of Stan Petrov and Maciej Zurawski.

There was a dream start for the much-changed Celts as the returning Hartson opened the scoring for the visitors within five minutes. Aiden McGeady's delightful curling shot from the edge of the box had looked a goal from the moment it left his boot, beating Dons keeper Ryan Esson all ends up only to crash back off the crossbar. The predatory Welshman showed once again why he was so valuable to Celtic, following up to nod the ball into an empty net. With Aberdeen pushing for an equaliser and enjoying the better of what few chances were created, it was another piece of quality which appeared to have sealed the three points for the champions. We had just reached the hour mark when Stephen McManus launched a clearance down the left touchline, to find Maloney lurking with intent. His sublime first touch left Dons defender Brian McNaughton for dead, Scotland's new Player of the Year duly striding on to beat Esson low at his near post for 2-0, for a classic counter-attacking goal.

As often happens with such leads, the next goal proved crucial. It was also contentious, the officials presumably the only people in the stadium who felt that Aberdeen substitute John Stewart was onside as he picked up a long through ball just eight minutes later. In fairness to the striker, he remained calm as he waltzed around David Marshall to reduce the deficit. With the home support reignited, we could write the script which followed, as Celts came under immediate bombardment. Within three minutes, a low cross from the right managed to evade defenders and attackers alike, before reaching Stewart at the far post, the Dons man with all the time in the world to pick his spot for an unlikely equaliser. A late Celtic flurry saw

Stephen Pearson given the opportunity to finish the campaign on a high, Esson this time getting his angles right to make a fine diving save, as the honours and points were shared.

The television pictures beaming back highlights afterwards did pick up an image to gladden the hearts of the Celtic family, as Tommy Burns was captured in a fleeting appearance pitchside at the end of the game, a first sighting of Tommy for most of us since the announcement of his illness five weeks earlier. It would be another week or so before we would hear him quoted in the media and, typical of the man, Burns was open and relatively upbeat as he supported a campaign by Cancer Research UK around the dangers of exposure to the sun's rays.

"It started with a mole on my leg, which I have had since I was very young – it was just like a big freckle. Then, more recently, it started to get bigger and darker in colour, but I didn't see any reason to go and see anyone about it. Only when it started to itch and get blistery did I go and see a doctor. It was two or three times the thickness of a normal melanoma, apparently. That was the thing that was really worrying. I had surgery to remove it, but then it came back seven months later further up my leg and I had to have more surgery. At this moment in time, all the tests have proved to be clear. But, with melanoma, it could come back again. It's difficult, but at the end of the day you do need to get on with it and stay hopeful. I think you push it to the back of your mind and try not to think too much about it coming back. I live a normal life as much as possible, but just stay out of the sunshine or cover up. A year ago, I didn't know what malignant melanoma meant. To be honest, even after the first time I went to the specialist and he told me what it was, I was just thinking it was something on my skin. But it is actually something happening under the skin as well. So, I was ignorant of it as well, not so much now but in the past. In football, you tend to go away somewhere hot for the first two weeks of June and get a lot of sun, but that is not good."

Tommy made those comments on 15 May 2006. That date would later prove to be very poignant.

With the competitive campaign now over, there remained just two fixtures for Celtic to negotiate in the midweek after Pittodrie before the collective feet could be put up for a well-earned summer break. These would involve trips to Old Trafford and St James Park to honour two of the greatest players to grace the English game over the previous decade, with current Celt Roy Keane and former England striker Alan Shearer both receiving 'bumper' testimonial matches against the new Scottish Champions.

The game against Manchester United in particular had captured the imagination of the Celtic support, with thousands snapping up tickets. There was some controversy in the media surrounding Gordon Strachan's decision to withdraw his players from the unofficial Kirin Cup tournament in Japan, involving Scotland, Bulgaria and the hosts, in order that they could take part in the matches in England. Strachan had initially stated that the decision was taken amicably after discussions with Scotland manager Walter Smith.

"If Walter had insisted the players travelled, then there would have been absolutely no problem. Likewise, if there was ever any prospect of the players' non-attendance jeopardising their future Scotland careers, then obviously they would have gone. However, having spoken to Walter, there is no problem at all and, as he said to me, having been an Old Firm manager, he is well aware of the demands which are on our players. Walter's co-operation is greatly appreciated by the club and we thank him for his support."

However, Smith was clearly unimpressed with the situation, dismissing the Celtic manager's claims that the players would have travelled should he have insisted on that.

"In the conversation we had, [Gordon Strachan] *stated to me he'd withdraw all Celtic players from the tournament. That meant the three players I had named* [David Marshall, Stephen McManus and Shaun Maloney], *plus Stilian Petrov of Bulgaria and Japan's Shunsuke Nakamura. When that is said to you, Scotland have got no right to take a player. Insist? I can't insist on anything. If somebody phones me up and tells me they're withdrawing them then I have no recourse because they are friendlies."*

Never one to miss an opportunity, Old Trafford boss Alex Ferguson weighed in with his threepence worth ahead of the clash with his old sparring partner.

"Gordon Strachan phoned Walter Smith to say he wanted them to play against United. I don't know what this game is coming to. But it shows they mean business."

As a postscript to this discussion, Scotland would go on to win the Kirin Cup that weekend, following a 5-1 victory over Bulgaria and a goalless draw with the hosts, who had lost 2-1 to the Balkan side.

There was no sign of Shunsuke Nakamura at Old Trafford and David Marshall was on the bench, whilst Stephen McManus, Stan Petrov and Shaun Maloney all started for Celtic in a carnival atmosphere. I had driven down with my three kids and United-supporting wife, taking our seats with the bulk of the 30,000-strong Hoops support in the imposing North Stand. There were patches of green everywhere in the stadium as almost 70,000 fans packed in to honour the Irish legend Roy Keane, a record for such a fixture. The pre-match build-up continued with an emotional rendition of Dirty Old Town, Jim Kerr, Jinky and a cast of thousands belting out the song near the very Salford home for which it was written.

Keane himself enjoyed the best of both worlds, on what was after all his day, captaining Celtic whilst being named as a substitute for Manchester United. Both clubs fielded full-strength sides, with a number of Keane's Treble-winning teammates from 1999 listed beside him on the United bench. Football theatre would be guaranteed tonight. Roy Keane emerged from the corner tunnel with his five children to a guard of honour from his current and former clubs and an incredible reception from the supporters of both. A highly competitive first half failed to produce a goal, Celtic's best effort a Shaun Maloney free-kick, palmed clear by Tim Howard after the striker had been brought down by a youthful Gerard Pique, whilst Artur Boruc did well to block a close-range strike from Giuseppe Rossi.

The interval brought the expected raft of changes, Stephen Pearson, Alan Thompson and Dion Dublin starting the second half for Celtic - the latter against his former club - with Keane, Maloney and John Hartson making way. Edwin van der Sar, Gary Neville, Paul Scholes and Ole Gunnar Solskjaer joined the proceedings to roll back the years for the Red Devils faithful, United with Ryan Giggs and Cristiano Ronaldo in full flow suddenly looking a different proposition. Those two would combine for the only goal of the game, 10 minutes in, the Welshman playing a perfectly-weighted pass with the outside of his left foot to find the young Portuguese winger running clear on Boruc, the ball nestling in the net two touches later. Celts refused to accept defeat, Dublin's header bringing out an instinctive save from van der Sar which deflected the ball onto the bar, forcing the Dutch keeper's fingers painfully back in the process. The big Englishman then missed another glorious chance to equalise for Celtic, side-footing the ball past the post after brilliant work from Pearson. Gordon Strachan then gave two of his young players an experience they would never forget, Charlie Mulgrew and Rocco Quinn tasting the big-time as the night ended early for Paul Telfer and Stan Petrov. And then suddenly it was all over.

With the traditional stadium walkaround complete, most players by now wearing the jerseys of their opponent, it was an emotional Roy Keane who summed up his feelings afterwards in the centre circle.

"I'd like to thank everyone who has turned up. I hope you all had a great night. This is something I'll remember for the rest of my life."

Back in the relative sanctuary of the media suite at Old Trafford, Keane then faced the inevitable questions regarding his future.

"I have an appointment in the next week or two with a specialist and I will see what he says. If I am going to play it's got to be 100 per cent. It's all or nothing. I will speak to the manager at Celtic and the doctor and I am sure I will make the right decision. I am sure I could carry on at a decent level, but I am about giving my best every game. It will be difficult next season, with Europe as well, and I have got to weigh up a lot of things. But I am relaxed about it. What will be will be and I am not fearful of it."

As Roy Keane was considering and discussing his own options for the future, the whole fragility of life was brought home once again to me. As we left the ground to make our way back to the car for the long journey back to Glasgow, I took a call from a pal who had both worked with me at ScottishPower and succeeded me as the treasurer of our supporters' club, the Cairn CSC. Joe was calling with bad news in that a lad I knew had passed away. I actually knew two folk of the name he gave me, and, for whatever reason, I immediately assumed it was the former work colleague. A second or two later, I realised that he was talking about someone I had known pretty much my whole life. We had started school together at St Aloysius Primary in Springburn, some 40 years earlier, going through the whole programme over the next decade or so at St Stephen's, Sighthill then St Roch's in the Garngad, playing for the school and boys guild teams together before retaining that friendship when we left in the late 1970's. Then there were the teenage parties and the introduction to 'the dancing,' turning up at Shuffles in Sauchiehall St on one unforgettable night wearing matching Scotland tops as the country enjoyed the mania surrounding Ally's Tartan Army, and somehow managing to 'cop' with two lovely girls from Lenzie. The girlfriends would last longer than the jerseys after the humiliation of Argentina.

He would join our supporters club and meet his future wife there, as the group of pals moved on to the next phase. As the eighties progressed, there were the weddings followed by the first flats and the first children, before life got in the way and our contact became much less frequent. Even so, I was taken completely aback by the news as I hadn't realised that he had been struggling. Turns out neither did he, a short and unexpected illness ending his life at just 45. In a poignant twist, I find myself writing this on Tuesday, 29 September 2020, the day on which he should have turned 60. Rest in peace, Davie.

The month of farewells continued two nights later, as we once again headed south in the car for a high-profile match involving Celtic and a superstar from the English Premier League era. This time it was former England captain Alan Shearer, the latest to invite the Hoops to provide the opposition for his testimonial game. The Geordie legend had been a world-record £15m signing a decade earlier, having partnered our own Chris Sutton to win the English title for Kenny Dalglish's Blackburn Rovers in 1995. He was making a final appearance for his boyhood side, having suffered an injury three weeks earlier, shortly after scoring for Newcastle in a 4-1 win at the Stadium of Light against fierce rivals Sunderland. I guess as career endings go, it doesn't get much better than that for someone beloved by the Toon Army. Shearer would be fit enough to kick-off and not much else, replaced immediately by Michael Chopra before watching the remainder of the match from the bench. More on that later.

He wouldn't be the only one living the dream in front of over 52,000 fans in St James Park on Thursday, 11 May 2006. Celtic youngster Charlie Mulgrew followed up his late appearance at Old Trafford by getting a first start for his idols, coming in at left-back with Mark Wilson moving across to replace Paul Telfer, whilst Alan Thompson's final appearance for the Hoops would come at the venue and against the team he had adored as a kid growing up on Tyneside. There was no sign of Roy Keane, the Irishman presumably carrying out his tongue-in-cheek threat *"to find a wedding or a christening"* rather than attend the game honouring Shearer, or, more likely, resting his body ahead of his big career decision.

For the second time in three nights, a vast Celtic support played its part in a wonderful occasion in one of THE great football amphitheatres. As three-quarters of the ground waved black-and-white scarves in the air, the Hoops army up in the gods finished off the colourful mosaic, their songs ringing out across the Newcastle evening air. A magical experience. Sadly, the football was less spectacular. The highlight of a forgettable first hour was the good-natured abuse dished out to another Geordie hero, Paul Gascoigne, by the visiting support, as he appeared for the half-time penalty competition.

In fairness, the game did pick up hugely after the break, despite a wave of changes. Gordon Strachan withdrew his skipper Neil Lennon, Maciej Zurawski, Alan Thompson and Dion Dublin, the latter two having seen action in the colours of Celtic for the last time. On came Paul Telfer, Stephen Pearson, Paul Lawson and John Hartson. With 20 minutes remaining, the hosts took the lead with a superb goal. John Ramage's deep cross from the right evaded everyone to drop perfectly for Albert Luque at the far post, the Spaniard blasting the ball past David Marshall on the volley for 1-0. Back came Celts, 10 minutes later, Shaun Maloney beating Ramage to a long diagonal ball and being hauled down for his trouble, a stick-on penalty awarded by Newcastle United fan and referee Mark Clattenberg, following a comical moment when he raced fully 20 yards to red card the offender, before remembering the context of the evening. The spot kick was duly converted expertly by Maloney, the young Celt rifling the ball into the top corner with some aplomb. Within three minutes, the game had completely turned around, this time John Hartson rising majestically to direct a downward header past Steve Harper into the bottom corner of the net for 2-1. It would prove to be a very special goal for the big Welshman, unbeknown to the spectators that evening, and perhaps even to himself at that point.

With the game won at 90 minutes, we then had a pantomime episode which spoiled the night and the occasion for many of us, albeit I'm open to criticism that we're taking it all a bit too seriously. Firstly, Mark Clattenberg signalled that there would be an extra three minutes stoppage time, surely a first in a testimonial game, then awarded a free-kick at the edge of the Celtic penalty area for no apparent reason. The ball was played quickly to veteran Newcastle United guest Les Ferdinand, the man who had scored the first visiting goal at the revamped Celtic Park almost 11 years earlier. He made his way unchallenged along the byeline before his low cross entered the net via the leg of the unfortunate Paul Lawson, his last touch as a Celt being one to forget. With the Hoops defence presumably in on the plan, the next move verged on the farcical, this time Ferdinand crumbling in a heap at the edge of the box under no challenge as Clattenberg pointed to the spot. This was the cue for Michael Chopra to make way for Shearer as the legendary striker ran on to the pitch to a tumultuous welcome. A quick word in the ear from the referee saw David Marshall dive to his right as Shearer placed the ball firmly in the other corner, a goal for Newcastle United in front of his beloved Gallowgate End the perfect way to finish his remarkable playing career.

With the match over, the man of the hour conducted an emotional interview in the centre-circle with Geordie television presenters Ant & Dec. Shearer paid tribute to the Newcastle fans, commenting several times that he had been fortunate to *"live his dream"* by coming back to his home city to pull on the black-and-white jersey and score a goal at St James Park. And then he couldn't stop scoring, stating that his career highlight had been beating the record of Toon hero Jackie Milburn just three months earlier, against Harry Rednapp's Portsmouth. It seemed fitting that Shearer mentioned that tonight, on what would have been 'Wor Jackie's' 82nd birthday, with his widow watching from the stands. Then there were some lovely words of appreciation for the Celtic players and support, which once again caused the cheers to ring out across the famous old ground. I felt privileged and proud to be wearing my colours and to bear witness to such a wonderful occasion. We'll forgive the pantomime.

EPILOGUE

"We'll always have Paris." A final gift from the King of Kings

Two days after the match in Newcastle, on Saturday, 13 May 2006, the curtain came down on the top-flight domestic football campaign as Hearts finally received some reward for an outstanding season by lifting the Scottish Cup, following a 4-2 penalty shootout victory over third-tier Gretna at Hampden. With the Tynecastle men having already qualified for the Champions League, the Borders outfit would now find themselves playing in the UEFA Cup that autumn. Having enjoyed two successive promotions since their entry to the Scottish League in 2002, replacing the liquidated Airdrieonians, it was an incredible rags-to-riches story, which would continue to soar before the perhaps inevitable 'bubble-burst' just a couple of years later, by which time they had reached the Scottish Premier League.

The attention of Celtic supporters, though, was focused on a more glamourous football occasion which was taking place in Paris on the Wednesday, the final of that season's Champions League. With the match involving Barcelona, featuring a certain Henrik Larsson, that would not be unusual in itself, but there was more riding on this game for Celtic than just the hope that the King of Kings would do well.

As things stood, Celts were due to enter the following season's elite European club competition in the third qualifying round where a number of dangerous teams would lie in wait, including representatives from Spain, Italy and Russia. Given the events in Bratislava the previous summer, this was probably a scenario best avoided from a Celtic perspective. A potential escape route was available, depending on who won the 2005/06

Champions League. The semi-final pairings had divided neatly into a positive or negative scenario for the Bhoys. Arsene Wenger's Arsenal would face Celtic's old friendly foes Villarreal for a place in the final. Neither were likely to qualify for the automatic Champions League places allocated to England or Spain, meaning that a trophy success for either club would secure the slot set aside for the Champions League holders in the forthcoming competition. Conversely, the other last-four clash would see the European aristocrats of Barcelona and AC Milan meet, with both virtually assured of one of the automatic placings already assured for their country's top two. Put simply, should Barca or Milan win the Champions League in the Stade de France in May, then the slot allocated to the current holders would not be required and would pass to the highest-ranked of the qualifiers – Celtic. Otherwise, the Parkhead club would have to take its chances in the third qualifying round.

Celtic chief executive Peter Lawwell had, perhaps rather unusually, gone public with his support for the Catalan and Italian giants, given this scenario.

"We'll be cheering on Barcelona or AC Milan, as they look like qualifying [from their domestic leagues]. We'll only be there if this year's winners qualify directly from their league. Hopefully, that won't annoy Arsenal, but we have to be self-centred."

As it transpired, Barcelona would eliminate Milan, whilst Arsenal would overcome Manuel Pelligrini's *Submari*. In Italy, rumblings were increasing over a domestic football scandal which would come to be known as *Calciopoli*, I guess 'Footballgate' is the best translation for that. The charges involved would eventually see the Italian champions Juventus stripped of their title and relegated, whilst AC Milan's punishment included a points deduction which removed their automatic qualification for the 2006/07 Champions League. So only a Barcelona win in Paris would do for Celtic. Over to you, Henrik. Thus, the football script could not have been written any better for a man still hero-worshipped by the Celtic support to help out again. Larsson being Larsson, the smart money said he would have a part to play.

Henrik had enjoyed a fine Indian Summer in Catalonia since his move from Glasgow on a free transfer on 30 June 2004. He would be joined by a few familiar faces, as Barcelona regrouped from a season where they had failed to win a trophy. The Blaugrana had finished in second place in La Liga, five points behind a Valencia side who had also won the UEFA Cup under the stewardship of Rafael Benitez. Barca's hopes of glory in that same competition had been ended by Larsson's Celtic in the fourth round in March, the Swedish hitman setting up Alan Thompson for what would prove to be the only goal of the tie. The goalless return leg in the Camp Nou had seen teenage Hoops keeper David Marshall produce a performance which would ensure he would never buy a drink in a Celtic bar again, albeit he was quickly brought crashing back down to earth by Martin O'Neill's post-match comment that *"it would be all downhill from here!"* I had enjoyed or endured that night from a vantage spot next to the clock at the highest point of the stadium behind one of the goals. With our sombreros acting as emergency drainpipes to mitigate the incessant downpour, my nephew and I watched the matchstick Celts below being dragged all over the huge playing surface for what seemed like an eternity, before experiencing that most magical of all Celtic feelings, the European away win over a top-ranked side.

As Hoops fans prayed for an emotional Gothenburg Final farewell for their talismanic striker, perhaps against Newcastle United, the Celtic European dream was ended in the quarter-final by another La Liga side, Villarreal, despite Henrik Larsson's equaliser in the home first leg. Villarreal would then lose out to near-neighbours Valencia in the last four, whilst a Didier Drogba double ensured it would be Olympique Marseille rather than the Geordies who would meet Benitez and co in the Ullevi final, where the Spaniards won 2-0.

Jose Mourinho's FC Porto had followed up their 2003 UEFA Cup victory over Celtic in Seville by winning the Champions League 12 months later, with a 3-0 victory over AS Monaco in Gelsenkirchen. Midfield star Deco was again the dominant personality in the final, as he had been against the Hoops, this time adding a goal, whilst Dmitri Alenichev scored for a second successive European final. It would be the last hurrah for that Porto side and their manager as they moved on to the continent's richer clubs. In Deco's case, that would be to join Henrik Larsson at Barcelona in a £20m deal, after a last-minute change of heart saw the collapse of an agreement for him to follow Jose Mourinho to Chelsea. Barca's spending power was reinforced when they brought Ludovic Giuly, captain of losing Champions League finalists Monaco, to the Camp Nou, together with another three players who had faced Larsson and Celtic in Europe in recent seasons, Brazilian defenders Edmilson from Olympique Lyonnais, Sylvinho from Celta Vigo and Juliano Belletti from Villarreal. Another £25m saw the Catalans snatch Samuel Eto'o from Real Mallorca, whilst one of the three promoted youngsters from Barcelona B was a diminutive Argentinian forward called Lionel Messi, following in the footsteps of Xavi, Andres Iniesta and Carles Puyol. Oh, and did I mention Ronaldinho was already there, together with Henrik's old Feyenoord pal Giovanni van Bronckhorst? It was a fearsome array of talent, which the King of Kings would now enjoy and enhance.

Henrik was one of five debutants as Barcelona commenced their 2004/05 La Liga campaign against Racing in the northern port city of Santander, the Swede wearing number 17 on a smart navy away kit and spearheading an attacking three with Giuly and Eto'o on either side, the midfield support provided by Deco and Xavi. Not too shabby. The King was replaced just after the hour by Iniesta, Barca scoring twice within the next 10 minutes through Giuly and an Eto'o penalty to seal a 2-0 opening night win.

The opposition in Larsson's first game had been wearing green-and-white and the Celtic connection continued for his home debut, two weeks later. This time the opposition was Sevilla, as it had been in his last appearance in the Hoops. His direct opponent in the Camp Nou was a certain Sergio Ramos, however, Henrik would have the last laugh, volleying home his first Barcelona goal with 15 minutes remaining to complete a second successive 2-0 win, after Giuly had opened the scoring in the first half.

If those two co-incidences had raised a few eyebrows, then Henrik's third game for Barcelona was off the scale. The football Gods had decided to twist the knife after the King's departure from Glasgow by deciding to make Celtic's next European tie a home match with his new club! Celtic were drawn in a Champions League 'Group of Death' consisting of Barca, the 2003 winners AC Milan, and the powerful Ukranians Shakhtar Donetsk. So, six months after his involvement in knocking Barcelona out of the UEFA Cup, the Swede would be returning with a Catalan superclub with revenge very much in its mind. If there was any consolation – for us at any rate – it would be that the return of Ronaldinho from injury would see Larsson start on the bench for the first time. Maybe, hopefully, they won't bring Henrik on.

With Barcelona's Argentinian forward Javier Saviola now sent out on loan to Monaco, the Return of The King would see him again wear the number seven jersey in the arena where he had made it his own. Celtic's new No.7, Juninho, had excelled in his Hoops debut two weeks earlier, an Alan Thompson screamer with five minutes remaining beating Rangers, making it a day the little Brazilian would never forget. Perhaps he was telling his World Cup-winning teammate Ronaldinho all about it, as they chatted cosily in the Parkhead tunnel before the teams emerged to the cacophony of noise that only the iconic east end ground can generate on these Champions League nights. The maestro Larsson then slipped into an unfamiliar dugout seat as the main stand crowd around him rose to welcome him back.

Larsson's old partner-in-crime Chris Sutton had been struggling for the past month with injury, the big Englishman deemed fit enough only for a place in the opposite dugout as John Hartson started up front with Henri Camara. With 20 minutes on the clock, the star-studded Catalans took the lead with a sublime goal from an old foe, Deco taking Ronaldinho's perfect through ball in his stride to lash it past David Marshall. With Celts still that goal down at the break, Martin O'Neill gambled, introducing Sutton for Juninho. A huge turning point then followed, as Jackie McNamara's clumsy challenge on Giuly allowed Ronaldinho the chance to put Barca out of sight from the spot. Martin O'Neill's prediction that Marshall's career could only go downwards after his performance in the Camp Nou six months earlier would now happily come home to haunt him, the Celtic keeper diving to his left to save brilliantly from the Brazilian superstar. As the crowd roared, you sensed the momentum change, and five minutes later the stadium erupted as Camara's fine run and cross down the right was met first-time by the charging Sutton. There was only winner for that cross as he barged through to crash it high into the net past Victor Valdes for 1-1.

Barcelona coach Frank Rijkaard's immediate response was to send for Henrik Larsson, the ex-Celt replacing Ronaldinho to a strange mixture of cheers and boos from the support who had adored him. The jeers and chants of *"Bobo's gonna get you"* did not sit well with me, so God only knows what Henrik was feeling at that moment. Valdes then kept his side in the game, as a delightful interchange between Sutton and Stan Petrov produced the move of the match, the Bulgarian midfielder's flick and volley looking a goal all the way before the Barca keeper stretched up a hand to tip the ball over the crossbar. It was sensational stuff, as the Celts chased for a winner roared on by the huge crowd.

An evening of twists and turns then swerved again. With the Hoops now well on top, there was anguish followed by silence as McNamara's night went from bad to worse, a horrible deflection off the Celtic captain allowing Giuly's shot to squirm past Marshall for 2-1, then an ankle injury sustained in the build-up forcing his eventual replacement by Mo Sylla. But the coup de grace was saved until the 82nd minute. Alan Thompson, the hero of the Glasgow Derby just a fortnight earlier, had sensationally volleyed Henrik Larsson's headed knockdown home for the winner when the sides had last clashed there in March. The duo would now combine again, Thompson's inexplicable misplaced header back towards his own goal pounced on by the deadly Swede, a chested touch around Marshall allowing him the simplest of tap-ins for perhaps the unhappiest goal of his football career. As his new colleagues clambered gleefully all over him to celebrate, Henrik looked like he would rather have been anywhere else on the planet. The game finished 3-1 to Barcelona, and Celtic's long, proud unbeaten home record in the Champions League had gone, the final blow struck by one of its favourite sons. *"Et tu, Henrik?"*

The Swede provided an honest assessment of his feelings in a post-match interview.

"There were mixed feelings. I have had seven great years here, but I know what I have to do now. I'm a Barcelona player. It felt good but it was very difficult to celebrate when I had such a great time here. But I'm happy we got the three points. It was a good result for us. I saw Alan Thompson head the ball back and I just gambled. Celtic will always have a big place in my heart, but life goes on. You have to do what you have to do."

On the eve of his 33rd birthday, Henrik would be back on the bench for the weekend trip to Madrid to face Atletico, the Swede replacing Samuel Eto'o at the break as the teams fought out a 1-1 draw, his long-term friend Giovanni van Bronckhorst opening the scoring before 'El Nino' Fernando Torres equalised for the hosts. Having missed out on the 4-1 midweek victory over Real Zaragoza at the Camp Nou, Larsson would start up front with Samuel Eto'o as the Cameroon striker returned to Palma to face his old side, Real Mallorca, Henrik's early tap-in followed by a double from his strike partner as the points were secured before half-time. He would reprise his Parkhead cameo on Champions League Matchday 2, coming on again as a substitute and setting up the third Barcelona goal as they beat Shakhtar Donetsk 3-0 in the Camp Nou. The King's excellent start to his post-Celtic career then continued four nights later, his fabulous trademark leap and header with 20 minutes remaining proving to be the only goal of the game against Numancia in the same stadium, sending 80,000 happy Catalans home and Barcelona to the top of La Liga. They would not relinquish that winning position.

Following the international break, Henrik experienced his first Catalan derby on Sunday, 16 October, an early Deco goal proving decisive as an Espanyol team featuring Mauricio Pochettino were beaten in the Olympic stadium on Montjuic. The match is perhaps more memorable for being the senior debut of Lionel Messi, the youngster replacing goalscorer Deco for the final seven minutes. Larsson was then given his first European start for the Catalans against AC Milan in the San Siro in midweek, the Swede hitting the crossbar early on. Substitute Andres Iniesta would repeat that feat in the dying moments as ultimately it would not be their night, a first-half header from Milan's own Number 7, Ukrainian star Andriy Shevchenko, enough to send Barcelona to a first defeat of the season and the Italians to the top of the group. Some 1,500 miles or so to the east, Henrik's old Celtic colleagues were being beaten heavily in Donetsk.

Having missed out on the 3-0 home victory over Osasuna, Larsson would start his first Copa del Rey match in midweek, albeit he would probably have preferred to sit this one out. The superstars of Barcelona made the short trip to the north-western outskirts of the city to take on the questionably named UDA Gramenet, a third-tier side who normally competed with the B teams of the major clubs. Familiarity with such surroundings might explain the selection of 17-year-old Lionel Messi in an otherwise full-strength Barca side, the boy who would be king lining up for the first time beside Henrik Larsson. In front of 3,500 at the other Nou Camp, the tiny municipal stadium in Santa Coloma, an extra-time goal would send the giants tumbling out of the competition. In terms of the magnitude of this result, I guess it would be akin to Clyde's defeat of Gordon Strachan's Celtic in the Scottish Cup in January 2006, albeit perhaps an even greater upset like a hypothetical loss to an Albion Rovers at Cliftonhill, given the collection of world-class players on view. It would provide a stark contrast to Henrik's previous national cup-tie, his second-half double against Dunfermline Athletic securing the Double for Martin O'Neill's Celtic, in his final competitive match for the Hoops, just six months earlier.

Barca's domestic campaign continued the following Sunday with a 1-1 draw with Athletic Bilbao in the Estadio San Mames, Henrik replacing Ludovicv Guily after an hour. And he began on the bench for the return match with AC Milan, the Swede looking on helplessly as Andriy Shevchenko again opened the scoring for the Italians, although Samuel Eto'o would restore parity before the break. With 10 minutes remaining, Larsson entered the fray in place of the Mexican defensive midfielder

Rafael Marquez, as Frank Rijkaard went for broke. He would be rewarded as the game entered its final minute, Henrik's decoy run creating space for Ronaldinho to crash home a sublime winning goal. Larsson then had the chance to grab his own moment of glory in stoppage time, a Xavi cut-back uncharacteristically blasted over the crossbar as the match ended 2-1 to Barcelona.

Henrik's first season at Barcelona continued with another 10-minute cameo from the bench, this time for Samuel Eto'o as the *Blaugrana* closed out a 2-1 home win over Deportivo La Coruna. And his return to Seville was a disappointing one, six days later, Larsson's introduction for Ludovic Giuly after an hour failing to prevent a first La Liga defeat, as Barca lost 2-1 to the green-and-white stripes of Real Betis.

The biggest game in world football was up next, El Clasico, as Real Madrid visited the Camp Nou on the evening of Saturday, 20 November 2004. Earlier in the day, a match to which some assign that tag had taken place in Govan, Neil Lennon racially abused from start to finish as the hosts beat 9-man Celtic, the Irishman marched up to the Free Broomloan by his manager Martin O'Neill at full-time, in a gesture of support and defiance. The Spanish clash would be more about the football thankfully, the calibre of player on view reflecting the cream of football talent on the planet. *Los Galacticos* Zinedine Zidane, Raul, David Beckham and Luis Figo all lined up for the visitors, the latter, a former Barca hero, almost two years to the day from the infamous 'pig's head' incident at the same venue.

Whilst the majority of the 97,000 crowd would be ecstatic by a dominating performance from the hosts - goals from Samuel Eto'o and Giovanni van Bronckhorst sealing the points before the interval - Henrik's first taste of *El Clasico* would prove to be a bittersweet experience. Ten minutes before the break, he fell to the ground clutching the left leg that had been the cause of such misery for himself and Celtic in Lyon five years earlier. With the stretcher wheeled on, it looked ominous for the Swede, however, thankfully, he resumed play after treatment. Then with 20 minutes remaining and the score still 2-0, the striker crashed onto the Camp Nou turf writhing in agony for a second time, having played a one-two at the edge of the box before his knee gave way. It would transpire that he had damaged his anterior cruciate ligament. Having been replaced by Andres Iniesta, Henrik would presumably still be on a stretcher in the bowels of the giant stadium a few minutes later as Samuel Eto'o teased Guti into a rash challenge, Ronaldinho clipping the ball expertly past Iker Casillas to end the contest at 3-0.

Keyhole surgery was carried out on the Monday, the initial prognosis being that a six-month absence from football would be likely, as was the case for fellow new signing Edmilson, who had suffered the same injury in September. Curiously, Thiago Motta and Gabri had also suffered from studs catching in the Camp Nou turf recently, suggesting either dreadful bad luck or an issue with the playing surface. Whilst Henrik's cartilage damage had been repaired by this procedure, the club's medical staff advised that *"definitive surgery on the torn ligament had been postponed at the player's express wish."* It seemed an unusual decision or agreement to reach, creating only further uncertainty. 'The player' himself was in low spirits when he spoke to the Swedish media 24 hours later.

"I can't say if I will continue or quit before I have all the cards on the table. Right now, everything is just so grim and tiring. There are a lot of thoughts moving through my head. I had really hoped it would not be so serious."

Football being football, the first game Henrik would miss would be the Champions League return leg with Celtic on the Wednesday. The Catalan club had shown a touch of class by immediately offering a 12-month extension to his existing contract, Barcelona president Joan Laporta explaining their stance.

"I have offered [Henrik] a contract renewal so that he can put his mind at rest during this difficult time. We want him to concentrate on recovering without having to worry about his contractual situation."

By matchday, Henrik was more philosophical about his situation, having initially feared the worst.

"I'm feeling much more upbeat. It's a serious injury I've suffered, but it's part

of the game. Football's a physical game and these are things that can happen. I always knew something like this could happen. The most important thing now is to ensure my knee gets better. I need to speak to the doctors and make the best decisions about my recovery and how we're going to deal with it."

The battle between his current and former clubs would end in a 1-1 draw at the Camp Nou, a strike from Samuel Eto'o midway through the first half cancelled out by John Hartson's far post finish on the stroke of the interval, as Celtic finally secured a Champions League point away from home at the ninth time of asking. That left the Hoops with a decent chance of claiming third spot in the group and the prize of UEFA Cup football after Christmas for the third successive season, following a 23-year wait to achieve such a feat. However, with Celts needing only to match Shakhtar's Matchday 6 result against Barcelona on to progress, the Ukrainians upset the odds by winning 2-0 in Donetsk, meaning that the Bhoys' creditable goalless draw with eventual finalists AC Milan in Glasgow the same night left them bottom of their European group for the first time. That would be that for another year.

The November assessment made by the Barcelona medical team would prove to be spot on. Almost exactly six months to the day, on Sunday, 22 May 2005, Henrik Larsson left the bench to recommence his career at the Camp Nou, the third of three long-term Barca absentees to do so that evening, following the reappearance of Edmilson and Gabri for the *Blaugrana* in the second-half of the clash with Villarreal. It would also be a special night for visiting striker Diego Forlan, who joined an exclusive group of players to score a hat-trick at one of football's great cathedrals. The match itself, the penultimate La Liga fixture of 2004/05, would end 3-3, however, most of the 85,000 spectators had turned up for a party. Eight days earlier, Barcelona had claimed a first Spanish title of the millennium, ending a six-year drought. Henrik would join his teammates as the huge trophy was presented on the pitch. There was not a little irony as the great man lifted his prize just a few hours after one of the darkest days in the history of his old club. As mentioned at the start of this book, the events of Black Sunday at Fir Park, Motherwell will haunt me forever.

Henrik would then end his first campaign in Barcelona colours six days later, not far from where it all began, in San Sebastian on the northern coast. The new champions would bring the curtain down with a goalless draw against Real Sociedad, Larsson replacing Sylvinho at half-time to continue his recovery. Earlier that afternoon, his old boss Martin O'Neill had ended his own spell in Glasgow by winning the Scottish Cup, as our own recovery from the heartbreak of that last-gasp title concession commenced. On Tuesday, 31 May 2005, Henrik Larsson confirmed that he would be taking up the offer of a contract extension and would be playing for Barcelona in 2005/06.

"It is a flattering offer and I have decided to accept it. I expect us to solve all things this week."

Henrik would begin his second season in Catalonia once again used more as an impact substitute than a regular starter, seeing the last 20 minutes of action as the champions opened their campaign with a goalless draw away to Alaves and getting half an hour in the Vicente Calderon as Barcelona lost 2-1 to Atletico Madrid. He would make his first start in the fifth round of matches, a few days after turning 34, finally a happy return to Seville for Larsson as Barca beat Real Betis 4-1 on Saturday, 24 September 2005. He had remained on the bench at the same venue the previous month, as the Catalans won the first leg of their Supercopa de Espana play-off by 3-0 against the green-and-white club of the Spanish city, Real Betis being the holders of the Copa del Rey. Henrik would come on for the final six minutes of the home return leg the following week, duly claiming a second domestic winners medal for his new club in the space of three months, despite Barcelona suffering a surprise 2-1 defeat on the night.

Having watched Barca's opening Champions League victory over Werder in Bremen from the dugout, Henrik would get 10 minutes of Matchday 2 action as the Catalans comfortably beat Udinese 4-1 at the Camp Nou, followed by 20 minutes in the weekend draw with Real Zaragoza at the same venue, Larsson's introduction triggering a fightback from two goals down to salvage a late point. The Swede would start against Panathanaikos in Athens' Olympic stadium on Tuesday, 18 October 2005, making way for Lionel Messi in the 67th minute, as the match ended goalless.

The following midweek would see the King score his first goal in over a year for Barcelona. Once again, he received the call from the bench, with the hosts tied at 0-0 against Malaga. After Ronaldinho had controversially won and converted a penalty kick with nine minutes remaining, the Brazilian slid Henrik through on goal in the dying seconds, the Swede producing an exquisite scoop over the Malaga keeper to seal the three points. And he netted again in the Camp Nou on the Sunday evening, heading home at the far post just six minutes after joining the fray, to complete a 5-0 win over Real Sociedad. Those goals would not be enough for Henrik to force his way into the starting line-up for the home return with Panathanaikos in midweek, Larsson remaining an unused substitute as a Samuel Eto'o hat-trick and Lionel Messi's first-ever Champions League strike helped Barca to another 5-0 victory.

Messi was becoming an increasingly important part of the Barcelona team, the brilliant youngster awarded a start in the Estadio Santiago Bernabeu as the anniversary of Larsson's injury approached. The Swede would watch from the bench as Ronaldinho produced a masterclass, his second stunning goal of the evening provoking a standing ovation from the home fans as the Catalans went top of the table following a comprehensive 3-0 victory. Henrik did mark his second Champions League starting slot of the campaign with another goal in midweek, sent clear again by Ronaldinho before slipping the ball under keeper Andreas Reinke for Barca's third as they beat Werder Bremen 3-1 at the Camp Nou.

December 2005 opened with a 2-0 win over Villarreal, Larsson's return to El Madrigal consisting of a 10-minute cameo from the bench with the game already secured. He would then start the Champions League Matchday 6 fixture in Udine, as the Catalan's completed an impressive first stage with another 2-0 victory, courtesy of Ezquerro and Iniesta strikes in the final five minutes. And normal service was resumed at the weekend as Sevilla came to town, boasting a strike force of Frederic Kanoute and Javier Saviola. Kanoute had allegedly been lined up as Henrik's replacement following his injury in Lyon in October 1999, the French-born forward who represented Mali at international level eventually joining West Ham United, whilst Saviola had worn the number seven jersey at the Camp Nou prior to Larsson's arrival, the Argentinian now on loan to Sevilla having completed a similar season-long arrangement with AS Monaco in 2004/05. Canoute would open the scoring in the Camp Nou, within seconds of Larsson replacing Lionel Messi, before goals from Samuel Eto'o and Ronaldinho turned the game around within 15 minutes, Henrik setting up the Brazilian superstar for the winner. The King's final appearance before the Christmas break would again be from the bench, Henrik replacing Ludovic Giuly for the last 25 minutes of the Catalans' comfortable 3-1 win in Cadiz.

The festive break allowed Henrik to take stock, the Swede taking the opportunity to announce that he would be leaving the Camp Nou at the end of the season, despite the offer of a further year's contract.

"My wife and I have spoken about this for a while now and it's a decision that has grown on me over the course of the season. If I had played more things might have been different, but the fact that I'm not playing regularly is not the main reason why I'm going back to Sweden. The time is right. It's as simple as that. I'll see what offers I get and after that I'll make my mind up. I'm not ruling anything out, but I'm not promising anything either."

2006 began with the short trip across the city to face Espanyol, Larsson a late substitute for Messi as Barca held on for a 2-1 derby win. Henrik marked his return to the starting line-up for the Copa del Rey clash with third-tier Zamora by scoring his first double for the club, both goals coming within 60 seconds midway through the first half in the Camp Nou, as the Blaugrana ensured there would be no repeat of last season's shock cup exit at Gramenet. He then got just seven minutes game-time in the 2-1 home victory over Athletic Bilbao the following Sunday, again replacing Lionel Messi, regaining his place as the second half of La Liga fixtures commenced with the visit of Alaves. Larsson would open the scoring early in the second half before making way for Lionel Messi with 17 minutes remaining, the Argentinian teenager continuing his excellent breakthrough season by scoring a late second goal.

The quarter-final of the Copa del Rey saw Barcelona paired with Real Zaragoza, a remarkable five-minute spell in the away first leg seeing the Catalans lose three goals. A classic Larsson header followed by a Ronaldinho penalty kept Barca in the tie before Diego Milito's late goal gave Zaragoza a 4-2 lead to take into the return. Henrik would come off the bench to score a late winner in the Camp Nou, six days later, however Real would progress to the last four on aggregate despite their 2-1 defeat on the night, Ronaldinho earlier shown a red card. Larsson had also played the first 73 minutes of the League match at Mallorca the previous weekend, albeit his replacement had then helped himself to two goals as Barcelona won 3-0. No prizes for guessing that Henrik's replacement had been Lionel Messi.

The next visitors to the Camp Nou were Atletico Madrid, the match a personal triumph for visiting striker Fernando Torres as his double helped secure a 3-1 victory. Henrik's deft finish just after the hour had briefly revived hopes of a Barca comeback at 2-1, before El Nino added his own second goal. The following week saw Henrik return to the Mestalla, a little over four years since the UEFA Cup clash involving Celtic. Just like that night, Valencia would edge it by a single goal, David Villa's strike just before half-time, just three minutes after Larsson had replaced Ludovic Giuly, deciding the contest and consigning the champions to a second successive La Liga defeat.

Barcelona would get back on track six days later, Henrik Larsson sliding in to open the scoring in the 5-1 home win over Real Betis, before making way for Lionel Messi with 15 minutes remaining, the substitute promptly scoring the final goal. Henrik would be back on the bench for the midweek trip to Stamford Bridge in the Last 16 of the Champions League, as Barca sought revenge for their defeat at the hands of Jose Mourinho's men at the same stage of the competition the previous season. It was a game of own goals, Thiago Motta beating Victor Valdes before John Terry did likewise to Petr Cech at the other end. By that time, Motta had made way for Larsson, the Swede instrumental in setting up the winning goal on the night for Samuel Eto'o. Henrik would yet again replace Lionel Messi in the weekend fixture in Zaragoza, and to great effect, racing to get on the end of Samuel Eto's superb cross to seal a 2-0 win, just minutes after Ronaldinho's penalty had opened the scoring. Larsson then ended speculation by confirming that he would be returning to Sweden to rejoin his former club Helsingborg at the end of the season, signing an 18-month contract. It had not been a difficult choice in the end.

"I'm Helsingborg through and through. I played with them for two seasons and I've even built a house in Helsingborg. There was no other alternative for me. I'm really happy. I've been away since 1993 and had many good years there but everything must come to an end. Moving back to Helsingborg in the summer doesn't change anything on my position with the national team. I'll keep going. There's no age limit for the national team. I get a lot out of it. I still want to play and as long as I'm playing top-level football then I want to play in the national team."

March would see the King receive a starting role for the home clash with Deportivo La Coruna, Frank Rijkaard's faith rewarded with another Henrik Larsson goal, the Swedish striker rising expertly to meet Ronaldinho's corner and level things at 2-2. Samuel Eto'o would grab the winner just before Ludovic Giuly replaced Henrik on 64 minutes. Three days later, Larsson came off the bench within the first half-hour in front of 98,000 in the Camp Nou, as Lionel Messi collapsed on the turf during the second leg of the Champions League tie with Chelsea. A moment of Ronaldinho magic would increase the aggregate lead to 3-1, the Brazilian swerving past defenders before leaving Cech flatfooted. There was a certain injustice about the stoppage time penalty awarded to Chelsea for what appeared a legitimate tackle on John Terry. After a few minutes of heated discussion, Frank Lampard stroked the ball home to give the Londoners an undeserved draw on the night, but Barcelona progressed to the quarter final.

Before that, there would be domestic business to conclude. Henrik would again come off the bench the following Sunday in Pamplona, with Barcelona already trailing 2-0 to Osasuna. Larsson would take a Ronaldinho pass to score a superb goal within seven minutes of his arrival, however, the hosts would hold on to inflict a surprise defeat on the champions. The two men would again combine brilliantly six days later, the Swede opening the scoring within eight minutes of a tricky match with Real Sociedad in San Sebastian. Samuel Eto'o would seal the points with a second goal early in the second half, before Larsson made way for Ludovic Giuly with 20 minutes remaining. Henrik would get a rare 90 minutes for the trip to Malaga, neither side able to score as another point was secured in the race for the title.

Larsson would retain his place for the Champions League quarter-final match against Benfica in Lisbon, the former Celt playing for 75 minutes then replaced by Giuly, as once again the match ended goalless. And having played against the second side to win the European Cup - the Eagles having beaten Barcelona 3-2 in the May 1961 final - he would be selected against the club who had monopolised the competition in the early years three days later, Real Madrid. The latest instalment of *El Clasico* saw the Catalans in an extremely strong position, 11 points clear of their great rivals with just eight games remaining. The must-win scenario for Madrid looked less likely after Roberto Carlos was shown a second yellow card within the opening half-hour. Having conceded a penalty-kick, which Ronaldinho converted, the Brazilian then hauled down Henrik Larsson, the referee showing leniency until Roberto Carlos continued to voice his disapproval. Despite being one man down, it would be Real who would score next just 10 minutes later, a heavy-looking Ronaldo showing wonderful composure to clip the ball over Victor Valdes for a Larsson-esque finish against his former club. Speaking of the Swedish legend, he passed up two great chances to add a goal in this fixture to his magical scrapbook. With 12 minutes remaining, we witnessed one of football's less likely substitutions, Zinedine Zidane making way for ex-Everton midfielder Thomas Gravesen. El Clasico would then end with honours even at 1-1, the Swede philosophical afterwards about his failure to find the net in the world's greatest fixture.

"It was just one of those nights when things didn't go for me. It was disappointing because we had enough chances to win the game."

The return fixture with Benfica at the Camp Nou would again see a starting role for Henrik, Barcelona being a Ronaldinho goal to the good before he was withdrawn with just four minutes remaining. His replacement Ludovic Giuly would hardly have had time to warm up before Samuel Eto'o confirmed a semi-final place for the Spanish champions with a second goal. Larsson's run in the side continued for the weekend visit to Santander, the Swede sliding the ball home neatly to give Barca an early lead with what would prove to be his last goal for the club. Racing would turn the game around with two quick goals before Samuel Eto'o completed the scoring at 2-2, just after the half-hour.

Friday, 14 April 2006 would prove unlucky for Henrik as he limped off the Camp Nou pitch with a thigh injury after just eight minutes of the clash with fellow Champions League semi-finalists Villarreal. Samuel Eto'o scored the only goal of the game a few minutes later, as Barca closed in on another title. Larsson would miss out on the midweek trip to the San Siro, as Ludovic Giuly's goal beat AC Milan to give Barcelona one foot in their first European Cup or Champions League final in 12 years, however, he would come off the bench to replace the same player with 20 minutes remaining of the goalless second leg. Barca's opponents in the final the following month would be Arsenal, the Gunners having eliminated Real Madrid, Juventus then Villarreal without conceding a knockout goal to become the first London club ever to play in European football's showpiece event, 50 years after its inception.

That match would mark a final opportunity for Larsson to wear a Barcelona jersey before returning to Sweden. There was an indication of the esteem in which he was held when Ronaldinho, currently the world's greatest player, spoke of the man he considered more than a teammate.

"With Henrik leaving us at the end of the season, this club is losing a great scorer, no question. But I am also losing a great friend. Henrik was my idol and now that I am playing next to him it is fantastic. He is a real friend and that is a pleasure. I just want to enjoy the remaining time he has with us rather than

dwell on what we will be missing when he's gone. I haven't tried to convince Henrik to stay in Barcelona. I respect him so much that I can't try to influence his decision. It's something he has thought about for a long time. I'm not happy he's leaving but I'm not going to pressure him at all. At Henrik's age, many players announce their retirement from international football but no-one I know of his age is at the great physical level Henrik is at right now. He could play at the highest level for a long time."

The last game in the calendar month of April saw another early goal - this time from Ronaldinho - settle the home clash with Cadiz. Ludovic Giuly again made way for Henrik Larsson for the final 25 minutes of the match. The King regained his starting slot as May opened with a visit to another old haunt, the Balaidos stadium in Vigo, for the midweek match with Celta. A goal 10 minutes into the second half from Samuel Eto'o – his 25th of a wonderful personal campaign - would give Barcelona a third consecutive 1-0 La Liga win, however, more importantly, Valencia's 2-1 defeat at Mallorca earlier the same evening had confirmed the Catalans as Spanish champions for the second successive season. Having been sidelined with injury as the previous year's title had been clinched, Henrik would no doubt savour his 90 minutes of action and the celebrations afterwards in Galicia. This was a fifth national title in six seasons for the phenomenal Swedish striker.

Three days later, Saturday, 6 May 2006, it would be local rivals Espanyol who would provide a guard of honour for the new champions in front of 88,000 in the Camp Nou. Frank Rijkaard selected Henrik for what would be his final home appearance for the Catalans, the only thing missing being a Larsson goal. He had several great chances to score, not least five minutes into the second half, Henrik sent through one-on-one with the Espanyol keeper Gorka Iraizoz, who pulled off a save only to see the ball drop to Ronaldinho, the Brazilian making no mistake. That finished the contest at 2-0, Samuel Eto'o seeing his first-half effort deflected into the net to keep the early party atmosphere going. With 20 minutes remaining, Henrik left the Camp Nou pitch for the final time as a player to a huge ovation. The King would be in the group presented with the giant trophy after the full-time whistle had blown, celebrating the moment as the Barca anthem rang out loud and proud to the cheers of their support.

There was another celebration in full swing in Sevilla the following Saturday, as Barcelona played their last domestic fixture before the Champions League final with Arsenal in Paris. This time, though, it was the hosts receiving the guard of honour from the champions, following their 4-0 UEFA Cup triumph over Steve McLaren's Middlesbrough in Eindhoven in midweek. Henrik Larsson's former Celtic strike partner Mark Viduka had been part of that defeated side, as the Andalusian club secured the first of its record-breaking sequence of UEFA Cup/ Europa League wins, having commenced that campaign by eliminating a Bundesliga side, Mainz 05, managed by a young Jurgen Klopp in his first coaching role.

Henrik would depart proceedings on his final start for Barcelona – his last domestic involvement for the club - with 20 minutes remaining and the sides tied at 2-2. Sevilla had surrendered an early two-goal lead, future Barca star Dani Alves opening the scoring with a fierce shot before the hosts were awarded and duly converted a dubious penalty. Two goals within a minute from Ezquerro and Sylvinho would see the Catalans level before the interval, however, Sevilla would eventually edge a five-goal thriller, thanks to a header from Kepa, scored just five minutes after the King had left the building.

The showpiece event of European football took place four days later in Saint-Denis, on the outskirts of Paris. For the 50th anniversary of the first European Cup Final, the match would return to the city where it all began back in 1956. As expected, teenage Barcelona star Lionel Messi would not recover sufficiently even to take his place on the bench. His time would come. Thus, the fates again decreed that Henrik Larsson would be the attacking option for Rijkaard, should the Barca coach require an impact substitute in Paris. The Arsenal team included Belarusian midfielder Alexander Hleb, who had been part of the VfB Stuttgart team eliminated by Henrik's Celtic on the Road to Seville, albeit Larsson himself had missed both legs whilst recovering from a fractured jaw. The

Gunners also featured two future Celts in their starting line-up, Kolo Toure and Freddie Ljungberg, whilst their fearsome options to attack from the bench included star trio Jose Antonio Reyes, Dennis Bergkamp and Robin van Persie.

The match got off to a pulsating start in front of 80,000 in the Stade de France, Victor Valdes twice saving well from Thierry Henry, before his opposite number Jens Lehman became the first big story of the final. With 18 minutes on the clock, the Arsenal goalkeeper came charging out of his box to bring down Samuel Eto'o, the ball breaking to Ludovic Giuly who stroked it into the empty net. Had the Norwegian referee awarded the goal, then the story of the 2006 Champions League final may have been very different, however, Terje Hauge chose to send Lehman off, the first player ever to be dismissed in this fixture. On came Manuel Almunia between the Arsenal sticks, with Robert Pires the outfield player sacrificed in his last game for the club before joining semi-final opponents Villarreal.

The game then took another twist, 10 minutes before the interval, Sol Campbell rising unchallenged to bullet home a header from a Thierry Henry free-kick, giving the Londoners a lead they would fight to defend for the rest of the match. Barcelona replaced the defensive Edmilson with Andres Iniesta at half-time, however, it would be their second substitution which would change the course of the game. On the hour mark, Henrik Larsson received the call to duty, as he had so often during his two years with the club. He replaced Mark van Bommel, as Frank Rijkaard went all in, the gamble paying off in spectacular style. Within 15 minutes, Larsson's cushioned pass sent Eto'o through for the Cameroon striker to beat Almunia at his near post, with Arsenal defenders claiming offside. And four minutes later, the turnaround was complete, this time the Swede's delightful clipped pass inside the Gunners defence found Juliano Belletti charging through in the inside-right position. The Brazilian full-back took one touch before rifling the ball through Almunia's legs to score his first goal for the club. It would prove to be the winner, as Barcelona became European champions for the first time in 14 years. I remember thinking that there was a certain justice in how this match had played out, that Henrik was receiving the medal in Paris that night which his performance had earned three years earlier in Seville.

It was a fitting way to end his spell with another of the great clubs in world football, Henrik Larsson revealing afterwards the role he had been asked to carry out.

"My job was to come on and try and move and open up the defence. Frank Rijkaard's instructions were to stay central and move and try to win it."

Job done then.

And what next for the man who has given me most pleasure as a Celtic supporter in more than five decades of following my team?

Henrik advised that his decision to turn down a new contract offer from Barcelona to return to his old Swedish club, Helsingborg, was due to a combination of family and football reasons.

"I'm almost 35 years old. I've got kids and they need to understand how we live in Sweden. My house there is finished, and we need to go back there. I want to play football. I feel I haven't played as much as I would love to because of the great players we have at Barcelona. I maybe have one or two more years playing at a decent level and I want to do that playing for 90 minutes."

There was then an incredible post-match interview with Arsenal striker Thierry Henry, who in between questioning whether the referee should have been wearing a Barcelona shirt, made it clear who he believed had made the most telling contribution to the final outcome.

"All the time you talk about Ronaldinho and Eto'o and people like that. Let's talk about the proper people who make the difference, that was Henrik Larsson, who made two assists. He came on and changed the game. That is what killed the game. I didn't see Ronaldinho and I didn't see Eto'o. I saw Henrik Larsson. Two times he came alive, that was the key."

Two touches from Henrik Larsson in the grey Paris rain had transformed the Champions League final, and, in turn, sent his old club Celtic directly into the Group Stage of the following season's competition. Even in the colours of Barcelona, the King of Kings was still delivering for his beloved Hoops. A parting gift, if you will, for the Celtic support.

To quasi-paraphrase the four-person pop phenomenon from his homeland during my teenage years…

Thank you for the magic, Henrik.

Appendix 1: Celtic FC Fixtures 2005/06 – Scottish Premier League

Fixture	Date	Opponent	Score	Scorers	Goals	Points
1	Sat 30 Jul 2005	Motherwell	4-4	Hartson (3), Beattie	4	1
2	Sat 6 Aug 2005	**Dundee Utd**	2-0	Hartson, Beattie	6	4
3	Sat 13 Aug 2005	**Falkirk**	3-1	Hartson, Thompson (2)	9	7
4	Sat 20 Aug 2005	Rangers	1-3	Maloney (pen)	10	7
5	Sun 28 Aug 2005	Dunfermline Athletic	4-0	Zurawski (2), Hartson, Nakamura	14	10
6	Sat 10 Sep 2005	**Aberdeen**	2-0	Zurawski, Petrov	16	13
7	Sun 18 Sep 2005	Hibernian	1-0	Petrov	17	16
8	Sat 24 Sep 2005	**Inverness Caledonian Thistle**	2-1	Beattie (2)	19	19
9	Sat 1 Oct 2005	Livingston	5-0	McManus, Maloney, Zurawski, Sutton, Beattie	24	22
10	Sat 15 Oct 2005	**Heart of Midlothian**	1-1	Beattie	25	23
11	Sun 23 Oct 2005	Kilmarnock	1-0	Petrov	26	26
12	Wed 26 Oct 2005	**Motherwell**	5-0	Petrov (3), Maloney, Nakamura	31	29
13	Sun 30 Oct 2005	Dundee Utd	4-2	Hartson, Sutton, Archibald o.g., Pearson	35	32
14	Sun 6 Nov 2005	Falkirk	3-0	Maloney, McGeady, Hartson	38	35
15	Sat 19 Nov 2005	**Rangers**	3-0	Hartson, Balde, McGeady	41	38
16	Sat 26 Nov 2005	**Dunfermline Athletic**	0-1		41	38
17	Sun 4 Dec 2005	Aberdeen	3-1	McGeady, Petrov, Telfer	44	41
18	Sat 10 Dec 2005	**Hibernian**	3-2	Hartson (2), Maloney	47	44
19	Sun 18 Dec 2005	Inverness Caledonian Thistle	1-1	Hartson	48	45
20	Mon 26 Dec 2005	**Livingston**	2-1	Maloney, Nakamura	50	48
21	Sun 1 Jan 2006	Heart of Midlothian	3-2	Pearson, McManus (2)	53	51
22	Sat 14 Jan 2006	**Kilmarnock**	4-2	Nakamura, Maloney (pen), McManus, Zurawski	57	54
23	Sun 22 Jan 2006	Motherwell	3-1	Zurawski, McGeady, Hartson	60	57
24	Sat 28 Jan 2006	**Dundee Utd**	3-3	Hartson, Zurawski, Petrov	63	58
25	Wed 8 Feb 2006	**Falkirk**	2-1	Keane, McManus	65	61
26	Sun 12 Feb 2006	Rangers	1-0	Zurawski	66	64
27	Sun 19 Feb 2006	Dunfermline Athletic	8-1	Petrov, Hartson, Zurawski (4), Maloney, Lennon	74	67
28	Sat 4 Mar 2006	**Aberdeen**	3-0	Petrov, Maloney, Zurawski	77	70
29	Sun 12 Mar 2006	Hibernian	2-1	Maloney (pen), McManus	79	73
30	Wed 22 Mar 2006	**Inverness Caledonian Thistle**	2-1	McManus, Maloney	81	76
31	Sun 26 Mar 2006	Livingston	2-0	Zurawski, Maloney	83	79
32	Wed 5 Apr 2006	**Heart of Midlothian**	1-0	Hartson	84	82
33	Sun 9 Apr 2006	Kilmarnock	4-1	Nakamura (2), Hartson, Dublin	88	85
34	Sun 16 Apr 2006	**Hibernian**	1-1	Zurawski	89	86
35	Sun 23 Apr 2006	**Rangers**	0-0		89	87
36	Sun 30 Apr 2006	Heart of Midlothian	0-3		89	87
37	Wed 3 May 2006	**Kilmarnock**	2-0	Zurawski, Varga	91	90
38	Sun 7 May 2006	Aberdeen	2-2	Hartson, Maloney	93	91

Appendix 2: Celtic FC Fixtures 2005/06 – Scottish FA Cup

Round	Date	Opponent	Score	Scorers	Goals
3	Sun 8 Jan 2006	Clyde	1-2	Zurawski	1

Appendix 3: Celtic FC Fixtures 2016/17 – Scottish League Cup

Round	Date	Opponent	Score	Scorers	Goals
3	Wed 21 Sep 2005	**Falkirk**	2-1 (a.e.t)	Zurawski, Hartson	2
QF	Wed 9 Nov 2005	**Rangers**	2-0	Maloney, Klos o.g.	4
SF	Wed 1 Feb 2006	Motherwell	2-1	Zurawski, Maloney	6
Final	Sun 19 Mar 2006	Dunfermline Athletic	3-0	Zurawski, Maloney, Dublin	9

Appendix 4: Celtic FC Fixtures 2016/17 – UEFA Champions League

Round	Date	Opponent	Score	Scorers	Goals
Q2	Wed 27 Jul 2005	Artmedia Bratislava	0-5		0
Q2	Tue 2 Aug 2005	**Artmedia Bratislava**	4-0	Thompson (pen), Hartson, McManus, Beattie	4

*Home fixtures shown in bold

Appendix 5: Celtic FC 2005/06 – Record of individual appearances & goals

Squad No.	Player	Premiership		Scottish Cup		League Cup		UEFA		Overall	
		A	G	A	G	A	G	A	G	A	G
1	Artur Boruc	34	0	1	0	4	0	1	0	40	0
2	Paul Telfer	36	1	1	0	3	0	2	0	42	1
3	Mo Camara	18	0	0	0	3	0	2	0	23	0
4	Adam Virgo	10	0	1	0	1	0	0	0	12	0
5	Du Wei	0	0	1	0	0	0	0	0	1	0
6	Bobo Balde	28	1	0	0	3	0	2	0	33	1
7	Maciej Zurawski	24	16	1	1	3	3	2	0	30	20
8	Alan Thompson	16	2	0	0	1	0	2	1	19	3
9	Chris Sutton	8	2	0	0	1	0	1	0	10	2
9	Dion Dublin	11	1	0	0	1	1	0	0	12	2
10	John Hartson	35	18	1	0	3	1	2	1	41	20
11	Stephen Pearson	18	2	1	0	1	0	0	0	20	2
12	Mark Wilson	15	0	0	0	0	0	0	0	15	0
14	Jeremie Aliadiere	0	0	0	0	0	0	2	0	2	0
16	Roy Keane	10	1	1	0	2	0	0	0	13	1
17	Didier Agathe	4	0	0	0	0	0	0	0	4	0
18	Neil Lennon	32	1	1	0	3	0	2	0	38	1
19	Stilian Petrov	37	10	0	0	4	0	2	0	43	10
22	David Marshall	4	0	0	0	0	0	1	0	5	0
23	Stanislav Varga	10	1	0	0	2	0	1	0	13	1
25	Shunsuke Nakamura	33	6	1	0	4	0	0	0	38	6
29	Shaun Maloney	36	13	1	0	4	3	2	0	43	16
33	Ross Wallace	11	0	1	0	1	0	1	0	14	0
35	Paul Lawson	3	0	0	0	1	0	0	0	4	0
37	Craig Beattie	13	6	0	0	1	0	1	1	15	7
42	Michael McGlinchey	1	0	0	0	0	0	0	0	1	0
44	Stephen McManus	36	7	1	0	4	0	1	1	42	8
46	Aiden McGeady	20	4	1	0	2	0	1	0	24	4

**The following article was featured in The Celtic View issued in September 2023*

The Celtic family loses one of its own – a sad farewell to the wonderful David Potter

It was with huge sadness towards the end of July that we learned about the unexpected death of legendary Celtic author and historian David Potter, following a short illness. David passed away in his hometown of Kirkcaldy on 29 July 2023, just one month short of his 75th birthday.

As you pass through life, you inevitably meet so many different types of people, but it would be fair to say that David - or DP as he signed off every email - was a quite unique character. A lifelong Celtic supporter, a gift passed down from his grandfather then his own dad, Angus, David combined his passion for sport – most notably football and cricket – drama and history with an excellent academic career. Born in Forfar on 29 August 1948, he was educated in the Angus town but spent much of his adult life in the neighbouring kingdom of Fife, David graduating from the University of St Andrews then teaching Latin and Spanish in Glenrothes. And the teacher never left him. Bumping into David outside Celtic Park with my daughter a year or two back, he was immediately interested in her own career in education and engaged her in conversation, imparting advice and good wishes as a matter of course. That was DP.

Of course, most readers of The Celtic View will know David as the prolific writer and authority on all things Celtic. For the past 30 years, he has covered the characters and events from every era in his own inimitable style, bringing history to life whilst making it highly enjoyable in the process. From early 'Bould Bhoy' heroes Sandy McMahon and Dan Doyle to the first legends to wear the iconic Hoops, Jimmy Quinn, Alec McNair, 'Napoleon' McMenemy and 'Sunny Jim' Young, and the man who built great Celtic teams around them, Willie Maley. Through dazzling wingers Jimmy Delaney, Charlie Tully and Willie Fernie, who entertained our supporters either side of a horrific second world war, to those who would follow them, Yogi and Jinky and the other immortals who brought David and his fellow, long-suffering Celtic fanatics out of the darkness to share in the greatest moments of all in Jock Stein's incredible 1960s Rising, Bobby Murdoch, John Fallon and Charlie Gallagher. From Jimmy McGrory to Henrik Larsson, David Potter told the stories of the men who filled our hearts and the headlines, of the many triumphs and occasional tragedies in which they took centre stage. And he told them brilliantly. It is a litany of Celtic writing quite unsurpassed in its quality and depth and which ensures that their exploits will live well beyond those who witnessed them to pass into folklore. And no surprise that, David being David, he had just finished writing another Celtic book prior to his illness. Watch this space.

David leaves behind a loving family, his wife Rosemary, three children and five grandchildren, an infant grandson having tragically pre-deceased 'Grandy' some years ago. He would have been a proud man indeed listening to the love and humour with which his kids described their beloved dad at his funeral service in Kirkcaldy's Old Kirk. Then again, they had learned from the master storyteller, each managing to have the congregation in smiles on that saddest of days. He would have enjoyed the sight of Celtic colours dotted around the church, colleagues and friends who shared his passion, or travelled with him on the Joseph Rafferty CSC bus. He would have been quietly honoured by the attendance of senior Celtic officials in the church, and his old friend John Fallon, the original Holy Goalie. I suspect that DP would also have been delighted with - if a tad embarrassed by - the beautiful tribute paid by Celtic during the recent match with Ross County. The image smiling down from the big screens at Celtic Park at half-time that afternoon as the club acknowledged his own place in our history was of David celebrating like a teenager after the Treble Treble had been secured at Hampden in May 2019. This academic, a teacher of the classics, this thesbian, cricket umpire and of too many other interests to list, perfectly captured at his happiest as he witnessed yet another piece of that long and unbroken history being secured. He was full of surprises. Just last season, I watched him bouncing around behind the goal at Easter Road as the latest men to wear the jersey took a bow after another win. A one-off. Forever young, always full of fun and Celtic to the core.

Rest in eternal peace, DP. An incredible man, who meant so much to so many and who leaves behind a huge gap in our hearts but such a tremendous legacy. For his family and friends, a thousand memories of a life so fully lived. And for everyone else, an unbelievable catalogue of published work to enjoy.

David once said that Heaven will never be dull with two men who had inspired him - his father Angus and that other great Celtic writer, Eugene MacBride - around the place.

Well DP, you've just raised the ante!

You will truly never walk alone.

Words by Matt Corr